MY AFFAIR WITH STALIN

By the same author
King's Parade

MY AFFAIR WITH STALIN

Simon Sebag Montefiore

Weidenfeld & Nicolson
LONDON

First published in Great Britain in 1997
by Weidenfeld & Nicolson

The Orion Publishing Group Ltd
Orion House
5 Upper Saint Martin's Lane
London, WC2H 9EA

A catalogue reference is available
from the British Library

ISBN 0 297 81924 0 [Hardback]
ISBN 0 297 82011 7 [Paperback]

Typeset by Deltatype Ltd, Birkenhead, Merseyside
Printed in Great Britain by
Clays Ltd St Ives plc

Grateful acknowledgement is made for permission
to quote from the following sources:
Eastern Approaches, Fitzroy Maclean, Penguin, 1991
Twenty Letters to a Friend, Svetlana Alliluyeva, Hutchinson, 1968

To my parents

CONTENTS

'You can't make a Revolution with silk gloves.'

'One death is a tragedy; a million is a statistic.'

PROLOGUE

All true historical quotations by Josef Stalin
and others appear IN ITALICS

1

THE LOVE AFFAIR

My affair with Stalin surprised both of us. I was still a child and he was already one of the most powerful men in the world. When we fell in love, we were just dedicated revolutionaries, devoted to building a brave socialist paradise for the workers of the world. When there is an international revolution to ignite, there is little time for trivial passion. Love is just a bourgeois indulgence. The Party, especially Stalin himself, frowned upon human frailty of any sort.

It was an era of violent struggle. We were fiercely vigilant against traitors. Yet love crept up on us and caught us unawares, that balmy summer in the early years of the Revolution. A *'sentimental ambush'* – that's what Stalin called it.

I am tempted to pretend that I did not know what was going on in the torture chambers of Lubianka and the icy wastes of Siberia. But I did know. Stalin was my hero for making a home for the honest toilers. Now I am older. I live in obscurity in England, far away from the Kremlin. I work in a humdrum office. It is just a job. I've done it for years, decades, the rest of my life. After Stalin. At work, no one knows about my old life in the East. But my friends – the few that know – sometimes ask if I am ashamed of my passion for the Man of Steel. I should be; but I am not.

No one was kinder to me than Stalin. His beautiful yellow eyes often filled with tears at the mere thought of the suffering of working people. He lent me his favourite books on Peter the Great and Ivan the Terrible. He did not come home drunk. He never beat my cat, Engels, never goosed the maids. His only domestic sins were watching capitalist Charlie Chaplin films, dropping pipe ash on our Samarkand carpets and working until the early hours: he never came to bed before dawn. Then he slept until midday. The entire Soviet government had to follow the same hours.

He was just a busy man with a big job to do. Many people depended on him. Don't expect the sort of sordid psycho-sexual revelations that ooze like slime from modern biographies. There have been many vicious lies written about this gentle man. So let me tell you now that he was not a cross-dresser, a trans-sexual or a foot fetishist.

None of that, comrades. Only Ilyich himself (as those in the know called Lenin), when he took the chair at the Council of People's Commissars in the early days, equalled Stalin's modest but warm authority. I never knew Ilyich myself but Stalin often told me about him. Sometimes he talked about Lenin in his sleep – with respect, but a breed of anger too.

Stalin lived with the austerity of a monk. He slept fitfully on a rolled-up mattress in his office. He never noticed his salary: when he died, they found thirty years of salary envelopes left unopened in his desk at Kuntsevo, his dacha. When he died ... that day of agony when the sycophants who had pretended to worship him showed their true colours. The day they cut me adrift was the day my ordinary life began.

Stalin was so modest: when his pious old mother, Keke, told him in 1935 to get a proper job (nominally, he was just Secretary-General of the Party), he already ruled the Soviet Union. But he just laughed. *'Remember the Tsar?'* he asked, visiting the lady in her tiny room in the Viceroy's Palace in Tbilisi. She nodded. *'Well, I'm like the Tsar.'*

If you had known Stalin as I did, you would never have guessed that such a patient, sensitive lover was the self-created master of the greatest empire the world has ever known.

Some memoirs claim that when people actually met Stalin, they were disappointed because he was small with wolf's eyes. His torso was pot-bellied; his skin pockmarked. His left arm was slightly shorter than his right. (His toes were webbed. I was one of the few, privileged to gaze upon such state secrets.) His hair and his famous moustache were greyer and thinner than they appeared in the pictures that I saw everywhere.

That bald oaf Khrushchev – a peasant clod who did his best to ruin Stalin's legacy – wrote in his memoirs, *'when you were summoned by Stalin, you never knew if you would go home to your wife or a prison cell.'*

When I was summoned to serve Stalin at last, I knew exactly where

I was going – and what for. I was awakened by three secret police generals at four in the morning. The troika of nervous and swarthy Chekists stood on the doorstep, with their shiny boots, leather pistol holsters, bemedalled chests and NKVD shoulder-boards. The one with a face as livid with sleeplessness, crusted with sweat and swollen with vodka as a Baked Alaska pudding, coughed and said, 'The Central Committee requests you.'

The 'Central Committee' always meant just one man.

My parents thought I was being arrested. But I knew. Who could resist being rushed through the empty streets of Moscow in a long sleek ZIL limousine, black as jet, surrounded by secret police outriders, straight through the medieval ramparts into the forbidding Kremlin? It was far more of an honour than merely playing for the First Eleven at cricket or coming first in history.

I want to tell you what happened that remarkable night with Stalin, Secretary-General of the Communist Party of the USSR, Chairman of the Council of People's Commissars (that's 'Prime Minister' in our language) and Generalissimo of the Soviet Union.

But at home, my parents often criticise the 'guttersnipes' who kiss famous people and then sell their story to newspapers. Mr Trevelyan, my Headmaster, told me that such monsters are 'beyond contempt'– wherever that is. This is no Kiss 'n' Tell. As Mr Trevelyan, who is frightfully honourable, said, 'If you're hoping for that sort of nonsense, we might as well stop right now.' This is just my story. You might call it *A Study in Tyranny* like Alan Bullock's famous biography of Hitler. Perhaps. But I don't think so ... Never was a better man more sinned against than Stalin.

I had no rivals for Stalin's favours, though anyone, east of Berlin and west of Vladivostok, would have been honoured. But I was just eleven years old and youth conquers all. Stalin's first wife had died of TB in 1907. His second had committed suicide in 1932 (not strong enough for the struggle!). He liked his jolly Russian housekeeper; her jam was good but she did not understand Leninism.

Most nights, Stalin held rumbustious dinners, hearty affairs for his comrades. There was dancing, teasing and practical jokes until the early hours. When they departed in their limousines, I would come out of my room in my Azeri dressing-gown and Cossack slippers to calm him so that he could sleep at last. He did not trust a single one of them. Just me. *'Every one of them hates me,'* he used to sigh, as I stroked his greying moustache, pulled off his leather boots, brushed down his favourite old tunic, filled his pipe, laid out his nightshirt. *'But they are just innocent kittens. There are enemies all around us. They'd be lost without me.'*

'Now you're safe, Soso, safe with me,' and I massaged his neck.

'Perhaps ...' he would answer.

I was the only person alive, except his mother, who called him by his childhood nickname − Soso.

Once, after a marathon banquet, at the end of a glorious Party Plenum, when he had been drinking his favourite Khaketian red wine and singing his beloved Georgian folksongs with his Politburo colleagues in his noble tenor voice, we were sitting in the dining room at the dacha. The sun was rising. No Politburo, no secret police, no generals. Alone at last. Just a table loaded with empty bottles, soiled glasses and the gramophone. I had him all to myself.

A rare, tranquil, loving moment in a lifetime of strife. He put his pipe down, caressed my tousled blond hair and whispered − I can still hear that curdled Georgian accent which he never lost: 'What precocious Leninist purism, Stakhanovite industriousness and diligent vigilance against Trotskyite wreckerism, you have for an eleven-year-old.'

He really did have a romantic turn of phrase.

2

STALIN'S EXILE

Whenever I hear the crunch of majestic cars on golden gravel, I can see Coverdale School at eight o'clock on a Sunday evening. We are living in the middle years of the Nineteen Seventies. It is suffocatingly dark as my parents' Volvo motor car trundles along the potholed drive towards the school, parting the gravel like an icebreaker.

Coverdale is an over-sized Gothic folly, lit up by lanterns in silent drawing rooms, rising up out of the gloom. It has domes and towers. The school's own little chapel, as twee as a Swiss peasant's chalet, stands to the right of the front door. Its wooden spire is silhouetted. My parents are sitting in the front. I have been cheerful during the drive but suddenly, I see it there, and my throat tightens. I can no longer speak because I do not want to cry.

The drive is crowded with cars. Their headlights are blazing. It is an army decamping. Everyone is unpacking and carrying bundles like wealthy refugees in a time of turmoil. The cars are parked carelessly on grass or gravel with their doors open. You cannot see too much: just glimpses of small boys in grey trousers, tweed jackets and v-neck sweaters – their pale cheeks glow like masks. They are sometimes accompanied by Englishmen in pin-striped suits – their fathers – or women in elegant winter coats of camel hair and cashmere. I can still smell the Tower of Babel of perfumes mingling from the fine wrists of mothers and the acrid aftershaves of fathers. A couple of boys are left by chauffeurs in uniforms who step out of Rolls-Royces and are probably kinder than their parents could ever be.

The majority of the fathers are tired accountants, overworked solicitors, and gruff landowners. Then I spot the two most exotic parents. There ARE only two interesting ones: beside the stretch-Mercedes with bulletproof glass stands the father of my friend,

5

Mendoza. Mr Mendoza is a stocky, white-haired gorilla with a bludgeon nose. Tonight he wears a pin-stripe: it looks as if it has been painted on with a flame-thrower. He owns a casino in Marseilles. Mr Mendoza is loudly supervising the chauffeur who is pulling a tuck box out of the boot.

Mr Mendoza is accompanied by a blonde girl in hotpants, formerly Miss Israel: I recall that she shies and whinnies like a racehorse. But Memory has a way of turning characters into cartoons – and girls into racehorses. Her brown legs are fluorescent tubes of coffee in the dusk. She is my friend's latest stepmother. All his stepmothers are former Miss Israels. I envied Mendoza his stepmothers: they were far more exciting than my mother. My poor mother wore face cream and a hairnet at night.

'Look, darling,' says my mother to my father, 'doesn't she look sophisticated?'

My mother always points out more attractive women: it is a way of discounting them before my father sees them himself and can be impressed. We all know that when my mother says 'sophisticated', she means the girl is what dad calls 'free and easy'.

Dad does not answer. He says only a few kind words at a time. He picks up my tuck box and bears it past the chapel into the school.

We pass the only other interesting parent, Mr Rafferty, the Hollywood film producer, who almost never drops his son back at school. He sports a bushy beard beneath Red Indian cheekbones as sharp as tomahawks, cowboy boots and a khaki safari suit. He is dressed like Montezuma on safari: this looks silly in Dorset in midwinter. He is talking to Mr Mendoza. Both men hold cigars, nonchalantly watching the columns of shabby schoolboy bric-à-brac carried past them, like Panzer generals callously observing the human detritus their phalanxes have wrought.

'How do they know each other?' I ask my mum.

'They all know each other at the top,' she says, neither jealously nor reverently, just anthropologically – as if they were creatures of a different species from us.

When we lift my trunk out of the car, my mother says, 'Darling, now think. Have you got everything?' Across the gravel, I can hear every mother in the same clothes asking the same question in the same tone. The cars shine and catch the strips of light as their doors open and close under the lanterns of Coverdale. The scene has an air of melancholic suspense.

Darkness is traditionally hostile. But at Coverdale on a Sunday night, the darkness outside is comforting. It is the light inside that represents unhappiness.

Suddenly, we are in the light walking towards the front door which is wide open. There are two vast pillars on either side like the portico of a Greek temple. Inside, there is a grand hall with red carpets. Without even thinking, I look for her. If only she can be there, it will be easier. Mr and Mrs Trevelyan stand inside. They are most welcoming. But Miss Snow is my dear warm consoler. She stands beside the Headmistress.

Dad shakes hands with old Mr Trevelyan, Headmaster for forty years, who always wears the same green blazer that strains at the buttons. His stomach is a neat red football that sometimes peeps cheerfully though his shirt buttons. His pink flesh overthrows his check shirt as if his skin is just one size too big for him. My mother kisses the tiny, bird-like Mrs Trevelyan who wears a florid dress that reminds me of rhododendron bushes. She's antique too – fit for her age – over seventy, like Mr Trevelyan. The American Miss Snow, fetching in a brown suede jerkin like an archer at Agincourt, envelops me in her cloud of musky perfume. It is so overpowering, it is almost visible. She knows how pleased I am to see her. I look up at her dark saturnine face as a smooth-headed golden labrador dreamily greets its master.

The reassuring Mrs Trevelyan, whose cheeks are as concave as her husband's are convex, greets me and puts her hand on my shoulder to make me feel better. It works.

'Did you have a good hols?' she asks kindly. Her little muddy eyes peep out from a wispy brown fringe.

'It's the winter,' I answer, convulsed with panic. 'I DREAD playing rugby. I won't play. I can't!' Fear makes me dizzy.

'You won't have to,' she whispers before I am overcome. Then to my parents: 'He really doesn't have to.' My mother and Mrs Trevelyan take a few steps aside and talk quietly though I can hear mum saying, '... rugby ... upset ... worked himself into a real state ...'

And Mrs Trevelyan nodding and promising, '... really won't have to ... we've thought of something ...'

'You're so kind. I don't know HOW you do it, thinking of something for every one of them,' says my mother, out loud again.

I want to stay there but there are other parents, other boys behind us who want the same attention. We boys never catch each other's eyes because they are tearful. It is easier to see nothing. Some parents are more nervous than the children. So we move on and carry my paraphernalia upstairs to my room. It is a cavernous dormitory: rows of black-framed steel beds. Mum arranges my teddy bears and gushes: 'What a lovely cosy room, isn't it, Alexander?'

'Oh yes,' answers my father, who is not articulate. 'Very. Yes.' His handsome, stormy face with its blue eyes and dimpled chin is not built for white lies: he does not look convinced.

Then we go down to my classroom, blackboard, desks and potted plants – that drab race of droopy plants that haunt classrooms as wreaths haunt graveyards. My father leaves my tuck box beside the wall. It contains my tape recorder, my tapes by Queen and Abba, my mother's homemade coffee cake and a bag of mini-Mars Bars.

'If anyone bullies you,' whispers my mother, 'he's probably just having a sugar shortage. So give him a Mars Bar and he'll stop.'

This practical advice is well-meaning but misguided. Still, it passes time. Glimpses of my friends quieten my fears.

But then we are back in the lobby again. Mum and dad are saying goodbye to me. My friends and enemies are saying goodbye to their parents too, all around me, but I don't notice them because I am so involved in this last pitiful rite. Miss Snow, who is my best teacher, starts talking to me in her languid, deep, Yankee voice so I don't notice my parents have gone. I forget everything when I talk to Miss Snow: she is a divorcee from Pennsylvania, an American in the heart of Englishness. The very word 'divorcee' makes me shiver with its tarnished glamour. My mildewed parents are happily married; only enthralling women seem to be divorced.

'I went to a bullfighting school in a loft in Manhattan during the hols,' she says in that husky voice. She is not like the others. I imagine she has seen disturbing, wicked sights. Her eyes dart, her jet hair has a strand of grey like Indira Gandhi and her face is drawn as if she has stared once too often into the rays of the sun. I am her favourite. She has chosen me for something. Or does she say that to everyone? 'I wore a toreador's silken costume of olive green and ...' She hesitates and I remember where I am.

I look up and see the kindly crown of my father's balding head and his professorial jacket just going out into the darkness, and I long to run and follow him and kiss him goodbye all over again.

The parents have gone. It is only boys and masters left. But I can't speak to them. I sense the activity outside on the drive as the doors of an armada of cars slam shut. The engines start, the headlights illuminate those glistening chips of gravel and they begin to move. Parents are controlled but brisk because they fear that if they rush, we boys will panic and give chase; if they linger, we will see it as weakness and hope they are coming back for us.

I break away from Miss Snow and run to a window. The glass is cold but I press my hot face against it until my nose is squashed and my glasses mist up. There, amongst the reflections on the windscreens and the rumbling movement, THERE is my parents' car, turning slowly. It accelerates on the thick, sugary gravel. I hear it crunch under the wheels.

The gravel under my father's wheels sounds different from every other sort of crunching gravel in that car park, in the whole world. My throat constricts. I want to run after that car and stop it! I bunch my muscles ready to sprint with every breath of strength down the drive. But then I stop myself. Shame restrains passion. Thank God, it often does. Without shame, we'd just be beasts. The tears arise in my throat like a spring and my sobs shake me: a storm of electric spasms.

At that time, I could not place this sensation of desperate, frantic sadness when I was capable of any wildness to get my beloveds back to me. Later I understood how the broken-hearted throw themselves under trains, over bridges.

There are other boys at the window too. As the cars become flickering lights behind the woods and then disappear, our breaths and squashed noses make islands of condensation on the glass. For a long and terrible moment, those islands of loss are our only home in the world. But then we stir as if we had been asleep. We peer at one another as if discovering other life forms on the planet. We realise we are not alone. I wipe my eyes briskly as the others are doing.

There are more boys around me than around anyone else. There are hands on my shoulders and arms. For a moment, I fear that I am outnumbered again and about to be attacked: an infantile Ides of March? But those days are long gone. The imploring hands are soft and respectful.

9

One boy steps forward reverently from this array of supplicants. He leans over and says, 'Welcome back, Comrade Stalin.'

Another voice declares, 'Long live Comrade Stalin! Long live Stalinism!'

'Comrade Stalin,' petitions a third. 'May I ask a favour?'

But Ormonde raises his hand and announces officiously, 'The Secretary-General will answer questions after the first Central Committee meeting tomorrow.'

My comrades-in-arms, Petty, Ormonde, Ogleton and the other Politburo members, link arms to form a guard around me. The revolution is safe. Stalinism is triumphant. I want to project a grim authority yet, against my will, my face breaks into a victorious smile.

Sometimes, in my office in the Kremlin, I take a moment from the sixteen-hour days of receiving ambassadors and apparatchiks, marshals and secret policemen, to remember how it started. It is easy to forget how far I have travelled.

Bless you, Stalin, who makes even going back to school less painful!

3

CRIME AND PUNISHMENT

'Conroy, Conroy! Are you awake?'

'Of course,' I whispered back.

'Conroy, tell us – who is the Murderer of the Day?'

'Well ...' I began. The draughty dormitory was silent as a sepulchre. Every week at Coverdale I received a magazine called *Celebrated Murderers* in the post. Each issue told the story of a mass murderer. By that summer when I began my affair with Stalin, I had already read every gruesome detail of the following stellar murderers: Acid Bath Haigh, Hanratty, Christie of Ten Rillington Place, the Monster of Düsseldorf, Brides in the Bath Smith, Fatty Arbuckle and Doctor Crippen. Crippen was the most boring because he only poisoned his wife, which seems almost routine in some marriages.

I was an exuberant schoolboy but inspired by paranoia, macabre obsession and unbreakable optimism, hence my fascination with monsters. The other boys, especially my friends like Ormonde and Petty, were also interested in murderers. Who isn't?

After Lights Out, when we were not allowed to talk, I often used to tell my dorm the story of Jack the Ripper or Acid Bath Haigh. I always uttered those infamous names portentously. So that night I announced into the breathless darkness of my audience: 'Today, chaps: the MONSTER of DUSSELDORF.'

'A Hun! Schnell! Schnell! Achtung!' they answered because they had read too many of those imbecile war comics that reduced the mind to pulp fiction and corn ball. Unlike mine: I never read comics.

Then I seized their fetid imaginations like this: 'On Christmas Day 1925, the Dusseldorf police found a woman aged twenty-three in the cellar of a German beer hall ...' pause '... drained of all blood, beheaded and sliced into twenty-seven pieces.'

'Crumbs!' whispered the clear voices loudly in the baroque gloom.

11

Everyone listened except the sluggish St John, who slept throughout my stories, with his sloppy mouth wide open and dribbling: a repulsive sight of the basest indignity.

The case of Fatty Arbuckle, the comedian of the Keystone Cops, was a most intriguing one for us. He killed a woman, whom my magazine called a 'showgirl' but my mother would call 'sophisticated', by pushing a big block of ice 'up inside her'. What did this mean? How did it kill her? How could a comedian be a murderer? None of us dared ask.

Money-Banks, a weakling (Mr Eye called him 'a *soi-disant* Stalinist'), used to have nightmares after my stories.

Even Beaconsfield, the Head of School and our dormitory prefect, who let me tell the stories against the rules, said, 'Conroy, you really tell good stories.'

Diggle-Johnson, the outstanding liar in the school and a bed-wetter too, usually claimed that 'his uncle' knew anyone we talked about. For example, after we saw a film called *Gone With the Wind*, which made us cry at the end, Diggle-Johnson said, 'Actually, my uncle knew Rhett Butler. Scarlett O'Hara was his first wife. I'm not swanking! It's only the truth! I swear on my father's death.' His poor father must have died a million deaths for all his lies.

We believed it at first. But when he claimed his uncle also knew Crippen and Acid Bath Haigh, we decided he was lying.

Still, these murderers did not impress me, because they didn't achieve anything except ruining people's lives for no reason. They were quite brainy, yet they always got caught.

One day in June I received the new issue of the magazine. It was high Coverdale summer. Mum preciously called it a 'rustic idyll' but no other phrase catches it so well. All my friends, except Petty, were playing cricket on the Farm Ground right beyond the school's cowsheds. They wore white trousers, cricket boots and white shirts. The sportsmen were the *crème de la crème* of Coverdale. It was a dazzling, dizzily hot day. The bees, the birds and boys' voices shouting 'Howzat!' formed a fuzzy wall of massaging sound.

When I gazed at the buildings, I could see every detail in the bright sunlight: gargoyles, open-mouthed with stone tongues retching out through fangs from just beneath the roof. There were pillars and busts and buttresses, and a green onion dome right in the middle. Coverdale was extravagantly creepy.

As I stood on the steps with my friend Petty, we observed the game for a moment. Mr Holly, the history teacher, was the umpire: he had a bovine, loose jaw and a meagre prickly beard that stood up like the spikes of a rather stunted porcupine.

Petty, who spoke with a lisp and agreed with everything I said, would have liked to play but he had asthma. He wheezed hideously when he got out of breath. Petty was clever, ambitious but feeble and nervy at the same time. He was my comrade-in-arms, even in those early days, long before the Revolution, long before we had ever heard of Lenin and Stalin.

So I was not lonely. But I hated hearing the high voices of the boys appealing, 'Not out, sir!' I was jealous when they returned with raffish grass stains on their whites, spinning yarns of cricket heroism, tossing the red ball to one another with practised ease. If they threw it at me, I always dropped it, afraid of its hardness and spectacle-shattering speed.

In the winter terms, it was even worse. Often, at about four, I would be walking along the Long Corridor with my books when the rugby players poured in, like a horde of Visigoths, towards the showers. They overflowed with a dogmatic confidence that is the savage result of the worship of physical exercise, an evil religion. They would brush past me, as if I didn't exist, with lips smirking, wild-eyed savages intoxicated by the chase, mud on their knees, stinking of sweat, bearing coldness and force, bragging about their games. The cruellest leader of this bullying elite was a nasty brute named Crabbe. He knocked me over whenever he came across me. I was grazed by the old parquet floor.

'You're nothing but a Cabbage,' he said, laughing, showing his gums like a breathless dog. 'A Cabbage isn't even worthy to live in the same school as us. You'll never be anyone.' When I tried to get up, he knocked me down again. 'Get him!' he said. 'Plant the Cabbage!' Many hands lifted me, carried me. Then I was dangling like a piece of masonry from a big crane until they dropped me, face first, into the rampart of nettles near the cowsheds. My glasses fell off somewhere. It took many stings to find them again. I was bruised and swollen but, more than that, I was hurt. Crabbe and his Sportsmen ruled. So no one helped me. No one dared – except my friend Steady Pelham. He pulled me up from amongst the nettles, risking punishment to help me find my glasses.

A Cabbage was the slang for someone who did not play sports. Crabbe, that charismatic Neanderthal, was a Blood, which meant he was in the first team for all three major sports.

I hated their sporting panache. I didn't just want revenge. I admit that I wanted to destroy their world. And more than that, I yearned to win their respect and then, when I had it, to wipe them off the face of the earth. Let the Bloods bleed a bit.

I was determined to find a way in which I could be a hero. Certainly, it was not in sports. I was afraid of the rough 'n' tumble of rugger. I was pale, frail and thin as a rail. My Buddy Holly glasses were thick tortoiseshells. I had blue eyes, speckled with yellow and a thick mop of very blond hair. In my grey trousers I always carried three little books: a biographical dictionary, a gazetteer and a biblical dictionary. The sportsmen like Crabbe laughed at my bulging pockets, but I knew the names of the twelve Caesars, the sons of Jacob and the capital of Upper Volta (indeed: Ouagadougou) – and I'm not swanking – while they could only grunt and scrummage. Mr Trevelyan said my bulging pockets were not elegant. This irritated me. I wanted to be as elegant as a cockatoo at a masked ball.

'None of the other boys keep so many books in their pockets,' said Miss Snow. She understood me.

'I don't want to be like the others,' I replied. 'I despise ordinary lives. I would rather perish at thirteen than live a boring life. I will gamble everything for it!'

'Hunky-dory. You ARE a card.' She laughed as she walked away down the corridor, boots creaking.

Anyway, since I was not good at sports, I didn't want to play them. I was only interested in triumph.

Mr Trevelyan was a sportsman himself, in spite of his age and neat paunch. But he was kind enough to invent a special duty for Petty and me which did not involve sports. It was called Odd Jobs. We had to go through what was called the Inner Sanctum, where Mr and Mrs Trevelyan lived in a house of dignified grandeur. The Inner Sanctum, usually Out of Bounds to us, was a still museum of monumental ticking clocks and sepia photographs of plump Mr Trevelyan with his halo of fuzzy blond hair that stood like spun sugar at the centre of cricket teams. Then he would tell us to sweep the leaves, pointing past the blue-gabled wooden chapel right outside the Inner Sanctum, to a certain part of his private garden, with its noble oaks and sweeping green lawns.

Later, we would burn the leaves. We discussed murderers until the sun went down. Petty lisped to me about his parents who lived in Scotland, which was a fashionable place to live in those days. His parents were not like mine. They beat Petty if he was naughty which MY parents regarded as 'primitive savagery'.

Petty also talked about his elder brother, Petty major. My friend Petty was Petty minor. (If there were four brothers at Coverdale, they were known as Maximus, Major, Minor, Minimus. Latin was a dead language but it was alive at Coverdale.)

Their family performed what Petty called 'country pursuits', so Petty always saluted magpies with one finger raised to his temple. If he saw any bird in the sky, except a magpie, he pretended to shoot it with a shot gun, which he claimed to have at home. I never believed him of course: who would give a boy as young and wet as Petty a real gun? When I suggested this to Petty, he revealed that his parents called people like me 'townies'.

I did not want to be called a towny because most of the boys at Coverdale seemed to follow country pursuits in the Scottish countryside where they could salute magpies, talk about being Scottish and shoot everything except magpies. I did not pretend to be Scottish, but sometimes I stooped to fib that I went to Scotland frequently to salute magpies.

I did not like fibbing and was dying to find a different order to turn this around to my advantage. One day, I found a way.

Petty went to start on the leaves. I went into my classroom – we were then in Class C – and got my *Celebrated Murderers*. I was sick of reading for the third week about Christie, though I was appalled and intrigued that, when he killed the old women, he 'collected their pubic hair in a tobacco box'. I was looking forward to the issues on the Boston Strangler.

When, later that night, I briefed my dormitory about Christie's tobacco box, half of them giggled with an unhinged sort of morbid mania while that fool Diggle-Johnson suggested I had misread the article. 'It must have said "pubLic hair",' asserted the imbecile.

I then came to an article on 'STALIN and his perverted secret police chief Beria'. There was a beautiful photograph of Stalin in the austere splendour of his daily uniform: peasant boots, baggy green trousers and a grey tunic. It took my breath away. I loved his expression, which was pervaded by evil, cunning and cruelty: a combination that meant his orders would be obeyed – and no one would jeer at him after rugby. Just as young Stalin, then called Djugashvili, a teenage Georgian ruffian, discovered Lenin, so I discovered Stalin. The thunderbolt!

Beria, on the other hand, was superlatively sinister in his NKVD* uniform and his glinting rimless glasses, which the magazine called 'pince-nez'. I at once noticed that this monstrous Beria looked the very image of our friendly maths master, Mr Humphries. What a coincidence!

The best photograph showed Stalin dead, which the magazine called 'lying-in-state'. He looked absolutely marvellous dead. He 'went to Lenin' wearing the fine black uniform of a Marshal of the Soviet Union, with big epaulettes (Russians call them 'shoulder-boards') and medals. If I had to die – and I found that most unlikely in those days – I wanted to 'lie in state' too.

Stalin's friends, a villainous bunch of 'henchmen', guarding his 'bier', looked as shifty as my murderers. I imagined having my best friends like Petty and Ormonde standing around me. I noticed, too, that one of Stalin's friends, who was called Molotov, looked like my French master, Mr Eye. A series of coincidences had linked me to Stalin and Beria: fortuna!

The article was really about Beria and how he would 'cruise the streets of Moscow, pince-nez glinting, with his nose pressed to the window looking for young women to ravish. He feasted on young flesh.'

The words are for ever imprinted on my heart ... Ravish? Feast? Was he really a Marxist vampire? Did werewolves and Stalins really exist? I had thought they lived only in legends. 'No,' Miss Snow replied

* The Soviet secret police was known by ever-changing acronyms. First it was called the CHEKA, which stood for 'Extraordinary Commission for the Struggle Against Counter-Revolution Speculation and Sabotage'. From 1922 to 1934, it was the OGPU, All-Union State Political Administration. Between 1934 and 1946, the dreaded initials were NKVD, People's Commissariat for Internal Affairs, until the security forces were hived off into a Ministry of State Security – MGB. In 1954 Khrushchev wished to pretend secret police were no longer so necessary after Stalin's excesses. So he demoted it to the status of a committee, the KGB. Actually, it remained as powerful as ever. President Boris Yeltsin changed the notorious initials again after the fall of the Soviet Union in 1991.

when I asked her, 'monsters really roam the earth and they look like you and me.'

Then I read on. After Stalin's death, Khrushchev and the Soviet marshals actually strangled Beria.

What a name: 'Beria'. As in 'Burier'. But he was a bit of a weirdo: he chased girls. When one girl did not agree to his 'attentions' – whatever that meant (I asked my brothers what every dirty word signified) – he threw a bunch of flowers at her.

'*Thank you for the bouquet,*' stuttered the terrified damsel.

'*It's not a bouquet!*' answered Beria. '*It's a WREATH!*'

Beria just was not a gentleman. Mr Trevelyan said often, 'A gentleman knows how to lose.'

But Stalin! What a moniker, what a *nom de guerre*: Man of Steel. I fell completely in love with Stalin. 'Coup de foudre, mon cher,' said Mr Eye. I at once wrote my feelings in my notebook.

> 1. Stalin's evil face – yellow wolverine eyes, low forehead, black hair and moustache – and magnificent uniforms: a Tartar tyrant.
> 2. Stalin was the most SUCCESSFUL statesman-tyrant of all. Intelligent. Creator of the greatest empire of today's world!
> 3. Stalin's ruthlessness: nothing stood in his way. I want to be as ruthless and witty, evil and cruel as him.

The romance of it made me momentarily dizzy which, mum said, meant I was short of sugar. So I popped over to my tuck box (the tuck boxes were arranged around the walls of our class) and cut myself a juicy slice of mum's coffee cake. I pigged out and then ran off down the main corridor towards the Inner Sanctum.

I bumped straight into Mr Allcock, the divinity master, who had a romantic lock of floppy brown hair hanging over his right eye and a funny, long-stepped way of walking. He called himself a 'sixties buff', always wore a corduroy jacket with corduroy flares and reminisced about Swinging London all the time as if he had been the only one there.

He was standing outside the dining room with Miss Deirdre, an under-matron with blonde hair and magnificent bazookas.

'I once met Eric Clapton backstage at the Lyceum,' he was just boasting to the under-matron. 'We had a simple name for Clapton in those days ...'

'What was that?' she said.

'God,' said Mr Allcock.

'Is that why you teach divinity?' asked Miss Deirdre as I turned the corner too fast.

When we collided, I said, 'Sorry, Mr Allcock.' Then under my breath: 'All cock and no balls!' and ran off, giggling, to find Petty.

'Conroy – What did you say?' I heard him calling after me. But I ran for it. 'I've had enough, Conroy. I heard you!' Poor Mr Allcock: sometimes he said he heard boys saying, 'All cock and no balls,' when no one had said a word. Schoolmasters tend to go mad after a while: they hear voices like Joan of Arc.

When I found Petty beside the bonfire, I told him all about Stalin and Beria and how a new era had started for us.

'Shouldn't you go and put on your wellington boots?' suggested Petty, peeling off the black leather gloves his parents had just given him. If you were in the garden at Coverdale, you had to wear the right footwear.

I did not answer Petty's trivial question. Couldn't I be gifted with a secret policeman of a bit more gravity than little Petty? I thought.

'Let's sit down,' I said.

'Magnifico!' spluttered Petty. 'Capital idea, revolution. Capital. Let's smoke some grass.'

4

THE TSARIST EMPIRE AT STALIN'S BIRTH 1879

My elder brothers smoked grass in their rooms at home in Pimlico while they listened to records by Grateful Dead and Pink Floyd. My parents did not know. My brothers did not give me any. But they told me that everyone 'groovy' smoked grass. They wore white bell-bottoms and velvet shirts: one sported Charles I's curls and beard.

My brothers told me that they PAID for their grass, which appeared foolish to Petty and me because there was grass all over the playing fields.

Now I quickly picked some grass and rolled it up in a page of newspaper which we used to light the fire. We lit it and tried to smoke it as we sat against a tree stump. It always tasted vile but if my brothers were doing it, why shouldn't I? Inhaling lawns was the *Zeitgeist* of the age.

That was when I said, 'Petty, you're going to be my secret police chief. I am going to take over the Camps. I am going to use terror to bear us to power.'

'You'll never take over Camps,' lisped Petty. 'Camps is controlled by the Dugganoes. You can't even play rugger. I can't even run (though I'm a damn good shot with the 4.10 Father gave me). You're never going to beat Duggan and Crabbe.'

'We'll thrash Duggan, Crabbe AND the Dugganoes.'

'But they're bigger and older, and they have deep voices,' said Petty.

'I'm sure Lenin and Stalin didn't let the deep voices of the Provisional Government put them off seizing power,' I said.

Petty kicked the bonfire with his boot but said nothing.

'The lights will go out again tonight,' I said. There was another strike: the Prime Minister was governed by the unions.

'I like these strikes,' said Petty. 'Exiting as war—'

'Better than murder! Prep by candlelight! You can tell Coverdale's ripe for revolution. Lenin knew the Great War made revolution inevitable. These strikes will do the same for us ...'

'But how, Conroy?'

'Coverdale, a continental empire of different nations, ruled by an autocrat, is just like a little Russia ruled by a little tsar. Listen, Petty, I sense glorious opportunities for Stalin and me, his loyal lover, disciple and alter ego, to save the school.'

Petty stared at me across the bonfire. 'Shall we go for a promenade?' he suggested.

'Geronimo! Let's view this lackadaisical empire of Tsar Nicholas the Second.'

We wandered off through the smoke, behind the chapel, around the school, towards the woods, exchanging tokes of grass from our foot-long tabloid-sized joint, coughing like miners ...

'Are your parents worried about the strikes?' he asked.

'Yes. Yours?'

The troll in the bonfire smoke nodded. The whole edifice of bourgeois liberal life was crumbling: no one grown up was remotely happy in the seventies. They did not know it, but even mum and dad were crying out for a 'dictatorship of the proletariat', which meant MY dictatorship.

Our parents did not like the strikes. Dad worked hard as a doctor. But he always scowled like a bloodhound when he talked about what was called the Money Situation. Mum used to say, 'Darling, don't ask Daddy about it because he doesn't like discussing money because his father didn't like discussing it.'

'Was that because HIS father didn't like discussing money?' I always asked.

Since she did not know the answer to this question, she answered, 'It's been a NICE day but you're OVER-tired so don't spoil it by SHOWING OFF!'

That was the Money Situation that hurt everyone's parents. Mr Trevelyan said that he had considered moving Coverdale lock, stock and barrel across the Channel to Switzerland. Lord Petty, my friend's barbaric beating father, was thinking about becoming a tax exile but could not bear to leave his hunting and shooting.

My parents had dinner parties, which were never a great success.

During the hols, I liked to listen to the conversation from the first floor. Oftentimes, I heard pompous men's voices denouncing Mr Heath and Mr Wilson as 'sell-outs', 'Communists' and 'weaklings'.

Our leaders in the Seventies were not a touch on Stalin. Prime Minister Wilson wore short shorts on the beach while smoking a pipe. His legs were white and stubby. He did not look like a hero to me. Communism was taken particularly seriously in those days.

Once I heard a man at dinner say, 'We're losing out to these bloody Reds. Watergate MUST be a KGB plot! And the unions are destroying England.'

'If only someone would come who dared stand up to them,' came my father's voice.

That was when I wanted to come in and say, 'Stalin would have stood up to the unions. They gave him no more trouble than a gnat during his noble reign ...' But I could not because I was supposed to be in bed.

So the other man said, 'Someone's got to do something. We need a short sharp shock. You know, I wouldn't be sad if the army did something ...'

Then, in far away America, President Nixon had mentioned whitewashing the White House but had done nothing about it and so had resigned – perhaps to go on an interior decorating course in his retirement. My dad said he was a crook. But my mother said Nixon had resigned because he needed to shave three times a day and sweated on television.

It was confusing to be young at a time when the Government could not keep the lights on and presidents fell because of their six o'clock shadows.

As Saigon moved towards its fall, we watched our televisions to see the banknotes blowing in the apocalyptic streets and helicopters hovering over embassies. Then the Commies tried to get hold of a place called Angola. I read in the school library about a blood-soaked mercenary called Colonel Callan – and his spine-chilling massacres. Strange times, the seventies ...

Watching, aged eleven, from Coverdale, I was sure that the world outside was falling to pieces.

5

JOE STALIN'S SCHOOL DAYS 1879–99

While the empire tottered, we lay on our bellies in the woods coughing from Mr Trevelyan's narcotic lawn: 'We're SMERSH* spies, observing the secret life of the school,' said my secret policeman.

'You do learn fast, Comrade Petty.'

Our mission led to an event of world-historical importance in the development of Leninist-Marxist dialectical materialism: I underwent such class oppression that I became not merely Stalin's lover, but a revolutionary of iron-ore resolve.

Coverdale Preparatory School was set in the rolling Dorset countryside, pine forests and downs, that my English master Mr Fitzroy-White mysteriously called 'Wessex' – though I could never find a county of that name on the map. My overwhelming memory is of an exhilarating greenness of fields, bushes and lawns.

Its owner, Mr Trevelyan, may have been the Tsar; but a gentle one, more Nicholas II than Ivan the Terrible. His teddy-bear face was devoid of cunning or impatience: it glowed benignly. That helmet of thick fuzzy fair hair, which bounced when he nodded, was the weather vane of his temperament. When he walked outside, the wind made it swim to and fro as the tentacles of underwater plants wave with the current. When he became angry, his hair seemed to stand up as if electrified. Then we would say, 'Beware! He's going electric!'

Mr Trevelyan strode out onto the manicured lawns in soft suede shoes that Mendoza inexplicably called 'brothel-creepers'. He then turned right, across that painfully crunching gravel (that percussion

---

* The Soviet acronym for the secret police's counter-intelligence organisation during the Second World War. The name SMERSH derives from the Russian words that literally mean 'death to spies'. SMERSH was popularised by Ian Fleming in the James Bond books.

of homesickness), past the chapel, and headed off towards the farm. Like a little empire, Coverdale had its farm, its own cricket grounds, a veritable village of pavilions and its own chapel.

Hiding in the woods, loping like apes through the rhododendron forest, we shadowed the Headmaster, watching his every move. Outside the cattle-sheds, he stopped to talk to Merke, the grey-haired Baltic loo cleaner who sometimes helped with the milking.

They shared a glass of frothy fresh milk which Merke poured from a churn. Merke was a funny ('not funny-ha-ha, but funny-queer' as mum put it) character whom Mr Trevelyan said had 'just arrived at Coverdale during the war. He just walked across the cricket fields and stayed.' He was a Lett from Latvia, which Mr Allcock, in one of his biblical references, said was like being a Git from Gath. When I read what Stalin did to the Letts in 1940 and 1945, I wondered if poor Merke had run all the way from Riga to Coverdale ...

Merke shouted, 'Tovarish! Tovarish!' at the boys who tormented him. Later we learned it meant 'comrade'. We thought him barking. But who was he really?

Mr Trevelyan left Merke and walked gaily on past the farm towards Mr Hester's cottage: the masters, including the Deputy Headmaster Mr Blunt and the vigorous Mr Hester, lived around the estate. Mr Trevelyan walked on round the back, singing to himself in his open, happy way, as if he did not know the place was star-crossed with mysteries.

It was built by a millionaire in the reign of Queen Victoria. No one knew whence he came or how he made his fortune. He had some foreign title. I always wished he was the Count of Monte Cristo.

'But European titles are two-a-penny,' said Mr Trevelyan. 'Only British ones count.'

That millionaire lived for cricket. He had his own team, built the Old Pavilion. And he did it all for his one and only son.

One day, in a cricket game, the ball hit his son on the head. (Another good reason to avoid sports whenever possible.) He died in the Old Pavilion, which is why it is still haunted. There is a blood-stained mattress in there. I have seen it with my own eyes. The blood is black now.

The millionaire sold the house the next day. And died of a broken heart. As you will see, it brought us all bad luck.

'Good game on Ground Three? Did Lamb bowl well?' Mr Trevelyan asked Mr Hester, who had appeared out of his cottage.

'Damn well. Pelham and Bridgewater batted well too. I think we should put them in the Second Eleven, Oliver. It's worth the risk,' snapped Mr Hester in his acidic Irish accent. Mr Hester was of a different ilk to Mr Trevelyan: his sheer physical mass was terrifying – he seemed almost a giant. He was a lofty, tough, muscular Ulsterman with dense ginger curls oiled down and a ruddy moustache the shape of a reversed horseshoe that extended all the way down to the edge of his jaw. His eyes were bloodshot. He taught chemistry eloquently. Since he was from Ulster, we called him the Orangeman.

But his sadistic streak was as clear as the weals left by his beatings. The Orangeman was the enforcer of the *ancien régime*, boss of the tsar's secret police. Mister Orange looked towards the farm fields.

Boys in T-shirts and shorts were jumping and throwing javelins on the athletics grounds which were nearer than the cricket grounds. They fancied themselves as musclebound heroes. I saw them pointing at Petty and me. Were they laughing at me? In gym class that day, I had run up to the horse three times. And three times I had not been able to vault over it. I suddenly realised that Stalin would help me liquidate the Sportsmen.

'Shall we go and see how the Second Eleven's playing up at the pavilion,' said the Headmaster to Mr Hester.

'Second thoughts – better check the Camps and Gardens first.'

Just then, Mr Blunt appeared from the direction of Camps, accompanied by his younger colleague, Mr Selwyn. Mr Blunt, the Deputy Headmaster, was the aged classics pedagogue who seemed seriously to believe he was some sort of Roman emperor. The foetal-faced twenty-one-year-old Mr Selwyn, who had returned to teach straight from Cambridge, taught geography. The other masters were a parade of charming freaks whom we studied with zoological zeal.

'Avé, Headmaster,' intoned Mr Blunt, using the Roman greeting.

Again, they discussed the game.

'Listen to these degenerate tsarist officials – they never mention the wellbeing of the proletariat. Just corrupt cricket!'

'Sport is the opium of the masses,' whispered Petty.

We could hear Mr Selwyn's high-pitched giggle before the masters parted again. We followed Mr Trevelyan and Mr Hester towards the Camps and Gardens.

Petty and I scurried clumsily through the bushes, galumphing from tree to tree in our wellington boots, circumventing the school.

As we passed the cottages behind the chapel, we heard voices and crept up to the window. There stood Mr Allcock, the Clapton-worshipper, facing Miss Deirdre the under-matron. They both held glasses of red wine and were looking at each other so intensely that I wondered if their faces were joined by invisible threads. Mr Allcock was examining Miss Deirdre's necklace with his left hand.

'What a lovely stone: may I look?' Then he spotted a ring on her finger. 'That's a striking ring ... may I?' He took her hand so that it rested in his and stared intently at it ...

'Why's he so interested in jewellery?' whispered I, smelling a rat.

'I reckon he wants to steal it. A highwayman!'

'A dastardly footpad! A dacoit!'

'Shush, Conroy. He must be short of money. She doesn't seem to suspect a thing!'

'THE SWINE! If he does ANYTHING, we'll jump in and rescue her!' I said.

Just then Mr Allcock slipped the ring off her finger ...

'What did I tell you? He's robbing her ... Shall we save her?'

I was just considering a heroic SAS rescue of Miss Deirdre's jewellery when someone tapped me on the shoulder. It was Petty major, my friend's jealous, priggish elder brother.

'What are you two doing SKULKING?' asked the Leper. He suffered from dry, flaky skin – hence his cruel nickname – the Leper. Matron called the brothers 'the Sickly Pettys.'

We quickly moved away from the window.

'Nothing much,' said Petty minor.

'Mind your own beeswax! Get lost,' I sneered. 'Buzz off.'

'I'll talk to Father if you're up to high jinks,' said the Leper who was like an over-grown version of my secret policeman. His hair was not so much blond as almost white like an interloper from Mars. The Leper was hugely tall for his age, which only seemed to make his awkwardness and his skin troubles more obvious. He was such a hulking size that I wondered if, when he was a child, he had fallen into the fertiliser vat on his father's farm. 'Or else I'll have the Dugganoes teach you respect. Father says, "Manners maketh man"'

'SHOO', hissed Petty minor to his elder brother.

The Leper wandered off – so tall he seemed to bend uncomfortably in the middle.

We glanced back into Mr Allcock's window. They were once again just looking at each other without saying anything.

'God, adults have boring lives,' I said. 'Let's go.'

We crept back to the path, laughing uproariously, and caught up with Mr Trevelyan and Mr Hester towards the Camps. We followed surreptitiously.

The two masters walked on up the Flower Walk that led to the gardens. Each boy was allowed a small allotment to grow vegetables. There were some Coverdalians standing around, hoeing, digging – and stealing other boys' radishes.

'Ahoy! Diggle-Johnson,' called Mr Trevelyan. 'How are those famous lettuces?'

'Fine, thank you, sir,' said the School Liar, holding a fork.

Petty and I kept our distance, hugging the hedges, watching diligently.

'These Gardens are the estates of the aristocracy and the richer peasants,' I told Petty. 'They must be collectivised right after the revolution.'

Mr Hester – or Major Hester as he really liked to be called – was admiring a boy's meagre vegetable harvest.

'Very fine,' said the Orangeman like an officer inspecting rifles. 'Good lettuces, men!'

'Thank you, sir,' replied the boys.

'On to the Camps, Oliver! What are the war drums saying?' said Mr Hester.

'All rather harmonious under the Dugganoes,' replied the Headmaster beside him. 'Building their little camps is such a good way for the boys to learn responsibility and community, property and tolerance. No milling for years.'

All that was about to change. In the Camps that day, the die was cast.

6

THE WINTER PALACE

The Dugganoes' Camp was a pine maze of fortifications built out of branches and tarpaulins. It looked impregnable. What military might the Dugganoes possessed! They were the dynasty that had ruled the Camps for generations like the Romanovs of Coverdale.

'Imagine the arsenals of pine cones and conkers in there,' mused Petty as we stood outside and stared reverently at it. 'What an empire!'

'That, dear Comrade Petty,' said I, 'is the Winter Palace.'

The Camps seemed tranquil. We boys were allowed to build fortifications and treehouses in a certain part of the Coverdale Woods but the Dugganoes' Imperial Camp, founded by the Duggan brothers beside the grass tennis court, had dominated them ruthlessly for five years. Beyond the Camps was the Outback and beyond even the Outback were the Corinthian Woods, which were Out of Bounds. We loathed yet instinctively respected the invincible Dugganoes.

That day, Crabbe was acting regent because Duggan was playing chess. Crabbe, that coarse Neanderthal with a bulging low forehead and baboon jaw, emerged with a posse of his men, Minto and Danby, bearing wooden spears and slings, all officially banned. Spanker Grimshaw swished his riding crop. 'Hark, Crabbe! A pair of Cabbages doth approach!'

Crabbe turned his bulk to laugh at us. 'You happy spastic, Conroy. You wimpy little drip. Don't even think of challenging the Dugganoes. You and that huffing and puffing Petty. You can't even spring over the horse, Cabbage!'

Suddenly he ran up to me by the grass tennis court. He flicked off my glasses so I was blind. Then he held my nose very hard. I felt I was suffocating. I thought I might die. When he let go and threw me onto the pine needles, I was desperate for breath.

'You almost killed me,' I spluttered.

'Snubs to you! Stop shamming, y' little rat. You could have breathed through your mouth, you spaz,' he shouted. His cohorts laughed more.

'I forgot,' I said. I burst into tears. Petty picked up my glasses. He put them on my face. We were like two old men.

Petty pulled me up and we ran towards the school, straight past the squash and fives courts, the gym and finally the chapel. I ran upstairs to my dormitory and lay snuffling on my bed. Petty sat on the windowsill.

This was not exactly heroism. Petty looked rather worried about the destiny of a regime led by a Stalin who forgot he could breathe through his mouth.

This would have to be rewritten when I commisioned the history of my glorious role in the Bolshevik Revolution.

I lay on my tigerskin blanket on my bed in dorm J, amongst my favourite teddy bears, until I had recovered. Petty gave me half a chocolate bar and two Nuggets to cheer me up. Bars and Nuggets were the only currency, the nearest thing to money, in that primitive empire. After some sugar, I began to feel better.

'I want to kill Crabbe,' I said finally.

'Really kill him?' Petty looked appalled. 'No way, José! I wouldn't dare.'

'We could use the pitchforks from the farm. Let's kill him. Let's crack his head. It'll be blamed on hooligans. I hate him!' And I broke into sobs. 'How can we ever beat them? Killing him is the only way. Not now. But one day, Petty. Later ...'

Crying was a luxuriant cleansing ritual of mourning, forgetting and purging unpleasant events that is not available to adults in the real world. It marked the end of an incident and the beginning of the rest of your life – afresh, like rain on a garden.

So now, esteem restored by chocolate and tears, I saw the future of the socialist revolution. Petty and I leaned out of the window and looked down on the empire.

'By Jove, this is a historic day, Petty. It is justice to humble the bullies. By the gods, I swear I'll wreck them. I'll bring down the Dugganoes and I'll destroy the whole Sportsman Class with a thousand times the thorough savagery that Stalin used to liquidate his enemies. Oh, Petty, let my teddy bears be my witness, all power to the Soviets!'

Coverdale and the USSR had similarities. That was not surprising because, as argued in Professor Tucker's extremely adult biography, Stalin was both a radical Communist and the most successful imperialist tsar since Peter the Great.

Stalin was my hero. Ivan the Terrible was Stalin's hero. Tamurlane was Ivan's hero. Genghis Khan was Tamurlane's hero ...

'I'm glad that horrible Crabbe and Grimshaw attacked us,' said Petty.

'There's no going back.'

'That is right,' he said.

'From now on, we devote every waking moment to our cause. The NKVD will crush opposition. Tonight, Petty, after supper but before prep, gather Ormonde, Ogleton, Money-Banks, Archeamboye, Weeping Wharton, Steady Pelham and Nonsuch in the Black Shoe Room.'

'What's the NKVD?'

'Shut up, Petty. It's the secret police that was first called the Cheka, then the OGPU, then the NKVD and now is called the KGB.'

'OGpoo?'

'Cripes, Petty, this is serious.'

'I know that, Conroy,' said Petty, eyes welling. 'By Jove.'

'I'm going to be the Stalin of Coverdale.'

7

YOUTH OF A CAUCASIAN REBEL

'Who do we have to shoot to get power in Coverdale?' I said at the first meeting of my Politburo in the Black Shoe Room. The Coverdale Kremlin was a yard of boiler rooms, chimneys and outhouses, which were supposed to be Out of Bounds. It was getting dark. There was an electricity strike as usual in those revolutionary days. The black room was lit by a single candle.

'Shoot?' said Archeamboye, our gentle Nigerian giant.

'Yeah, shoot!' shouted Ogleton, who was slightly 'touched' in the head. Mr Trevelyan said Ogre was 'easily over-excited', which was an understatement.

'Any ideas?'

'Yeah,' said Ogleton who spoke in a fake cockney accent. 'We gotta get the Camps.'

'Which bloodsuckers do we have to shoot?' repeated the trusty Petty, wearing his black leather gloves. We were sitting in a circle of stools – except for the prowling 'Transylvanian Gypsy', Ogleton. He just screamed, 'Duggan, Crabbe and the BUGGERS of the Dugganoes.'

I'd heard the word before, mainly under my father's breath. I wasn't sure what it meant, but I knew it was beyond the final degree of Dante's *Inferno*.

'I don't think we should shoot anyone!' said the courtly Pelham, known as Steady because he was fair and polite. 'It'll all end in tears.' Steady was ever cautious: he thought just about any activity would 'end in tears'. He was plump, with a long pale face, yet he looked most benevolent. He resembled an old-fashioned, stolid, worthy, locomotive engine – slow and reliable. Everyone, especially adults, trusted Steady Pelham. 'I certainly don't think we should use LANGUAGE like that if we want to join the Dugganoes. Why make enemies?'

Ogleton, who had no fuse on his dynamite, simply threw himself across the room to grip Pelham's throat, pressing so hard on the soft bits that he left white hand-marks. The pair of them hit the polish-soiled tiles with a thump. For a moment, Ogre just banged the floor with Pelham's wriggling body in time with his words as he shrieked, 'You fuckin' thick gumby! You heard Stalin! This is a revolution and we're gonna GRAB the Dugganoes and you're gonna help us ...'

'Archie,' I snapped. 'Get Ogre off him.'

Archeamboye lifted Ogleton effortlessly off the shaken Pelham, who was stained with black shoe polish and sobbing, 'Wuss! Wuss! Temper! Temper! I'm not having anything to do with this if brutes like him are involved. That's the long and the short of it. This is supposed to be anti-bullies, for the benefit of all.' Even then, Pelham seemed ageless – he looked older than any of us. Yet it was impossible to guess his age.

'Nor me,' sniffed Weeping Wharton, whose flat brown hair perfectly framed a sallow, morose face.

Money-Banks and my fastidious Persian friend Pahlavi mumbled agreement with Pelham and Wharton. Petty, Ormonde and Ogleton stood firm – the first Stalinists.

'Bunkum,' I said. 'We're talking about Stalin. We will rule by fear.'

'Only brutal force will beat the Dugganoes. Do we want to thrash the bullying Dugganoes or not?' asked Petty.

'Of course, we do,' said Ormonde, swinging his yo-yo, which was all the rage that summer.

'This is the way we will do it. Fear and force. Stalin's way. This will be a reign of terror,' I explained patiently.

As we argued in low voices by a flickering flame, I understood, for the first time, how exciting it must have been for Stalin and the Old Bolsheviks to lead the underground life.

'Sounds pretty jolly,' said the bluff Money-Banks without the slightest irony. 'Could be quite a wheeze.'

'Petty's the one with the wheeze,' said subtle but venomous Pahlavi, who was related to the Shah of Iran, the successor of Cyrus the Great. The Pahlavis had ruled for a thousand years and no one doubted they would rule for a thousand more. The Shah was the Kublai Khan of the seventies. My mother said he was the handsomest man she had ever seen – except for my father.

'Shut up,' said Ogre, bringing gypsy eyes right up against Pahlavi's exquisite figure that was as slim as a sad brown reed. His hair was jet

31

black, his nose aquiline and he spoke the poshest English in the school. 'What does the Shah think?'

'The Shah hates Communists.'

'So you can be our Red Shah,' said Ormonde, in his tuneful, deep voice. He was the most talented of my friends: tall and strong with a refined artistic face, he could play the piano; he wrote poems and stories; sang beautifully. Yet he had a breaking voice which we thought was supernaturally strange for an eleven-year-old.

'Hope we're not going to be the First Eleven of Terror?' noted Pelham sensibly.

'No, we're not playing cricket, Steady Pelham. We're planning a revolution, destroying a class and founding a Communist empire,' said I.

'So we better start with a Politburo,' suggested Petty. 'Comrade Stalin?'

'First, I wish to be called Koba from now on. Stalin changed his named from Djugashvili to "Koba". It was the name of a heroic, young mountain bandit who defied the Russians in the nineteenth century.'

'Groovy name, Koba,' said the streetwise Ogre. He lived near me in Pimlico, but his mother worked, so he wandered around on his own, getting into trouble in Biba and Kensington Market. Ogre claimed to have shoplifted a muskrat from Harrods' pet department and urinated in the corner of Asprey the jewellers without anyone noticing: were these atrocities possible? Oh yes. Anyway, Mum called him a 'Latchkey Kid' because he was always in scrapes.

'Comrades Ormonde and Petty have some proposals,' I said. Stalin always got others to suggest things and only supported them at the end of the discussion.

Ormonde pulled out his yo-yo, extended it twice and then kept it spinning at the bottom, vibrating like a UFO, while he said, 'Comrades, you, together with Nonsuch, who's playing chess with Mr Allcock, have been elected members of the Politburo ...' Everyone admired his yo-yo grace.

'Elected?' asked Pelham.

'Yes,' I said, 'in elections throughout the democratic Communist Party.'

'Sounds like Nigerian elections,' said Archeamboye, the over-sized African with no front teeth but the most incandescent smile, who never could have found Russia on a map or spelled 'Stalin' but could crush a complete rugby team under one hand. I would have regarded his opinions with far more respect had I then known that his father, Colonel Archeamboye, was the head of the Nigerian secret police.

'But there aren't very many of us,' protested Money-Banks.

'There were only five in Lenin's first Politburo,' I explained. 'Lenin's Bolsheviks were a small, tight-knit organisation dedicated to seizing power.'

'You will also be the Central Committee,' said Petty. 'I suggest some magnifico appointments, if Koba agrees: Ormonde to be Commissar of Defence and Ogleton to head SMERSH – Death to Spies. Pahlavi should be Foreign Commissar. Pelham and Money-Banks will work in Koba's Secretariat.'

'And you, Petty,' said Ormonde, 'will be the chief of the secret police. Lenin's Iron Felix, Stalin's Yezhov and Beria will have nothing on you!'

'The OGpoo?' joked Petty. 'Magnifico!' We all laughed but he knew that it was the paramount job: Monsieur Guillotine.

'What about me? Can I be captain of rugby?' asked Archeamboye with a pathetic expression on his round, shiny face.

'You will be my Molotov, my Kaganovich, my Beria and my Malenkov!' I told them, standing on a black stool.

They looked bemused except Petty and Ormonde, who nodded sagely.

'WHO?' asked Archeamboye.

'I salute your honesty in asking,' I said. 'They were like Stalin's Keeper of Golf and Captain of Football. Stalin was both Head of School and Headmaster.'

'Oh right, I see,' said Money-Banks.

I did not know what to do with Archeamboye. So I appointed him People's Commissar for Sport and Nigerian Affairs.

The Politburo was over-excited: they each began offering their particular services.

'Let's beat somebody up – or at least terrorise them,' said Ogre. 'How about Diggle-Johnson, Grimshaw or Lamb?'

'I'm the school's best spin bowler,' said Steady Pelham. 'I'd like to spin bowl and be wicket keeper for Stalin.'

'My best pop group's Queen – can I sing Bohemian Rhapsody for the revolution?' asked Ormonde, who knew all the words.

'By 1945, even Bohemia will be in Stalin's empire,' I said.

At first, my Politburo was more interested in cricket, comics and Glam Rock music: luckily, Stalin and Glam Rock fitted well together.

Stalin enjoyed uniforms – high boots and striped trousers – and loved to have his face illuminated by searchlights. Stalinist pageantry was pure Glam Rock. Even as an old man, his daughter Svetlana recalls, Stalin liked to do the Georgian dances. He performed the flamboyant Caucasian steps – though not as exuberantly as Freddie Mercury. Stalin suited Freddie Mercury: this was one reason that Stalinism spread so quickly at Coverdale. That is one of totalitarianism's great advantages: the music's always better.

The Politburo passed all the motions. Then the bell rang so we had to go to prep.

'So when's the revolution?' asked Ogre, who wanted some Aggravation as soon as possible.

'We are following Stalin's life,' I said. 'But now it's only about 1904. The Revolution is in ...'

'1917! That's years to wait. Can't we have the revolution in about 1910?'

'No Ogre. But it'll be this term, I promise.'

'Thank God,' said Ogre. 'Anything else?'

I paused, looking around the room at the Politburo with the cubby holes filled with black shoes behind them.

'Are you all with us?' I asked.

Each said yes – even Pelham. I examined their faces by the candlelight. Pelham's kind, lumpy face looked worried.

'No aggro,' said Pelham. 'We don't need aggro to beat the Dugganoes ...'

'Maybe not,' I lied.

But then Money-Banks, dangerously innocent, asked, 'What happens if we get bored and want to do something else?'

'You can't,' I said. 'This is for life.'

'If you try and escape,' lisped Petty, jumping off his stool and walking slowly over to Money-Banks, 'my secret police will arrest you and take you down to Lubianka Prison ...'

'Lubianka is the KGB Headquarters in Moscow,' explained yo-yo Ormonde.

'And there in the boiler room, our Lubianka, I'll torture you within an inch of your life!'

'Crumbs! Long live the revolution!' exclaimed Money-Banks quickly.

I looked at their illuminated faces. Which were really my Stalinists and which were concealing Fascist or Trotskyite heresies? How could I know which was which? Vigilance was Stalin's answer. Trust no one.

Petty carried the candle out into the Kremlin.

As we marched back into the school, Petty hissed, 'So what do we need before we can revolt and overthrow Duggan and Crabbe and their Dugganoes gang of tsarist capitalist roaders?'

'Money. A million Bars and Nuggets! To buy arms.'

'Wow!' said Petty. 'The Grub Cupboard.'

8

STALIN'S DREAM

All the Bars and Nuggets were locked in the Grub Cupboard next to the Carpentry Room. The boy who managed to raid the Grub Cupboard would earn a place in pre-pubescent Valhalla.

There were stories in the mythical past of dashing bandit-schoolboys breaking into the Grub Cupboard and stealing enough Grub to last a whole term. So as our Politburo meetings became more frequent, I urged extreme vigilance to find a way to raid the Grub Cupboard which would earn me the name 'Koba'. It would give us Bolsheviks more prestige than the First Fifteen or winning a prize. And we could bribe the moronic masses to obey our orders.

'But we might get caught. What then?' asked Steady Pelham.

'*We are Bolsheviks, not schoolgirls,*' I said.

'But if we were caught, we'd be beaten,' said Money-Banks.

'We could be betrayed by someone,' said Petty.

I should have remembered that he was the first to mention Judas.

'Traitors will be crushed,' I said.

'You'd actually hurt someone?' said Petty.

'*You can't make a Revolution with silk gloves* – Stalin,' I answered.

'Wow!' said Pelham. 'Was Stalin any good at bowling?'

'Doubt it: Stalin's left arm was shorter than his right ...'

'So he could bowl with his right?' said Pelham, a stellar cricketer, earnestly.

'Possibly, Comrade,' I said, 'and he used to keep his arm like this ...' I put my left hand hanging between the buttons of my shortsleeved blue summer shirt. 'Like Napoleon. I suggest we all walk around like this from now on.'

The Politburo agreed to carry its hands like Stalin at all times.

By that time, my affair with Stalin had been going on for weeks and

36

I had read many library books on the subject. I wrote to mum and told her to go to a Communist bookshop on the Charing Cross Road and buy me anything about Stalin. The books arrived in boxes. I learned as much as I could. I memorised so many of Stalin's actual sayings that my Latin grammar went to the dogs: 'Mensa, mensam ... STALIN.' Stalinist studies seemed far more useful for real life.

There were two 'truths' about Stalin: the first was the Gospel truth that he was an evil criminal, dictator and butcher. But the second was 'the Cult of Personality' – the swanking glorification of himself that was believed by everyone in his empire. Of course, my silly comrades did not know the difference between the two 'truths'. Only I did: I enjoyed both – especially the lies.

Most parents wanted their children to be like others. But mine were delighted I read history instead of cartoons. They gave the school the credit: 'Dad thinks the teaching must be excellent to get you so interested in Russia,' said my mum. Indeed, that morning, dad telephoned Mr Holly to thank him.

The master did not know what he was talking about – though he happily accepted the credit – until our afternoon history lesson.

'Cardinal Wolsey was an evil man!' declaimed Mr Holly. 'Comment!'

There was listless silence.

'OK, chaps. Was Cardinal Wolsey an evil man or not? Lamb? Conroy?'

I stood up and said, 'Stalin was the most successful statesman of the twentieth century.'

'Stop swanking, Stalin!' whispered dear Pelham, who was far too English to understand the Cult of Personality.

'Stalin really won World War Two,' I continued, 'because he ended up with an empire that went from Berlin to Vladivostok, bigger even than the tsars'. And that empire still exists and always will. Long live Stalin!'

The whole class laughed, banged their desktops. My closest comrades-in-arms shouted, 'Long live Stalin!' which was then copied by other idiots, bourgeois elements who slavishly follow any firm leadership. The more enterprising had learned Russian phrases such as 'Za Rodinoo, Za Stalina.' This meant 'For the Motherland; For Stalin.' It was the rousing battle cry of the valiant legions during the Great Patriotic War, far more potent than 'Geronimo!' or 'Tally-Ho!'

What power I felt at times like that.

Mr Holly was fed up. Finally, he rubbed his beard like sparse stubble on a burnt field and barked, 'Sit down, Conroy, and shut up! We're discussing Henry VIII wives. What the hell's that got to do with Stalin?'

'Everything, sir. Henry VIII was the British Stalin,' I answered. 'Stalin still lives, sir. His empire is beating the West, sir. It will last FOR EVER!'

'Za Rodinoo! Za Stalina!' shouted Petty, my comrade-in-arms.

'Oh Lord,' sighed Pelham under his breath, horrified by the ostentatious enthusiasm of Stalinism, embarrassed by any rumpus.

'You'll get a black mark with another word, Conroy,' said Mr Holly.

'Wrecker!' I said. 'I'll bet you're a Trotskyite, Mr Holly!'

'That's it, Conroy. Out. I'll speak to you later. Out! Go and report yourself to Mr Trevelyan NOW!'

So out I went, heroically I thought at the time.

The things I'd do for Stalin.

Reporting oneself was like the Communist way of admitting one's mistakes in the Central Committee.

When I found Mr Trevelyan he was coming out of the common room with a tennis racket over his shoulder like a marching trooper holds his rifle. He was talking to Miss Snow and laughing: 'Absolutely splendid! Hilarious!' He was always happy: all his geese were swans.

I was pleased SHE was there when I reported myself. 'Sir, Mr Holly has sent me to admit my mistake and report myself for praising Stalin.'

Mr Trevelyan did not take my Stalinism seriously. 'Has he indeed? Stalin – eh? That wicked pinko monster! No more of this horseplay, Conroy, you rascal. If you persist, you'll be SHOT by firing squad at dawn with ICE CREAM!'

Off he trundled, leaving me with Miss Snow, who watched me. She narrowed her eyes portentously like a fortune teller at a fair.

After reporting myself, I felt omnipotent.

She was rocking her head slightly from side to side so I knew she was going to say something funny. Her face had lines when she smiled. But they were interesting lines.

'So, Conroy, is it Love?' she asked. 'Do you "amo" Stalin?'

My confidence collapsed. I could not answer. 'Love' was a word we could not utter without giggling with fear. We knew it involved beauty and magic, which was why we were so afraid of it. Was she mocking me or just enquiring? I did not quite understand. Then I remembered ...

When we arrived at Coverdale, before we started Latin, Crabbe played a trick on me.

'Hey, Conroy, you runt,' he called. 'Go up to Miss Snow and say "Amo, Miss Snow."'

I hesitated. 'What does "amo" mean?'

'Oh, it's Latin, twit. It means "hello".'

So when I saw Miss Snow, I obediently trotted up to her, followed by a gaggle of smirkers, and declaimed, 'Amo Miss Snow.'

She laughed piratically. 'You hardly know me yet. "Amo" means "I love" in Latin.'

A burst of strangled giggles, squeezed from behind hands clamped over mouths, bubbled out of my audience.

I blushed. What a scurvy trick! The shame of it!

'Don't worry,' she said. 'I'm used to it ...'

But I ran away and hid in the woods.

So at last I understood. She was trying to make a joke of it. But was she what my mother called a 'spawned woman'? Did she think I had once loved her because I said, 'amo Miss Snow'? Bitterly spawned by my affair with Stalin! My mother was uncompromising about it – a spawned woman, she said, was the most dangerous of all.

9

STALIN THE BANK ROBBER 1907

Koba Stalin led a series of daring bank robberies, or '*expropria-tions*' as he called them, on the Tiflis banks. When Lenin heard about this '*wonderful Georgian*', Stalin's career was launched.

We walked around Coverdale with our left hands in our shirts like Stalin, while we observed the security arrangements of the Grub Cupboard. It was secure. On Tuesdays and Thursdays after lunch, Emperor Blunt personally opened the Grub Cupboard and gave out the Grub. The keys stayed on the one keyring. It seemed we were foiled.

But the politician needs luck. Stalin called luck '*the God of History*'. The God of History was about to smile on me.

It was a Tuesday. As usual the first bell went at 7.10. I was then in dorm J with its ten beds. My dormitory prefect, the Captain of the School, Beaconsfield, was 'jolly d.' which meant Jolly Decent. But he was a good friend of Duggan, who was a prefect and Captain of Rugby.

On this day, I was making my bed and arranging my teddy bears when Beaconsfield came over and said, 'Walk downstairs with me to brekka, Conroy.'

'Jolly d. of you,' I said.

The Head of School definitely liked me. Once he even told me that he thought I had the springiest hair in the school – except for Mr Trevelyan. I was proud to be the favourite of Beaconsfield. The other boys stared with ill-concealed envy. I was so honoured I almost forgot I was Stalin. He often asked me to walk down to breakfast with him. But on this occasion, just as the bell for breakfast was sounding, he said, 'What's all this about you thinking you're ... Satan or someone and wanting to take on the Dugganoes?' (Freudian slip or what?)

'You'll never do it, Conroy. I always thought you were the brainiest junior. Don't be a gumby, Conroy.'

'It's a joke about Stalin, Beaconsfield. Archeamboye and Nonsuch took it seriously, but they're gumbies.'

'I don't believe you,' said the Captain of School. He had a deep voice. His thick brown hair was centre-parted. He was a real school hero – that curse of childhood: the all-rounder. For a moment, I wished I was him. 'I hear Pelham's with you. If Steady supports you, others will follow. Steady she goes!'

'Who told you about Stalin?' I asked, wondering who in the Central Committee had sneaked. That was a job for Petty and the NKVD. We would have to beat confessions out of them!

'Come on, Conroy. I can't tell you that,' laughed Beaconsfield. 'Sit beside me at breakfast.' At the door, we showed our hands to Mr Trevelyan like everyone else (palms up; palms down – this was a rule at every meal) and entered the dining hall. We filled our plates with handfuls of Rice Crispies from vats of cereal and sat at the top table in the dining hall, lined with boards of cricket teams from the nineteenth century.

Alphonse the Filipino cook, who sported a neat moustache, brought out steel plates of bacon and fried eggs. We called him 'D'Artagnan' because he fancied himself: he wore patent leather shoes and a tie pin even in the kitchen. Whenever anyone grumbled he just smiled, 'No problem,' and did nothing. D'Artagnan was always helped by the obese Liala, his Brazilian wife. She looked years older than D'Artagnan because she did all the work.

Sometimes they were accompanied by their sulky daughter, Catalina, who was a bit older than us. She was known as the Cake Maker. Catalina never said anything. But she snarled like a Latino polecat when we asked her for extra toast or more marmalade. 'Not my department. Ask Liala!'

Each table went up, phalanx by phalanx, and received the food and returned to their table. I went with the Head Boy. He was twice my height. When we had sat down again, Beaconsfield asked, 'Are you homo on Stalin?'

'I don't know,' I said. 'What happens if I am homo on Stalin?'

'I don't know what happens to homos,' said Beaconsfield. 'I don't know if it counts when you're homo on a dead Russian Communist. He is dead, isn't he?'

'Yes. He was in the Mausoleum with Lenin but that idiot Khrushchev buried him under the Kremlin Wall. That peasant was a real gumby! Brezhnev's a better Stalinist.'

'I thought you Commies supported the peasants. But Bridgewater's in your Central Committee and his father's a duke.'

'All bunkum! This Stalin thing's just a joke ...'

It was true Bridgewater's father was the Duke of something, which we knew because his name appeared as 'Lord John Bridgewater' in the School List. But class was irrelevant amongst us. Sports were what mattered: either you were a Sportsman or you were not. Our revolution was against Sportsmen not noblemen.

Sport was a question of force. Force was about power. And power was all that mattered to Stalin.

Beaconsfield looked at me gravely, ignoring my denials. Perhaps he thought I was nuts. Then he said, 'You're really brainy, Conroy. But don't be a gumby about the Dugganoes' Camp. Everyone knows fighting isn't your forte.'

A bell tolled in my mind. Professor Riazanov once said to Stalin, *'Don't be a fool, Koba. Everyone knows that theory isn't your forte!'*

Big mistake.

Once, over a glass of pepper vodka in Siberian exile – I think it was 1916 – blabbermouth Kamenev and the Polish mystic Dzerzhinsky asked me, *'Koba, what is the greatest pleasure in the world for you?'*

I puffed on my pipe. I do not know why but I answered the question with naked honesty. I later learned to be more careful. But I said, *'The greatest delight is to mark one's enemy, prepare everything, avenge oneself thoroughly and then go to sleep.'*

Later, in the twenties, they would use my honesty against me; they called this 'Comrade Stalin's Theory of Sweet Revenge'.

So Stalin had that Professor shot twenty years later. Beaconsfield had slipped up. But in some ways, the parallel was a sign of good luck.

I hated him for disdaining me. I didn't care if he was Head of School or not. I had a good mind to arrest him myself, there and then, take him down to Lubianka so Petty could hammer screws under his fingernails. Would THAT convince him of what I was capable? Or would he have to be extinguished altogether to understand my God of History?

Luckily, the cold milk on my Rice Crispies calmed me: if you listened, they actually went, 'Snap, Crackle, Pop.'

After breakfast, the Politburo, except Pelham and Money-Banks (who had to play football in the courtyard), waited outside nervously. We walked down to the Black Shoe Room. We already had our books with us. As we entered the Kremlin, I spotted something, out of the corner of my eye, shining in the grate of the drain. Instinctively I dropped my books (which included Kennedy's *Shorter Latin Course*: our second class was Imperator Blunt's Latin), crouched, picked up the key and slipped it in my pocket.

In the Politburo meeting, I told them that there was a sneak amongst us. Stalin always played one secret policeman off against another so I said, 'Comrades Petty and Ogre will both make enquiries.'

'Together?'

'No, separately. Torture if necessary.'

Then the bell rang for 'All In' and we went to lessons.

I said nothing about the key. The next bell rang. We sat at our desks and observed silence. I was chatting to Petty. Goody-goodies like Cavendish and Lamb kept saying 'Shush!' They would learn respect one day.

Then young Mr Selwyn, the shamelessly weak geography master, came in, which meant that we would have thirty-five minutes of noise and naughtiness. Mr Selwyn's distinctive feature was the biggest Adam's Apple in Christendom – we were often amazed it did not block his windpipe. He was trying to teach us about fishing ports like Billingsgate and then about what a 'bottleneck' was. So boring! Mr Selwyn pointed at me. 'Conroy, what is the Continental Shelf?'

'Sir, it's where a Frenchman puts his books!' (Laughter.) 'But I can only answer your questions if you call me by the right name.'

'What?'

'My new name, sir, is Koba as in Koba Stalin.' (Spontaneous Applause is shown in the Central Committee records here.)

Mr Selwyn was not exactly brainy, which is why he taught geography.

'Fine. How many feet is a fathom?'

'Never mind that, sir, the revolution is coming and you know what Stalin will do to your family, sir?'

'What, Conroy?'

'Koba, sir. We will shoot them all, sir!'

The master looked for help at the class: a typical ploy of degenerate Tsarism.

'Has Conroy gone mad, Money-Banks?'

'No sir, Koba is our leader, sir. Za Rodinoo! Za Stalina!'

By lunchtime I was simply dying to tell someone about the key. But I respected Stalin's Byzantine secrecy, overcoming my longing to chatter.

At lunchtime Mr Trevelyan clapped his hands and announced in his jolly bass, 'This afternoon at two: chess team goes to Sunningdale to play. Money-Banks, Nonsuch, Duggan and Lamb to go with Head of School and Mr Allcock.'

'All cock and no balls!' came a voice I knew: Ogleton of course. Everyone started laughing. Mr Trevelyan's hair went slightly electric. He clapped his generous pink hands again and went on, 'Hush! Also, Torpids play Thirds in cricket on Ground B. Mr Humphries is umpire. Lastly, we have lost a key ...'

The whole school went silent. The word 'key' could mean anything. The school was full of doors. But no boy could hear it without dreaming of the Grub Cupboard. Every boy knew, too, that to be caught raiding the Grub Cupboard meant beating and rustication, if not expulsion. The beating machine was a cane which we called Widow Twanky – Twanky for short – because it twanged as it sliced through the air. And Twanky might be wielded not by the honourable Mr Trevelyan or the senile Emperor Blunt but by that strapping Goliath, Major Hester.

'... Silence, please. There will be a reward if anyone has picked it up. A rather splendid reward.'

I flushed from head to foot. Petty hissed through his little fangs; his watery grey eyes flashed, 'I read your mind, Stalin.'

We had Silent Rest in our classes for half an hour while I thought about the key. If it had been the key to the gym or the swimming pool, Mr Trevelyan would have said so. But he deliberately did not specify WHICH key. That suggested it had to be the Grub Cupboard. Mr Trevelyan must think we Bolsheviks were sub-gumby liberals or lily-livered Mensheviks not to work that out!

10

NAKED STALIN

Streaking was the most prestigious parade of Soviet power during the rule of Stalin.

As the revolution got closer, I realised I needed to raise the stakes of my revolutionary heroism: so far, my lack of sporting prowess, dense spectacles and pockets bulging with books did not give me the panache of a hero of the working class.

'What can I do?' I asked Petty as we raked the leaves that afternoon.

Petty understood this without exactly saying so. 'I think it is time for another streak,' he said. He knew that streaking was the perfect way to do it. In Soviet Russia, the regime raised its prestige with parades of tanks and missiles. But at Coverdale, streaking was the best way, if you did not play rugger or cricket. I was already Coverdale's most famous streaker: I had twice streaked around the Snake Path without being caught.

So that afternoon, after supper, when we had our free hour, we were standing by the tennis court when Ormonde boomed in his toastmaster's voice, 'Oyez! Oyez! I dare you to streak round the Snake Path!'

'Is it sensible, Koba?' asked Pelham quietly. 'I think it might end in tears.'

But everyone else was excited. We set up a system of 'Cave' (pronounced 'KayVee!' Latin for 'Beware') to watch for masters. Then we walked past the pine trees.

I checked there were no masters around, ripped off my clothes and ran the mile around the Snake Path stark naked. It was intoxicating: the wind and the dappled sunlight on my legs and arms, my feet padding on the mud and pine needles. It reminded me of how Stalin came to love the nature of Siberia during one of his exiles ...

When I returned, I was truly Koba Stalin: the Naked Commissar.
'A fine streak,' Ormonde declared to the Politburo.

When I had recovered my breath, I gave my orders to Petty.

'Top Secret: the Central Committee orders Ormonde, Ogleton and
you to meet me exactly three hours after lights out at the loo known
as the Slippery Quagmire in dressing-gowns and slippers. Ask no
questions. We will be beaten if there's a whisper. Also I want Pahlavi
to listen at the common room at gin 'n' tonic hour to see what the
masters are talking about.'

It was time for swimming: it was stinking hot that afternoon,
especially after the running around. The Politburo wandered along to
the pool. Steady Pelham knew the secret of course: he was utterly
discreet. But he naturally warned me that the end of the adventure
would surely be 'lacrymose – that's the long and the short of it,' he
said.

Normally I hated swimming because I loathed getting my face wet.
But that afternoon was an exception. Miss Snow was on swimming
pool duty. And in the summer, we could swim naked. This meant that
every boy in the school wanted a swim because she would see them
naked.

When we jumped in, we made sure that we did so from the end
where Miss Snow stood with her arms crossed. We would go as near
to her as possible and then jump in with our legs open.

This was a Coverdale tradition started by Duggan, who authorita-
tively told us when we were Berks (second formers; new boys were
called Twits; third formers were Scallywages), 'If Miss Snow sees your
ammo boxes, she'll fall in love! That's what courtship means! If she
loves you enough, she'll forget herself and jump in after you!'

As a result of this advice, every boy jumped in repeatedly with their
legs parted and then swam up and down on their backs, hoping to
catch Miss Snow's dark eye with this primitive display. The open-
thighed Politburo performed vigorously but Miss Snow never seemed
to notice our spread-eagles.

As we dried in the changing rooms, I went over the final
arrangements. Petty pretended to shoot an imaginary bird like his
father and then, as he dried his hair, he said, 'You've got the Grub
Cupboard key, haven't you? Magnifico!'

I smiled Koba's heroic Caucasian smile and rested my hand in my
buttons. Like Stalin at Yalta.

'I wouldn't miss the revolution for anything!' said Petty. And he celebrated by twanging the elastic on his y-fronts.

11

THE RAID

It was hard trying to stay awake for three hours after Lights Out. For a while, I pretended I was Stalin lying in state. I could hear every sound: it was so quiet that each muffled creak created the vision of a vivid scene taking place far away.

I listened to the footsteps of the Orangeman walking along the top floor turning off the lights of each dorm: clip, clip, then switch. Mr Hester had the most distinctive gait in the whole empire of Coverdale: the Major marched like a drill-sergeant. Mr Fitzroy-White, the scruffy and always-smiling English teacher, had just taught us the word 'martinet', which suited this walk. The Major was a giant who took tiny staccato steps like a little man.

Time passed as painfully as swallowing cough medicine. I hoped that the elite of my Politburo would manage to stay awake for this heroic escapade.

Matron clanked along the linoleum passageway, balancing on her high-heeled brown boots. The dissonance of her white nurse's polyester coat, rubbing against itself as she walked, put my teeth on edge: swish, swish, swish. I could smell her taint – scent and skin and surgical disinfectant. We hated matron. She was useless: when Spencer-Percival almost died of a fever, she told him to get back to his rugby game. When he collapsed, she somehow never took the blame. But that was only because he lived. Still, I liked Spencer-Percival and did not want to him to die, even to show up Mato.

Mato was good friends with Mr Hester: he liked to burn out verrucas. He said it was his hobby. Even as a young Stalin, I thought that was a little odd, so I told mum who told dad who said, 'Seems a harmless enough perversion,' in his absentminded professor way.

Just before Lights Out, Pahlavi reported diligently what he had heard: he had crouched under the bushes beside Mrs Trevelyan's blushing roses, under the window of the common room. Every adult in England was discussing the strikes, the unions and the blackouts. But after much grumbling about miners and Communists, Pahlavi overheard Mr Hester ask Mr Holly, 'You're our resident historian. Who or what is this "Koba" lark?'

'No idea. Why?'

'Conroy says he wants to be called it. Something to do with the Communists,' said Young Mr Selwyn.

'Oh, right-ee-oh,' said that quaint Mr Holly. 'Must be something to do with Stalin.'

'Of course it is,' interrupted Mr Eye. 'It was Stalin's underground name.'

'How do you know that?' asked Mr Hester.

'I know about a lot of things,' said Mr Eye mysteriously. The origins of Mr Eye were such an enigma, we used to chant, 'Salvador Eye. Russian Spy.'

Then the masters had a discussion about making sure the boys washed their hands after going to the loo.

Mr Eye muttered, 'In most cases, it would be better to wash their hands before they go.'

I asked Pahlavi if that was all they talked about.

'There was one other thing.'

I raised my eyebrows.

'The Grub Cupboard key is missing. But since no one's found it, they're not going to change the lock.'

'Bingo! Hurrah for Lenin!'

This passed a few more minutes but soon my heart was beating so fast that I could not sleep – even if I'd wanted to. All the lights went out at about ten. Midnight seemed to be so far away, so remote that it was even beyond Contempt.

Finally, it was one in the morning, probably the latest I had ever been awake. I got up with the key in my dressing-gown pocket, put on my slippers. Their rubber soles squidged on the lino but I walked carefully to the door. I looked left and right.

The long corridor lined with dormitories was lit every twenty feet with a single naked light bulb. The corridor seemed luridly, murkily brown by night, so I felt like a POW escaping from Colditz. I strolled nonchalantly along, while wishing I did not have to go through with this terrifying adventure.

Until I met the others and went downstairs, I could pretend I was visiting the loo. But once downstairs, we had, as Mr Blunt put it classically, 'crossed the Rubicon' like Caesar. I did not want to encounter Twanky but I wanted power and I needed vengeance on Crabbe. I would break the back of the Sportsman class who were worse than the capitalists of the Landlord class. Stalin's Theory of Sweet Revenge, again. But I never wanted terror for its own sake. That was forced upon me by traitors ...

As I passed each dormitory, I glanced in and could see the metal beds in rows like parked tanks. I could hear the muffled breathing of dozing boys, soothing as sighing cattle, lost in their oblivion of cricket games and cowboys and Indians – or whatever Mensheviks and White Guards dreamed of.

I reached the Slippery Quagmire outside dorm F, next to the staircase that came out right beside the carpentry room – and the Grub Cupboard. The trouble was that it was also close to Mato's bedroom. Hopefully, by this time Mr Hester would have martinetted out to his own house. So the main danger was Mato.

I retreated into the Slippery Quagmire's shadowy vestibule. It lived up to its name. It was smelly because Coverdalians did not appear to be interested in target practice. As soon as I stood still, I could tell there was someone in it – probably either Marshal of the Soviet Union Ogleton, NKVD General Petty or Politburo member Ormonde. Generations of boys had made little holes in the door, which had then been filled with balls of loo paper. I pulled one of these bits of paper out and looked in.

Mato was sitting on the loo in her white nurse's coat with her painted, ravaged face and dyed red hair. But it was the bright red hair between her legs that caught my eyes. It was as red and bushy as the hair on her head. I was gobsmacked: what was it for? Why there? My brothers had never mentioned THIS.

'Crikes,' I said aloud. She looked towards the door. I froze just as a hand rested on my shoulder. It was Ogre, wearing a Batman mask around his eyes. I had to chuckle at my valiant Transylvanian. Petty was right behind him, already wheezing. His eyes shone with the ruthlessness of firing squads and thumbscrews.

'Who is it?' asked Petty.

'Mato,' I whispered. 'She's definitely a member of the Red Army. Take a look!'

Petty and Ogre were so fascinated that they pulled bits of paper out of holes to ogle at Mato: one of those moments when history might have been distracted from its destiny by a triviality.

'She's already been awarded the Order of the Red Banner!' said Petty, which showed he'd been listening to some of my lectures on Soviet society.

'She must be a secret Stalinist,' I whispered. 'Come – let's get going! Where's Ormonde?'

'He's asleep in dorm Y. I didn't go in and wake him,' said our bemasked Dick Turpin.

'Well done, Comrade. Bistro! Bistro!'

'What?'

'It means "fast" in Russian.'

We set off down the stairs. We hoped that neither Mato nor Ormonde would suddenly appear. So it was now or never.

At the bottom of the steps we swam through impenetrable darkness. We could not turn on a light. It might draw attention to us. So we felt our way forward until we came to a fire door. We opened it and crept on.

There were two wooden doors. One was the carpentry room; the other was the prize of our Great Game. The Tsar's Own Imperial Bank of Coverdale.

I tried the key. My hand was shaking so much that I could barely get it in. Then it clicked, with a deafening jolt that seemed to echo down the corridor. Once it was in, it jammed. Petty was gasping. 'It doesn't work. Let's go!' His whisper was as loud as a bark.

But suddenly the lock turned with a jerk. The door opened. I switched on the light inside.

The sight was as rewarding to us as that cave must have been to Ali Baba. The light illuminated more radiant chocolate boxes than a sweet shop. Consignments of Mars Bars, Cadbury's Milk, Marathons and Hershey Bars like chests of gold and jewels. For a second, I forgot all about Stalin and imagined myself to be the Count of Monte Cristo finding his gold after escaping from the Château d'Ife. The other two were speechless.

The three of us stepped in and ran our hands over the boxes in a fever of almost sensual joy. I remember the feel of the bars inside the glossy wrappings. Mato's Order of the Red Banner was quite obscured by the heady aroma of chocolate.

Suddenly we heard a door creak. I switched off the light and opened the door and glanced down the Long Corridor with all its classrooms. There I saw the unmistakable colossus of Mr Hester, head down, heels-a-clicking, in a black suit, Ulster regimental tie, waistcoat and watch chain, stroking his red handlebar moustache.

The Orangeman was coming straight towards us. As I watched him for that split second, I could hear Mr Fitzroy-White declaim Byron: 'The Assyrian came down like a wolf on the fold ...'

I swivelled. Closed the door. Left the key outside.

'Cave!' I whispered. 'It's Orangeman!'

'Cave!' repeated Ogleton.

'Orange Alert!' said Petty.

'Don't say a word. He might go right past.'

'I hate you, Orangeman, I hate you!' said Ogleton.

'Silence!'

'Aye, aye, Stalin.'

The footsteps of the martinet grew closer. I could imagine the spark as his metal clips struck the stone floor like dragon flies in the darkness.

Inside the Grub Cupboard, we were almost suffocating with the musk of chocolate. Petty was wheezing again like an iron lung: he wouldn't last long in Siberian exile. I nodded at Ogre, who put his hand over Petty's face so that he could not breathe at all. Miraculously, Mr Hester did not look at the Grub Cupboard door and notice it was peaking open with the key in it. He just marched straight past.

We heard him slam the front door: he was on his way to his cottage. We were alive! Ogre released the puffing Petty.

'Now listen,' I whispered. 'These are the rules. Never call it the Grub Cupboard. Call it Operation Watergate ...'

'Why?' asked Ogre.

'After that American burglary in Washington, you dolt. We must never take more than a quarter of a box at a time. That way they'll never notice that we have the key. We raid the Grub Cupboard in twos twice a week for as long as no one is suspected. We will use the Grub to bribe the Dugganoes, lead the Russian Revolution and raise an army to beat Duggan and Crabbe and those spanners Grimshaw, Danby and Minto. That's the rules. Agreed?'

The Politburo, a full quorum, nodded.

'Aye, aye, Stalin,' said Ogre, gypsy eyes wild with chocolate fumes.

'Magnifico! Where will we hide it?' asked Petty.

'I've thought of that,' said Ogre. 'Under the cowsheds.'

We took the Grub and then we locked the Cupboard and walked along past all the classrooms into the dim world of the Kremlin whose shadows we knew so well.

What a triumph for the Bolshevik Party of V. I. Lenin! We all felt it. Just past the Latin classroom, the masked Ogre started to dance, jumping into the air. We joined in, doing foxtrots and Scottish reels. Ogre leaped and smacked his bare heels together in midair, singing, 'The Grub – tra-la-la – the GRUB!'

'Shut up, Ogre – or we'll get Twanky! You'll ruin the revolution.'

We hid the booty temporarily under the cowsheds, scampering out in the spine-chilling night, before creeping back upstairs.

My Politburo, those trusted comrades, were to raid that Grub Cupboard twice a week for long enough to fund the revolution. (Not me, of course. Stalin himself had to be protected. Others were as expendable as the extras who were always killed in *Starsky and Hutch* on television.) We built up a gleaming reservoir of Grub, worth billions in the currency of Coverdale.

We had to amass our Red Guards swiftly to storm the Winter Palace of the Dugganoes' Camp – or the God of History would pass us by for ever.

The nightmare was the most terrifying I had ever had. There was a brutal, shrewd man with a black moustache, pockmarks and yellow eyes. But I was not him. Stalin was not ME.

There was a brilliant, doomed man with wild fuzzy hair and rimless spectacles and HE was me. I had an icepick buried between my ears.

He was Trotsky. I was Trotsky. The flamboyant, vain, erudite ... loser.

The enemy of the revolution. Satan.

The exile.

The dead exiled loser.

'*Trotsky is a medieval handicraftsman,*' wrote Stalin, '*imagining himself an Ibsen hero destined to "save" Russia with an ancient saga.*' Was it me?

I awoke at dawn, covered in sweat. The dorm was still fast asleep. Outside it was light. But the room was draped in a sort of blue-grey gloom as if we were sleeping under a huge blanket.

I could not sleep again. How could I avoid being Trotsky? By strength. Subtlety. Barbarism. I lay awake until Mato came in and said: 'Rise and shine!'

12

MY HERO, LENIN

Mendoza was the only person in the world, except Clint Eastwood, who could throw a cigarette up in the air and catch it carelessly in his mouth.

'So you want to hurt somebody, my little friend Stalin?' Mendoza asked in his husky voice, stretching like a tiger, putting his velvety paws behind his glossy head.

'I need some bone crushers, Comrade Lenin,' I said with machismo calculated to impress the Great Panjandrum, Mendoza.

'I'm your Lenin, am I?' he asked, making no effort to conceal his amusement. Mendoza was above everything in the school. Everyone was afraid of him.

'When Stalin was dictator, he coined the slogan STALIN IS LENIN TODAY!'

'How clever of him. You don't want to be hurt yourself?'

'Certainly not, Mendoza. But it's already October 1917. We've got to storm the Winter Palace. There will be blood.'

He opened a pack of Silk Cut with a slash of a red Swiss Army knife and did a Clint with the first cigarette. He lit it with a steel lighter. 'The fuel is diesel. Smell it. Groovy. Smoke?' He offered me the packet.

'No, dad's promised me a hundred pounds if I don't smoke cigarettes before I'm twenty-one. But of course, I smoke lawn – you know, grass every day during Odd Jobs.'

Mendoza chuckled under his breath.

'Groovy, my Stalinette,' he sighed languidly. 'All right, so you need the Bovverboys.'

'But I'm scared of the Bovvers myself. I don't know how to find them ...'

'Hush, Koba, my friend. Hush. Listen to the birds and the Bovvers will be here.'

I hushed.

Mendoza was titanic, swarthy and hirsute, even though he was only about twelve. He reminded me of Shere Khan, the tiger in the *Jungle Book*. He was especially kind to me – my protector against the Sportsmen.

Mendoza had the same natural authority as Lenin. Like Lenin, he was never a swank. When Stalin first saw Lenin in action, he called him '*a mountain eagle*'. Mendoza was my mountain eagle.

When I told him this, he laughed loudly in his fearless way and ruffled my hair with one tigerish paw.

After lunch on Tuesday, we queued up for Grub outside the Cupboard. Mendoza was waiting there for me. 'Come with me,' he said.

Mendoza glanced around and then we walked out past the cowsheds and strode straight down towards the Lake, which was Out of Bounds, like Stalin's Closed Cities. Its water was 'as green and greasy as the Limpopo river', overhung by branches that curled like an old woman's fingers. I half-expected Excalibur to rise out of its forbidden waters in the white hand of the builder of Coverdale's dead, fast-bowling son. This was beyond the Pale: the Kingdom of the Bovverboys. They fished there, fought and carried knives. Only Mendoza was friends with these vandals.

Mendoza led me into the woods until we were at the water's edge. Then he reclined on a tree trunk that hung over the water, swung his feet in the void with his buckled Italian moccasins hanging off his toes and reached into his pocket for the fags.

While I was a Man of Steel before my comrades, I was a mere pupil and disciple before this Clint Eastwood-tiger-Lenin. Lenin never put on airs, never humiliated anyone and was happy to take criticism because he could win by argument. Mendoza was like that too. That was when we began to talk revolution. He listened, patiently holding the fag in one hand and a little radio in the other.

'So you want to storm the Winter Palace of Duggan's Camp?'

'Yes, my mountain eagle.'

Mendoza blew the blue smoke out of his nose. He smiled, as if to say that he was too grown-up to play Camps, but too kind-hearted to put me down. How I worshipped my Lenin.

'You need muscle to beat Duggan and Crabbe. Who's on your side?'

I told him about the Central Committee. He ignored drips like Petty and Money-Banks but approved Archeamboye, Ogleton and Steady.

'You have to pay Bovvers like Colonel Callan's mercenary army. Would you like this?'

He reached into his pocket and rakishly pulled out a banknote, scrumpled like a handkerchief. When I looked at it, it was £100! I had never seen such a big note. Even dad only had £50 notes. It must have been from his dad's casino in Marseilles.

'Do the Bovverboys like Grub?' I asked.

Mendoza sat up on the branch. 'Of course, but it will take more than a few Nuggets to buy a Bovver army.'

I was so proud. I did not hesitate to trust Mendoza. I said, 'I have boxes and boxes of Grub. I have raided the Grub Cupboard every day for the last few weeks.' I handed him back his £100.

'You are a dark horse,' he said. What a fantastical compliment from a boy raised by bodyguards in a casino in Marseilles!

He turned up his radio. I remember distinctly that it was playing the most fascinating and occultish song by David Bowie called 'The Man Who Sold the World'.

Then I heard a twig snap. The Bovvers were there. Two of them. I was scared of them. I backed towards Mendoza. Almost fell in the Lake.

But Mendoza did not move. He just ignored them until the song was over and then turned the radio down. They watched him in silence until he was ready. They did not pay the slightest attention to Stalin.

The Bovvers were probably Mendoza's age but they were creatures from another world, like Red Indians in a cowboy film. They wore earrings, army boots, T-shirts, blue jeans and denim jackets. Their denims were groovily faded. My jeans were never faded. How did they do it?

Both smoked cigarettes. One of them was the fattest boy I have ever seen. Gross actually, really gross. In his hand, he carried a big bag of salt and vinegar crisps. He had a plaster on his nose which was red and upturned like a sunburned pig. His ears were at right angles to his head.

The other was the leader. He was slim and tall with high cheekbones, brown hair that hung in his eyes. He had thin lips but his most striking feature was eyes of the deepest, brightest azure. They were the most beautiful eyes I had ever seen.

Mendoza nodded towards the boss of the Bovverboys.

'This is Barry. Barry Blue-Eyes. That's what I call him,' said Mendoza. 'And Jug Ears.'

'Heya!' said Barry. 'What's 'iz name?' He had a very different accent from ours: rough.

'Meet Koba Stalin,' said Mendoza, gesturing at me (it was so kind of him not to call me Conroy).

My Lenin tossed them each another cigarette which they lit with Blue-Eyes' lighter.

'What happened to your nose, Jug Ears?' asked Mendoza, who was not remotely afraid of them.

'Got into a punch-up with Darren's boys.'

'Fancy a fight with some Coverdalians?' asked Mendoza.

'Always nice to punch up some snobs,' said Barry, but then he smiled and nodded towards Mendoza. 'We don't count 'im as a snob. But we don't know about you, Señor Stalin.'

'He's a Communist,' said Mendoza.

'Yer what?' said Jug Ears as his trotter-fingers stuffed crisps into his gob. It was so cavernous you could toss a cauliflower into it – like feeding hippos at the zoo.

'It would cost ya,' said Barry.

I stepped forward, trying to speak as much like Mendoza as possible. 'I can pay ...' Here I paused for effect. '... Chocolate. Pure chocolate.'

Jug Ears cocked his walrus head. 'What sorta chocolate?'

'Mars, Flakes – you name it.'

Blue-Eyes and Jug Ears turned around and whispered to each other. Then they came back and Blue-Eyes said, 'Twenty Mars for me and twenty Cadbury's Fruit 'n' Nut per mercenary.'

'That's a lot,' I pretended.

'Half before and half after,' said Mendoza.

'Deal!' said Blue-Eyes, offering his hand. I gave mine and he slammed his into it. Useful comrade, that Barry Blue-Eyes.

'So what 'ave we gotta do?' asked Jug Ears.

I hesitated for effect again.

'This is the Russian Revolution. Tomorrow afternoon, we're going to storm the Winter Palace.'

'Winter Palace?' said Jug Ears. 'Sounds like the place me mum goes to play bingo.'

13

OCTOBER 1917 – THE RUSSIAN REVOLUTION

At precisely 0200 hours, Archeamboye, who was as big as an oak tree, yawned open his abyss of a toothless mouth and let rip a cry of revolutionary savagery. He threw Duggan out of his way and led his Red Guards towards the Winter Palace, waving a red flag.

'1917,' he shouted at the top of his Kilamanjaro-sized lungs. 'All Power to the Soviets!' The Dugganoes suddenly realised that this was no ordinary game of Hanks and Ties: it was a revolutionary coup d'état. Ogre, Ormonde and the rest of the Red Guards followed at a run, pelting the defenders of the Palace with a deadly fire of pine cones and stones. Ogre, running low on the ground, black eyes like Dervish pebbles, was a particularly fearsome sight. Unlike Petty and I: we followed nervously behind them, running from tree to tree, shouting the bravest slogans, then hiding again.

'Hanks and Ties' was the perfect cover. It is a team game that we used to play in the Camps. One side had white handkerchiefs hanging out of their pockets; the other side had ties. If you were a Tie you tried to grab your enemy's Hank. If you succeeded, he became a Tie too and joined you to hunt Hanks.

Archeamboye challenged the Dugganoes that morning to a gargantuan game: Dugganoes versus the Rest. If I had asked, Crabbe and Duggan would just have laughed at a presumptuous Cabbage but they suspected nothing about Archeamboye, a rugby ace and future Blood.

As usual the game began at the edge of the Outback. The Dugganoes ran off into the woods to hide. We waited briefly then returned to the grass tennis court.

It was an idyllic day for a Revolution: I had never seen Coverdale looking so green and beautiful, a sorcerer's palace in a magical forest.

Soon our Communists were milling, awaiting orders. But coups are always chaotic affairs ...

Crabbe did not follow the others: he stayed right with us, hopping around us with the swinging rhythm of a dancing ape. He never got too close, like Cassius Clay. Sometimes he actually waved his Hank in our faces. I sent Ogleton after him but they never locked horns, just shadow-boxed, bush to tree.

Archeamboye seemed to have forgotten why we were there and suddenly shouted, 'Let's chase 'em into the woods.'

Then Archie charged off into the Outback, followed by Money-Banks and Bridgewater. This was exactly what he was not supposed to do – the fool. I sent Petty over to get him back with a written order from the Central Committee that even he would understand: 'Comrade Archie: return at once to storm Winter Palace. Or the OGPU will torture you in Lubianka. Central Committee Secretary. Stalin.'

Archeamboye was running into the bracken in pursuit of Duggan when Petty finally caught up with him, wheezing of course. Comrade Archie was still almost illiterate. He paused to read it. 'Not the OGpoo!' he said.

Duggan ran up and grabbed it and ran off into the woods.

'Get back to the tennis green, you gumby,' spat Petty. 'You might have blown it already.'

Archeamboye burst into tears. 'I didn't mean to spoil Stalin's plans. Really I didn't ...'

Petty slapped his face with his leather gloves, which he insisted on wearing even on such a hot summer day. 'Then get back to Koba, you dunce!'

Archie, our version of Stalin's T-34 tank, turned and thundered at such velocity through the bracken and rhododendrons that he brought half the forest with him. This marauding elephant emerged onto the tennis courts with branches and leaves sticking out of his hair. He left a tunnel through the undergrowth. But Duggan, another Blood, his Hank flying like a flag from the pocket of his shorts, was close behind him, waving my written order, shouting, 'They're attacking the Dugganoes. Get back, Hanks, get back!'

I could hear them coming back from every direction in the Outback, so I screamed, 'Battleship Aurora: FIRE! FIRE! Ogre, Archeamboye, Ormonde, STORM THE WINTER PALACE!'

This order was greeted by high-pitched laughter from the young spectators. There were now at least thirty-five boys ruining the grass on the tennis courts – there was no enclosing fence. Most of them were Twits, Berks and Scallywags, whom we had invited to witness a 'historical event' and later provide cannon fodder for the Red Army. This might have been a little optimistic. We had also invited 'fellow travellers' like goody Lamb, Spencer-Percival and that craven bed-wetting liar, Diggle-Johnson (who claimed his uncle had been at the real Winter Palace in 1917).

That was when Archeamboye gathered himself, threw his arms around Duggan and literally tossed him aside. We all followed through the breach. As I scampered along behind, watching Arche-amboye's huge bottom filling his baggy white shorts, I thought breathlessly, 'This is It. We'll be in power by teatime!'

The pine cone hit me in the chin and I was down. Petty was hit too and was crying like a girl. It was pathetic. For a second, I could not see out of my eye. I'll wear an eye patch just like Moshe Dayan!

I was staggering around in no-man's-land. I was hit repeatedly by slingshots all over my body, especially my legs. They flew like arrows, stung like hell. I crawled behind a tree, rubbing the weals. When I looked ahead, I could not really understand what was happening.

Archeamboye, Nonsuch and even Ogleton retreated past my tree, running to escape. It was a rout. I did not want to be captured by Crabbe's boys. I retreated after the Red Guards, leaving the weeping Petty rocking himself in a bush. Wharton started to wail ...

'Told you it'd end in tears,' muttered unflappable and terminally sensible Pelham from his hideaway in a bush.

The Dugganoes' White Guards, at least twenty of their toughest, sharpest shooters, were pouring out in pursuit. They were disciplined and stopped every five yards to throw spears and shoot their slings like extras in one of Cecil B De Mille's biblical extravaganzas. All against the Geneva Convention; but this was war.

The revolution was over before it had begun. Back on the tennis lawn, I tried to regroup but cowards like Money-Banks and Bridge-water fled. Wharton did not stop running until he was in Siberia. They were not real Bolsheviks: they just wore the mask. They were probably White Guards, Mensheviks, British Imperialist spies, wreck-ers, Trotskyites, revanchists – or at least one of the above. But I said nothing then. I was not yet powerful enough.

Ogleton was so angry that he was throwing golf balls at the White Guards until he was hit in the face with a pine cone inkbomb. It made him look like an ancient Briton wearing woad.

Duggan stayed inside the Palace to lead its defence; the White Guards gave chase to my motley forces and their champion, Crabbe, stood on the lawn, with a dustbin lid shield, spears and slings, flanked by Minto, Danby and Grimshaw brandishing his riding crop.

'Snubs to you drips, happy spastics, odd jobsters,' screamed Crabbe. 'Hard cheese, you Cabbages! Come and get me! Right here! Now! You red bastards!'

Crabbe, the magnificent swaggart with his short hair, his bulging forehead and his biceps, terrified me.

There was only Archeamboye and Nonsuch left now. Archeamboye could look after himself, even against Crabbe and his henchmen, but Nonsuch was as much of a wimp as I was. He was even thinner and even fairer, though his hair was straight, almost like a girl. But he was devoted to me – and Stalin. His father was Admiral Nonsuch, a dashing man with twinkling eyes who took Nonsuch and me to the Royal Tournament every year. Now, poor Nonsuch, who tried to play rugby even though he was built for Odd Jobs, was taking one hell of a beating – our first martyr!

Minto and Danby tackled Archeamboye from different directions, hanging onto his elephantine frame like Lilliputians. He tottered and then fell. They lay on the beached whale, hitting him. Crabbe cornered Nonsuch, crouched, grasped one ankle with one hand and just pulled it away so hard that Nonsuch landed on his back. Crabbe tortured Nonsuch, putting handfuls of mud in his face. Grimshaw went from one to the other with his riding crop, thrashing them across the face and legs, saying, 'Little Communist bastards!' Slash. 'Bolsheviks!' Slash.

Nonsuch's crying was so shrill that Crabbe took an ugly pine cone and stuffed into his mouth. It made him retch.

I managed to get Ogleton to join Ormonde and me under a rhododendron bush at the edge of the Outback. If necessary, we would have to go underground in Siberia. Petty had been captured too and was being tortured by Duggan in the Winter Palace itself.

'Mr Trevelyan's coming!' whispered Ogre.

Mr Trevelyan was cheerfully striding up from the school in his baggy cords, hair bouncing like a haystack being used as a trampoline. The Headmaster was keeping watch over Camps that afternoon.

'Cave! Cave!' hissed Ogre.

Duggan, presiding over our destruction, saw him too. He jumped up, whispered at his gang and everyone threw their weapons into the bushes and stood up. Even Archeamboye and Nonsuch pretended to be sunbathing (which was hard because Nonsuch still had the pine cone stuffed in his mouth).

Mr Trevelyan said, 'All right, scoundrels?' He always called us that. 'Everything all right?'

'Yes, sir,' said Crabbe. 'Who's winning the match, sir?'

'The First Eleven's winning against Sunningdale WITH FLYING COLOURS!' The Headmaster looked at all the Berks, Twits and Scallywags: 'Why are you chaps milling? No loitering, scoundrels! Play cricket or look after your gardens! Stop ragging, you swinish multitude! Cease mooching!'

The Twits, Berks and Scallywags shuffled over towards Gardens and pretended to admire their radishes, tilling the soil purposefully with their trowels.

'What are you doing on the grass?' Mr Trevelyan asked my comrades.

'Sunbathing,' said Archeamboye bravely.

'Why has Nonsuch got a pine cone in his mouth?'

'He's hungry, sir,' said Crabbe with a demonic gleam in his eye.

'Take it out of your mouth, Nonsuch!' shouted Mr Trevelyan.

Archeamboye took it out, still striking a sunbathing pose. 'Have you been crying, Nonsuch old chap?' The Headmaster had a tender heart.

'No, sir,' said that Komsomol* hero.

'Are you hungry, Nonsuch?'

'Yes, sir,' said Nonsuch, spitting out bits of pine. 'When's tea?'

'In an hour, scoundrels,' said Mr Trevelyan gaily, heading back, via the farm, towards the playing fields. He loved watching the cricket and took team selection as seriously as the scriptures. We disappeared into the rhododendron bush and watched his feet go by, just a yard from us. He was humming 'Merrie England':

* Komsomol was the acronym for the Communist League of Youth in the USSR.

> There'll always be an England
> And England will be free
> If England means as much to you
> As England means to me.

The moment he was out of sight, Duggan and Crabbe jumped back onto their Bolshevik victims and stuck the pine cone in poor Nonsuch's mouth again. The Berks, Twits and Scallywags threw down their spades and ran back to watch.

'Oh well,' I said. 'It's over.'

I admit that I thought the October Revolution was not going to happen at Coverdale.

'Never mind,' said Ormonde. 'It was rather ambitious anyway.'

'Let's go back, listen to some tapes and I'll smash Crabbe's face in another time,' said Ogre.

The woods vibrated and the bushes rustled as the Dugganoes hunted for us, beating the nettles and bracken methodically: 'Bolshy manhunt! Bolshy manhunt!' they chanted.

'... Crabbe said he wanted to teach that Cabbage Conroy a painful lesson,' said one.

'And what about Petty?'

'Can't you hear him crying? Spanker's gonna whip him.'

'Golly. Where are they? Do you see anything?'

I was truly terrified: the skirmishes in the Camps always seemed as real to us as true war. The pain if you were hit or shot with a catapult was as petrifying as death and as close to it as we could imagine. That was why the revolution – and all that came after it – was as real as we knew.

The White Guards were so close now. We did not move in our bush. We did not speak. I barely dared breathe.

'If they catch us,' whispered Ogre. 'We don't run. We fight.'

'Hang on,' said Pelham. 'If we run now, we'll get away. Maybe October 1917 isn't the right time for the Russian Revolution. It'll end in tears.'

'That was what Zinoviev said. But Lenin disagreed. And Lenin was right. Then – as always.'

'Oh all right,' sighed Steady. 'But I still wonder if it's sensible ...'

They were ten feet behind us. I glanced out front towards the Outback and saw something that suddenly changed everything: a hand was raised from a bush wielding a knife. I had quite forgotten the Bovvers. I raised my tie and waved it.

There were seven Bovvers: a blood-curdling sight! They ran across the Gardens, leaping over the allotments; the Twits and Berks jumped out of their way. Jug Ears cavorted like a ballet dancer who had swallowed a Zeppelin. They had cleverly put on balaclava helmets – Coverdale's own Black September terrorists. They turned the battle like Marshal Blucher's Prussians at Waterloo.

The Bovverboys' orders were to smash anyone wearing a Hank who did not surrender – pronto!

They sprinted straight across the tennis court towards Duggan and Crabbe. The Grand Dukes of the Dugganoes looked up at them more with surprise than anything else. They were expecting us. Duggan and his Commander-in-Chief, Crabbe, left their victims to Spanker Grimshaw and headed towards the Bovvers.

'It's Cabbage Conroy and Asthma Iron Lung,' shouted Crabbe. 'Take your masks off, you Red cretins. You're not going to win the Camps that way. Long live the Dugganoes!'

The Bovvers did not understand this. But it sounded like aggravation. They loved fighting. But being Bovvers they did not fight with fancy sticks and twee pine cones like Coverdalians. They only used knives and fists.

They ran straight at Duggan and Crabbe. Jug Ears swung his fist right at Crabbe's face and then headbutted him. I heard the crunch. Blood shot out of Crabbe's already shapeless nose all over the tidy grass of the tennis lawn. Crabbe hit the net post with a thump. Jug Ears leaped on top of him, winding him outright, and went on punching him in the face. But Crabbe got up again, roaring like Rasputin rising from the dead. Several of the Bovvers fell on him: one had his switchblade out and slashed him across the face.

'Oh, s'truth!' I gasped. 'Oh dear.'

'The gods are thirsty,' laughed Ogre, smacking his lips. Then he quoted Stalin at me: 'You can't make an omelette without breaking eggs.'

Duggan and Barry Blue-Eyes rolled around until the Bovver swung a right and knocked him clean out. I feared he might have killed him. The third Bovver had got hold of Minto. Another was holding a knife to Danby's throat before throwing him aside like a sack of potatoes.

'Time of our lives! Let's scram,' said Barry Blue-Eyes. The Bovvers were just about to leave – without having even penetrated the Palace itself. 'Scram, Jug!'

Just then, an alarum was raised in the Dugganoes: they probably thought this was just another suicidal frontal assault by my Red Guards. Out they came in their Hanks, bearing sharpened spears and catapults, pelting the Bovvers with ink-bomb pine cones and stinging conkers.

The Bovvers' New Model Army formed up and ran at them with their daggers flashing in the sunlight: what a noble charge! When they reached the White Guards, they were angry and hurt from the barrage. They punched, beat with sticks and fists and slashed with their little knives with the bestial ferocity of Marshal Budyonny's Red Cossacks.

This was no time to hesitate. I jumped out and shouted, 'ALL POWER TO THE SOVIETS!' My Politburo ran forward.

'There's the Bolshevik Cabbage! There he is! Get him!' said the Dugganoes, who were close to catching us. But when they saw the Bovvers, they turned tail into the woods.

Archeamboye and Nonsuch were the first in and they came out with Petty waving his black gloves, as happy as those hostages from Entebbe. We ran across the green, past the bleeding Crabbe, towards the Winter Palace.

Knocking a few dazed Dugganoe camp followers out of our way, we charged over the ramparts and through the doorways into the once-impregnable stronghold.

Their weapons lay where they had abandoned them. One White officer was even boiling himself a cup of tea with one of those portable water-boilers in a mug. The water was still warm. It was only when we got there that I noticed that the Bovvers had disappeared. I ran out past the cheering Scallywags (they always support the winning side) and saw Barry Blue-Eyes on the edge of the fields that led round to the Lake. He bowed elaborately, wrist flopping like a French dandy – and then leaped over the fence.

The Duggan-Romanov dynasty was no more.

14

CIVIL WAR 1918–20

I could almost hear dogs barking, louder and louder – 'Stalin! Stalin! STALIN!' as the Cabbages hunted the Bloods. It was strangely satisfying for a wimp to run the Sportsmen to ground. We caught them one by one, Danby, Minto, Grimshaw, in the wilds of Siberia and the marches of the Crimea, just as the Bolsheviks defeated the White Armies of Kolchak and Wrangel. But that is what a revolution is all about. Justice – and vengeance. The Age of the Sportsman was over at Coverdale.

We led the three naked White warlords back into the Outback to the place further down the Ravine called the Rubbish Dump. The Dump was thirty feet below: a heap of old food, grass and branches, decomposing horribly in a steaming pile. Archeamboye and Ogre set up a plank and managed to jam it under the pythonic tree root of the fine tree we called the Corinthian Pillar. Archeamboye checked it was strong enough to bear his own Sherman tank tonnage.

We formed a revolutionary troika of the Extraordinary Commission – the Cheka that later became the KGB. Just like in 1918. We tried the tsarist counter-revolutionaries for crimes against humanity, the workers and our Soviet state. They were sentenced to walk the plank.

They walked it all right. Starkers. When Spanker Grimshaw hesitated on the edge, Ormonde gave his yo-yo an elegant 360 degree 'round the world' and hit him on the cheekbone, sending him flying. Their bodies fell like dolls. When they landed they squelched like a finger in goo: pop goes the weasel! So that was the end of the Russian Civil War.

Back at the Dugganoes, half the school was milling. We paraded our stinking prisoners through the jeering crowd, naked and covered in mould, baked beans and dog shit. Then we let them scamper back into the Outback to get their clothes. The whole swinish multitude wanted to join the Communist Party.

'If Pelham's a Communist, then I'm joining,' I heard one Scallywag say to another. We renamed the Dugganoes 'Stalingrad'. We named other camps 'Leningrad' (beside the chapel), 'Kiev' (near the cow-sheds) and of course 'Stalino', 'Stalinsk', 'Stalinabad' ...

Pelham, whom everyone so admired for his lack of vanity and his plain speaking, was beside me, waving at the crowd. But Steady was already worried about hurting people. 'Is this cruelty necessary?' he said quietly, beetling his brow.

'The Civil War wasn't romantic like the Revolution, Steady. It was an insane bloodbath.'

'Not good,' said Pelham.

'But it's over now.'

When he heard that, he smiled. I was proud of his popularity. It helped the revolution.

Crabbe and Duggan were not mortally wounded, but they were still lying, bleeding profusely on the green, trying to get attention. But no one understood what they had seen. No one could identify the Bovvers. No one was really sure if they were Bovverboys at all. Ignoring the wounded, I addressed the Scallywags and other waverers like Lamb, Diggle-Johnson, Spencer-Percival.

'Workers, you have witnessed the Coverdalian Revolution and Civil War. My name is Stalin. Welcome to our Socialist Workers' Paradise! Our Stalinist-Leninist Soviet empire. From now on, every one of you has equal rights. Never again will sports brutes like Duggan or Crabbe lord it over us, fellow workers. The Sportsmen will be destroyed as a class. From now on, all Camps will be a single Soviet Union ruled democratically by a Politburo and Central Committee, protected by our brave Red Army and noble Extraordinary Commission of secret police. Long live Lenin! Long live Stalin! Long live our Soviet Union!'

Surprisingly, the wavering Scallywags listened to this propaganda with credulous joy. Several times, the Official Soviet Archives show that I was interrupted by 'spontaneous applause'. I don't suppose they understood much. But they had seen Duggan and Crabbe beaten up and they trusted Pelham. I was under no illusion: terror alone would force the enemy to allow us to create a proletarian dictatorship on behalf of the masses.

'What a performance, Conroy!' declared a deep voice with an accent we never managed to place.

'Eek! Salvador Eye; Russian Spy!' exclaimed Lamb, unaware of the danger. The Scallywags giggled.

'Shut it,' I whispered, suddenly sweating. They went quiet.

There, under a tree on the Flower Walk towards Kiev, stood our fierce French master, Mr Salvador Eye, wearing a brown checked suit and a wide-brimmed white fedora hat. Over seventy years old but tall, broad and exotic, his black eyes burned through glinting round specs. His bald head had square sides with a brown dome rising on top like a mosque in one of the holy cities of Islam. Coverdale's Molotov had a grey moustache and a pointed goatee beard. Mr Eye really did have the air of an Old Bolshevik.

Luckily, he could not have seen Duggan and Crabbe, nor their besmeared naked henchmen marched through the Gardens. But I worried that he would walk over and see everything. I broke off my speech in the middle and gave the podium to Ormonde, who sang Queen's Bohemian Rhapsody, Number One in the hit parade. The Scallywags sang along to the operatic bits: 'Scaramouche, scaramouche ...'

'Come here, Conroy,' Mr Eye shouted. 'Run, boy!'

'Salvador Eye; Russian Spy,' said I under my breath. Then I ran.

A bridge of pinched skin crumpled across the top of his nose giving him a permanent scowl. In French he pulled our ears if we got something wrong. He revelled in teaching us risqué Gallic phrases like 'coup de foudre' and 'boeuf bourguignon'. 'La vice anglaise' became my favourite tool in carpentry lessons.

When I reached him, he courteously raised his fedora. There was a bright white dash of pigeon shit splattered across his head. Mr Eye's head seemed to be as accurately hit by pigeons as the target of the SMARTest intercontinental missile. It was most unusual to see Mr Eye's dome without a dash of birdshit. He never wiped it off. He believed it was lucky. When I saw it, I fought an irresistible urge to laugh hysterically. Not a good idea, since Mr Eye was a pedagogic grenade with a devastating explosive range.

'What the devil are you doing, you fool?' he shouted, as he replaced his hat. 'Are you holding a revolution, you childish numbskull?'

'Yes, sir. Mr Eye, we've seized power. It's October 1917 and I am

Stalin, sir. Luckily, there isn't really a Trotsky. So I am poised for supreme dictatorship.'

'The attack on the Winter Palace was orchestrated by Lenin and Trotsky. But the role of Stalin was dubious. Trotsky was the genius. He described Stalin as *the most eminent mediocrity in the Party*" – "*the gravedigger of the Revolution*".'

'That's hard to take, sir. I've thought about it a lot. One day, sir, I'll have to destroy Trotsky and rewrite the history books.' I hoped if I kept him talking, he would not notice Crabbe bleeding on the tennis court.

'Posterity must believe it was you – and you alone – who made the Revolution. Conroy, who were those ruffians in balaclavas? Who were you fighting? Duggan? If you are involving outsiders in your games, you will be expelled. Or as your hero might put it, "liquidated as an enemy of the People". Do you know what that means, Conroy?'

I shook my head.

'It means the day you go, no one will ever mention you again. No one will recall you. You will be a Non-Person. It will be as if you had never existed.'

'Sir, I'm a mere disciple of our great teacher, Lenin. What happens to me does not matter.'

'Are you crazy, Conroy?'

'No, sir. But I'm besotted with Stalin.'

Mr Eye's scowl throbbed. I feared a grievous punishment was coming. So I flattered him with an irresistible compliment. 'Sir, we Bolsheviks regard you as the Molotov of our revolution!'

I could not guess his reaction but he gave an undertaker's smile. 'Ah, Molotov the Hammer. You're a most unusual boy, Conroy ...'

I always suspected him of being a Bolshevik of some sort. In lessons, he'd point at Bridgewater and say, 'Dolt! Your family owns half London – how dare you be so STUPID as to not even know the French for WINDOW!'

'You don't understand the remotest iota about the tragedy and evil wrought by Stalin, but you will. I came looking for you to give you a present.'

'What, sir?'

He reached into the scarlet silk lining of his jacket and pulled out a book. He handed it to me. It was called *Conversations with Stalin* by

Milovan Djilas. I had heard of it, of course. But I was so happy to have it.

'Thank you. What a lovely present, sir.'

Mr Eye raised his hat, turned around and walked off without saying a word.

'Sir,' I said. He stopped. 'Sir, will you one day tell me about your life?'

Mr Eye looked back for a moment. 'No, little Koba,' he said. 'You're too much the egotistical child to hear my life. But suffice it to say that I have seen things in faraway places that would have shown up your games for the grotesque satires of reality that they are. Good afternoon.'

When I opened the book, Mr Eye had written in it: 'To the KOBA of COVERDALE.'

15

THE POLICE STATE

'Knives at Coverdale! What a sign of the times! England's in decay. Blackouts and three-day weeks. Strikes of miners and rowdies on the streets,' Mr Trevelyan said. 'Britain'll be like America before we know it. Knives at Coverdale! Perhaps we'd better ban Camps.'

Pahlavi and I were listening outside Mato's Surgery after tea that triumphant afternoon. Luckily, Bolsheviks like Bridgewater and Archeamboye had been hurt too so it could not be all our fault.

'Crabbe needs stitches,' said Mato. 'We've got four broken noses – that's Duggan, Crabbe, Minto and Grimshaw. Poor Harry Nonsuch and Gladstone Archeamboye look as if they've been whipped with a riding crop. Bridgewater, oh dear, and Petty is having an asthmatic attack ...'

'Bloody mayhem! We're going to have to watch the Camps more closely after this!'

I heard Petty accelerate his wheezing. Petty was the only boy in there: the others were in sick bay.

'Are you all right, old boy? Lady Petty – your mum's been on the phone. You can call her later. Mato, Mrs Duggan and Mrs Crabbe have been on the phone. The Mintos are in Barbados,' said Mr Trevelyan, checking off the names. 'I've had to call the police. We've got to investigate this.' Then he rounded on Petty: 'Who the devil were those yahoos with knives?'

Petty at once suffered another life-threatening asthmatic attack.

But the police! I went to see Mendoza who was smoking at the Lake. I was worried. But Mendoza, my tiger-Clint-Lenin, clicked his fingers and said, 'Beautiful, careless and neglectful mothers will make a fuss for a whole hour and then sashay off to their drinks parties. Fall back

into the adulterous arms of their lovers. Dogs bark. The caravan
moves on. Besides, Stalin had nerve, didn't he?'

What an exotic and wicked world he inhabited!

But it did not take Mr Trevelyan long to learn more details from the
Scallywags about his 'Yahoos in balaclavas'.

One Scallywag told the masters that Petty and I had hired a hit
squad of Bovverboys.

So that evening, during prep, Mr Trevelyan came into my class and
said, 'Conroy, will you come to my study, please?'

The word 'study' was pregnant with doom: not the Twanky! Ogre
fiendishly concentrated on his work. Even noble Pelham lowered his
eyes. But I felt their pitying gaze as Mr Trevelyan waited for me at the
door. He led the way. His hair had never been more electric.

I feared that the adventure had been betrayed: suppose he had
learned about the Grub Cupboard and the Bovvers? I would be beaten
and expelled. When I thought about my whole future life being
ruined, my stomach danced a giddy tango and I wanted to be sick.

We passed the Grub Cupboard but he did not glance at it. Mr
Trevelyan's study was reached through his drawing-room in the
Inner Sanctum. It looked out onto the chapel. Behind the door, there
were three shelves of books. On the top shelf rested Widow Twanky
with her silver handle.

Imagine my relief to see another man in the room: he was grey-
haired and middle-aged, much older than Mr Trevelyan, and he wore
a grease-stained anorak and brown slacks. His puce face reminded me
of a orang-utan's glands on a nature programme. He smelled of damp
fag ends and plastic car seats. But he had a sort of indestructible force
about him.

'This is the boy in question,' said Mr Trevelyan. 'His name is
Conroy. He is eleven.' He looked at me. 'Sit down, Conroy.'

I sat on the leather sofa. The Headmaster remained standing behind
the desk. He crossed his arms.

'My name is Inspector Arthur Dawson of Dorchester,' said the heap
of a man, sitting beside me on the sofa. The leather squelched like a
fart. If he had not been a policeman, I might have got the giggles. He
had a juicy Dorset accent that made me think of haystacks, cider and
Tess of the d'Urbervilles. 'I just want to ask you a couple of questions
about this afternoon.'

'Answer his questions, Conroy. You know that several Coverdalians were hurt this afternoon by boys whom we think were from the town. Since it involves outsiders and ... a knife—'

'At least one knife,' interrupted Inspector Dawson. 'Excuse me, Headmaster.'

'Thank you, Inspector. Yes, a knife. Or more than one knife. So we had to tell the police,' said the Headmaster, who, I could tell, was secretly ashamed of calling in outsiders.

I felt guilty because I so liked him. But the revolution was progress. Headmasters and imperial police were bound to be in cahoots.

'Right, lad,' said Inspector Dawson. 'Which football team do you support? Like Manchester United, I'll bet? A stonker of a team, eh? Roy of the Rovers and all that?'

I raised my eyebrows. Silly grown-ups always think they can soften up children with idiotic questions in comic-strip jargon.

'I hate football,' I said.

'So what are your hobbies, son? Cricket? Comics? Making Airfix models of planes? Come on, admit it: you live for soccer, eh? Where do you like to play? Goalie or are you a centre forward?'

There was silence.

'Does the name ... Stalin mean anything to you, Inspector?'

'No. Who does he play for?'

'Stalin. Josef Stalin,' I said slowly, like 'Bond. James Bond.'

The Inspector cocked his head. His eyes flicked over to meet the Headmaster's and then returned to mine. 'Oh right. Yes. I know the fella you mean.'

'My hobbies are Lenin and Stalin, revolution, secret policemen, mass murderers and international Communism.'

Mr Trevelyan was leaning on his hands. The Inspector looked at me for a long time. Then he said briskly, 'I'll try to be quick. One: you were at the tennis lawn this afternoon and you saw what happened.'

'Some of it, Inspector, sir.'

'Who were the Yahoos, Conroy?' ejaculated the Headmaster.

'Let him answer, Mr Trevelyan, please. Well, did you see the boys who were not from the school?'

'It all happened very fast. All I remember was seeing some boys in masks scarpering. I know Duggan was hit but I didn't see anything.'

'You know, son, that telling lies to the police is against the law.'

'Oh, yes, sir.'

'All right, so you saw nothing but you accept that these boys might be from the town?'

'Seems a bit unlikely, sir. I mean why would Bovvers want to play Hanks and Ties?'

'Bovvers?' asked Inspector Dawson.

Mr Trevelyan interpreted, 'Oh Inspector, it's the boys' nickname for the locals.'

'Hanks and Ties?'

'A game of pursuit favoured by Coverdalians,' said the Headmaster eagerly, his thick plumage in permanent excitement.

'Thank you,' said the policeman, writing it down. 'Well, young lad, did you invite these youths onto Coverdale property?'

This was the most dangerous question. I laughed. 'You mean a ... hit squad, sir?'

'In a manner of speaking, young man, yes.'

'Well, I don't think Coverdalians order hit squads, sir. Do I look like Lucky Luciano?'

I knew all about Lucky Luciano and his gangsters from *Celebrated Murderers* magazine.

The policeman appeared to be embarrassed by the mention of Lucky Luciano: perhaps he didn't know who he was?

'Did you see' – and here he hesitated for dramatic effect – 'the knife?'

'THE knife or A knife?'

'Good God, boy,' exclaimed the Headmaster. 'Was there more than one knife? At Coverdale!'

The policeman was perplexed by Mr Trevelyan's conviction that a knife at Coverdale was like sodomy in the Sistine Chapel.

'It's the real world, Mr Trevelyan. The most heartless crimes I have seen in a thirty-year career were committed by kiddywinks.'

'I didn't see a knife at all,' I said.

'Moving on swiftly,' said the Inspector. 'One last question: what were you actually doing at Camps?'

Mr Trevelyan's expression was rapidly losing its kindliness.

'Tell the Inspector,' he said.

'I was leading a Communist revolution. It was October 1917 and I was storming the Winter Palace. There is now a Leninist dictatorship of the proletariat. You called me "Conroy", Inspector. But I'll be known to history as Stalin.'

The policeman sighed: was it a clue? 'That fella again,' he repeated and reluctantly wrote 'Stalin' in his little notebook.

'Talking of which, sir, Mr Trevelyan ...' I felt suddenly loquacious after the ordeal of interrogation. 'Can I suggest that we rename the school "Stalin-dale"? After all, sir, Coverdale's architecture is early Stalin Gothic.'

Mr Trevelyan did not reply but shrugged meaningfully at the Inspector.

The Inspector sighed again and then stood up, simultaneously smoothing down his anorak with a crumpling sound and putting his notebook in his pocket. 'Thank you Mr Trevelyan. Not really much to go on, is there? I'll speak to some of the lads in town and down at the Lake. I'll call later, Headmaster, but that'll be it for now.'

Mr Trevelyan showed the policeman out.

'Stay here, Conroy.'

They hesitated at the front door. I heard the policeman say, 'It ain't right a boy that age knowing about Stalin and the Reds. I think you can have too much education, Headmaster.'

'I can assure you I didn't teach him about Stalin.'

'Lads that age should play footer and have train sets. Otherwise some of your boys are going to grow up to be right fruitcakes. I'm not a professional intellect like you sir, but ...'

'I'm more worried about the knife. We've never had a knife at Coverdale.'

'Really, sir,' murmured the Inspector, who sounded mischievously pleased that such a tool should penetrate toffee-nosed Eden. 'Like they say up North, where there's brass, there's muck. There's muck in plenty here amongst your Little Lord Fauntleroys, Mr Headmaster.'

When Mr Trevelyan came back, he looked more angry than I had ever seen him. His hair almost sizzled. He shut both doors of the study.

'I don't know what happened up there today, boy. But I don't like liars. Lying is the lowest perfidy of all. You've embarrassed me in front of parents and the police. How dare you trot out this nonsense about Russia?'

I did not know what to say. I wanted to cry because I was afraid of his anger.

Then slowly, he said, 'Conroy, I am going to give you six of the best. Bend over the sofa.'

I did so. I concentrated on the wrinkles in the leather sofa. I tried to estimate the number of bottoms that had left them. Then I noticed the creases seemed to form a face, a familiar face. Yes it was so like him ... Stalin. Mr Trevelyan reached up to seize Twanky and then hit me six times on the bottom with the cane hard enough to jolt me. But Stalin gave me strength: 'History has indulged us today,' he whispered across time.

When it was over, I did not cry. But I stood up and avoided Mr Trevelyan's eyes.

'You can stay in here for a bit and then go to your dormitory,' he said gently. His face cleared after the storm.

Oddly, I was grateful to him for his humanity in these circumstances and guilty that I had put him in the situation where he had to beat me. So I said, 'Thank you, sir.'

He said, 'Thank you, Conroy.'

We both stood ramrod-straight and almost bowed as if the formality of the beating had transformed us into medieval knights at a jousting tournament.

As soon as he was gone, I collapsed into tears. They passed quickly. I wiped my eyes and then I went upstairs to my dormitory. Everyone was lying in bed with the lights on. I appeared in the doorway. I was dying to smile but wanted to make myself look as brave and grimly heroic as possible: Stalin returning from Siberian exile.

The boys sat up.

'What was it like? What happened?'

'Long live Lenin! Long live Stalin!' I shouted.

'Get into bed NOW, Conroy!' ordered Beaconsfield curtly. 'Unless you want to get beaten again!'

I didn't.

That night, I had the horrible dream again.

I was NOT Stalin. I was Leon Davidovitch Bronstein, aka Trotsky, with an ice pick deep in my temple.

The bloodied ice pick was silver – made on commission for Stalin from Tiffany's.

Oh, Trotsky.

16

MY OWN TROTSKY

'I throw my men at your feet. I want to join the Politburo,' said Crabbe, towering over me in his whites, little eyes overshadowed by his Cro-magnon forehead, as we watched the end-of-term cricket competition.

'What on earth for?'

'I think I could help you.'

'How?'

'Security at Stalingrad. Enforcement of your Five-Year Plans. Collectivisation. Operation Watergate.'

'How the hell do you know about Watergate?'

'Never mind. But I am a Communist: doesn't everyone want to contribute to Stalin's Workers' Paradise?

'Of course.' He wanted the Grub. Well, who didn't?

'I place myself at the disposal of the Central Committee of the Communist Party. And the Party for me is you, Comrade Stalin.'

Coarse and athletic, Crabbe still had the stitches in his face and a plaster over his broken nose (we all loved wearing plasters and wore them as long as possible).

'Have you had a conversion on the Road to Damascus?'

Crabbe, who had not heard of that particular thoroughfare, twitched. 'Dunno about that. I admit I made mistakes. I wanted to lead the Dugganoes but I was never anti-Communist. I was always a Stalinist.' The Blood, a Sports Hero in his cricket whites, prostrate at the feet of a mere Cabbage! I was not afraid because he was defeated and humiliated. But he still had ambitions.

'*All that is in the past*,' I said, the forgiving Stalin, who forgave nothing, '*and the past belongs to God.*'

It was a clever move by Crabbe, because it would be hard for my Party to exclude him, especially when he said he wanted to be a real

Bolshevik with all his fit Sportsman's heart. He even said, 'Sorry for any hassle earlier.'

My hair stood on end. Surely this was like when that Menshevik Trotsky brought his Inter-Borough Movement and joined Lenin's Bolsheviks? Crabbe was the answer to my Trotsky nightmares. Now they were over. I had found my Trotsky.

'Who will you bring?' I asked.

'Duggan, Minto, Danby and Grimshaw and their friends,' he said.

There was a cry. Duggan was batting and had hit a four. The ball was rolling towards us. Crabbe stopped the ball with a white cricket boot resting on alligator-teeth studs and then threw it back. 'Thanks Crabbe!' Pelham called affably.

'Who is the leader of our Party?' I asked when Crabbe strode back.

'Lenin the great teacher and Stalin, the wise, firm, decisive pupil and disciple. The Lenin of today.'

'*You and me are the Himalayas – all the others are nonentities,*' I said, using Stalin's own words on a similar occasion. 'Let's reach an understanding.' I smiled. 'Come here and give me a Brezhnev bearhug,' I said. We had seen Brezhnev bear-hugging a menagerie of foreign leaders on the news. 'Fraternal greetings, Comrade Crabbe. Report with your cadres tonight right after supper. Science lab.'

'Will I join the Politburo?'

'That is not up to me,' I said. 'It's up to the Congress and later the Central Committee.' (Stalin always pretended that he was just another equal member of the Politburo.)

'Pax?' Latin again: 'Peace.'

'Pax,' I answered.

How had Crabbe known exactly how to hail me as leader up on the cricket pitch? Someone WITHIN the Politburo must have told him what to say. Could this be what Ancient Mr Blunt would call a 'Trojan Horse' to change the destiny of the Stalinist Revolution?

If Crabbe had once not understood that I was the natural leader of the Soviet Union, a historical giant and a sage of Marxist-Leninist theory, he must be masking his real views now. Once an enemy – always an enemy.

Why did I always return to war, blood and hatred? Why did I want physically to smash my enemies? They had to be destroyed. Their names had to be wiped from history. But who were they?

When Stalin was growing up in Georgia, there was a saying amongst the Caucasians:

> How long will blood flow in the mountains?
> Until sugar cane grows in the snows.

17

THE DESTRUCTION OF TROTSKY 1924–8

'Crabbe! He's Menshevik scum,' grumbled Petty at the Party Plenum in the science lab.

'We Communists can afford to be generous,' replied Steady Pelham. 'It's only sensible.'

Now there were thirty members of the Central Committee, the Black Shoe Room was too small. There was a national coal strike again: the school was in candlelight. Ormonde lit all the Bunsen burners so that we ruled the Soviet Union from a tunnel of blazing torches.

'We're civilised people,' continued Pelham. 'I believe in forgiveness.'

The lab stank of the sulphur of school experiments. It was dark outside; sinister within; flames flickering around glinting test tubes and rubber tubing.

'It makes us stronger having those Bloods inside rather than outside. If they cross the Party line, it will be easier to destroy them within,' said Ormonde, understanding the point precisely.

'Why don't we liquidate that class enemy right now? Weigh him down with stones and sink him in the Lake. Or at least hand him over to the Bovverboys.' Petty was becoming a fanatic.

'I agree with Ormonde and Steady,' I said. Pelham could always persuade comrades to be fair; his words could soothe acid. Steady was my Bukharin who then ruled with Stalin. Bukharin, like Pelham, was, in Lenin's own words, 'the darling of the Party'.

'Aye, aye, Stalin,' said Ogre. Now they all agreed with me.

'I move to suggest that Commissar Petty bring in Crabbe and his henchmen,' said Pahlavi.

'Where are they?' asked Petty.

'Outside.'

He led in Crabbe, the once-mighty Duggan and his three friends. The science lab was absolutely silent as they walked through the pathway of torches to the teacher's podium. There stood the Politburo.

It was not quite silent: the rats in the cages were wriggling on their wheels. The mice squeaked. The locusts, in their specially heated and illuminated steel case, which was designed to emulate the steamy clime of Egypt, jumped around, clicking their brittle limbs.

Crabbe and I cut our fingers with a needle and pressed together the two jewels of blood, fingertip to tip, to make ourselves blood brothers. I could tell that Crabbe and even my own followers thought this sanguinity really meant that we were now friends. The fools were pleased our war was over.

After another Brezhnev bearhug, I distributed Grub to everyone to celebrate our coming to power. Crabbe, Minto, Danby and Grimshaw held up Bunsen burners and shouted, 'Long live Stalin!'

During my short speech, there were frequent interruptions for 'thunderous applause'.

'Here I unite the efforts of the proletarians of the West and the peasantry of the East in order to SMASH the old world. May the God of History help me.'

Ormonde, Second Central Committee Secretary, was the perfect cheerleader. 'What achievements! Comrades, we have collectivised the Gardens. Destroyed the richer peasant Kulak class. And Production is up!'

(The chaps guffawed because at Coverdale, 'Production' did not mean the industrial capacity to produce steel but the biological capacity for boys to produce sperm. But whether it meant combine harvesters or semen, Stalin stressed Production and so did we.)

'So,' continued Ormonde in his smooth actor's voice. 'Rafferty, Mendoza and I can all Produce. I suspect it is not long before Pahlavi and Ogre join us. Therefore I am pleased to report that we are far ahead of the Production Quotas of Comrade Stalin's Five-Year Plan.'

'Hurrah Stalin! Jolly good chap!'

'Thank you, comrades,' I said. 'We have completed the Five-Year Plan in a mere two weeks.'

'Hurrah! Jolly d!'

'But we mustn't slacken our efforts. It is true that the loss of the Gardens means that the peasants are starving. When Churchill asked Stalin what was the most difficult decision of his life, he said, *"The death of ten million peasants. It was fearful. But absolutely necessary for*

Russia." Let us not be arrogant. Let us be vigilant against enemies from within and without. "*Comrades, we are dizzy with success. Let's dance. Ormonde!*"

Ormonde put the tape into the tape recorder. The Politburo used squash rackets to simulate guitars. I brandished a ruler as a microphone and strutted and kicked just like a cross between John Travolta and Freddie Mercury. Even the rats on their wheels and the vaulting locusts seemed to join in. The Central Committee whirled their Bunsen burners, flames flickering in this fanatical Stalinist ritual.

We Bolsheviks always ended a Plenum with Saturday Night Fever.

I wish it could have gone on like that for ever.

When I saw Petty scurrying along from the school through the telescope we kept at Stalingrad, I knew there was something seriously amiss. Lenin was gone; Trotsky and Stalin would one day have to fight for his crown. But when?

It was a sunny afternoon off lessons. I was sitting in my 'office' in Stalingrad, giving a seminar on 'Stalinism at Coverdale' to some younger cadres. Money-Banks brought up a tape recorder, once again playing Queen's 'Night at the Opera'.

'Have you noticed that Freddie Mercury has exactly the same moustache as Stalinist Politburo giants such as Kaganovich, Zhdanov, Voroshilov and Ordzhonikidze?' he asked, looking at one of my Stalin books.

'You're right. But Stalin's was bushier.'

The Twits gravely compared photographs of the Politburo and Queen. I handed out some Grub which we kept in hidden silos of conkers and pine cones within Stalingrad, which was now even more secure than in Dugganoe days.

But it just shows that, whenever we relax vigilance, our enemies use it against us.

Wearing those black leather gloves, Petty arrived looking most worried, huffing and puffing, saluting magpies as he hurried along. He saluted, clench-fisted.

Petty and I had become very close: we were best friends, superlatively best friends. It was hard even to imagine existing without each other. We were inseparable, though we never went anywhere without our bodyguard of Ormonde, Ogleton and Archeamboye.

I could see Petty had important intelligence so I told Ogre and Ormonde to wait outside. I dismissed the class of young cadres and sent Lamb, Minto and Danby to collect more conkers and reinforce vigilance in the border areas.

'What shall we do after that?' asked Minto.

'Come back here, Comrade Minto. It is time for us to create a Five-Year Plan.'

'We've just had one,' interjected Lamb – a sheep in sheep's clothing.

'The SECOND Plan will create a powerful state to beat the western imperialists and take us closer to true Communism.'

'Oh great,' said Nonsuch enthusiastically, though lost in the labyrinth of dialectical materialism.

Archeamboye asked a better question. 'Does it really take five years because we're leaving Coverdale in two years?'

'No, Archie, my Five-Year Plan will be finished before supper,' I answered.

'Wow!' said Nonsuch.

'Now, go!'

They went.

'Petty, jolly d. to see you. What's up?' I said.

'No time for small talk, Comrade Stalin.' He was as officious as the worst apparatchik hatchet man, the cruellest Lord High Executioner, my secret police chief nonpareil. 'It is now 1929, Koba: you must destroy Trotsky, Kamenev, Zinoviev and Bukharin. Like in history.'

'Do I really have to destroy anyone, comrade? I'm Stalin. The Soviet people look upon me as a little father. Isn't the time of struggles over?'

Petty had a little file with him, which he opened. It was addressed like this:

Letter to Komrad Stalin, Jenrel-Sectary, Commoonist Party of SU.
Stalingrad Camp.
this is from
Komrad Petty, Chereman of OGpoo
Lubianka Boyler-room.

I could see at once that like every good secret policeman, Petty understood instinctively what I wanted. Before I wanted it. It was fine work. In his spidery handwriting, ill-spelled, he had collected some informer reports that showed that Crabbe was telling everyone that I had raided the Grub Cupboard and that Operation Watergate was still continuing. Furthermore, this had reached the ears of Mato, who had heard him talking about it while he was having his hair washed, and she had told Miss Guinivere the Laundry Queen, who had told Mr Trevelyan. Pahlavi had heard the Headmaster talking about this in the common room.

'Strooth, Petty! Strooth! That's betrayal. What should we do to an imperialist traitor in our midst?'

Petty was taking his job in the OGPU seriously.

'Shoot the vermin!' he shouted, with a lot of spit flying because of his lisp. He had exquisite ivories. But they were tiny and sharp like a stoat. 'Shoot the lickspittle wreckers, rightists, spies and saboteurs.'

It did not take Comrade Petty and his torturers in the boiler room to see that Crabbe was deliberately sneaking on us.

'Anything else?'

'Yes, one thing, Koba. Crabbe has also been ... "claiming" that in the early days of the revolution, you weren't much of a leader. More of a blur really. And that once he made you cry by holding your nose. Then you fled like a scurvy coward. Lies that are a direct insult to Lenin and Stalin.'

'Trotsky calls me a "blur"? It was true you know: Stalin is not even mentioned in John Reed's *Ten Days that Shook the World*.'

'Trotsky this! Trotsky that! During Odd Jobs, I burned the library's copy of that book in the bonfire!' ranted Petty.

I thought carefully for a minute. I looked at Petty, who kept a straight face. Petty was clever – the cleverest of the Politburo. Tiny, asthmatic, awkward, with his chubby face pointed like a trowel and sweaty skin, he was a believer. A believer is always more dangerous than a cynic. He was a red-hot hater. He did not torture for sport like Ogre, but because Stalinism was the Gospel. Not as sensitive as Ormonde, nor as brave as Pelham, I loved his mind: it anticipated mine at every turn.

Petty pulled off his Gestapo gloves and pleaded, 'Let me get Ormonde, Ogre, Archeamboye and take Crabbe down the boiler room and shine a light in his eyes. Put him on what Stalin called The Conveyer. No sleep, beat, beat! Liquidate him!'

I raised my hand. '*We know a policy of chopping off heads is fraught with great dangers. You chop off one head today, another tomorrow ... What in the end will be left of our Party?*'

'Right,' smirked Petty. He knew that Stalin hadn't mean a word of it. 'Come on, Koba. You hate him. So do I? Why don't we kill him? Really kill him! You once suggested it yourself – before the Revolution. No one would figure out it was us. I've got the gun at home. I kill animals all the time. Wring their necks, blow them out of the sky. We could bury Crabbe in the Corinthian Woods. No one would know. Just us two, Conroy.'

I thought for a moment.

'Wait. But the time will come for you to act, Comrade Petty. The Grub Cupboard raids are continuing? Ormonde and Ogre are in charge?'

'Twice a week,' said Petty.

For an anxious moment, I enjoyed the nostalgic song 'Lazing on a Sunday Afternoon' on the Queen tape.

'Cancel all Operation Watergate raids. Forthwith,' I ordered.

'Right, Secretary-General. We're scientifically developing a new programme of tortures. You know the rats in the lab? Have you read *1984* by George Orwell?'

'Send me Comrade Crabbe. Now.'

Petty got up, saluted and marched out. When I say he marched, he had actually begun to march like a Russian – arms out.

Power does funny things to children.

'My uncle knew Stalin,' said Diggle-Johnson the School Liar, walking in step with me back from Stalingrad. Just then, I got downwind of him and caught a rich whiff of steamy faeces: silage in shorts. Poor Diggle-Johnson. 'But my uncle Humphrey knew EVERYBODY! Still does!' He was a precocious namedropper.

'I doubt that,' I laughed.

Diggle's hair always looked greasy; his face was a car crash of freckles. He had wall eyes like a mongrel. He always stank. There were often complaints about his excretory habits at Central Committee.

'No, I swear on my mother's life. I want her to die if I'm lying, Koba. Swear! Cross my heart and wish to die! Honest!'

'So how did your Uncle Humphrey know Stalin?'

'Stalin goes shooting at Uncle Humphrey's quite often. He was there a few weekends ago. Everyone goes shooting at Uncle Humphrey's.'

'Including Rhett Butler, Churchill and Stalin?'

'Honest, Koba. Why would I lie?'

'Who was the best shot?'

'Oh. Ummm. Not Churchill. Rhett Butler of course. Uncle Humphrey said Stalin peppered a beater and had to be sent back to the house.'

Somehow in those early days, we let Fellow Travellers like the School Liar into the Central Committee.

More fool us.

We only had to shoot them later.

18

TROTSKY EXPELLED 1929

Crabbe swaggered into Stalingrad and sat down in one of the wrecked chairs.

No salute.

He did not wait for me to tell him to sit. He just sat. He slapped my back, like a member of the liquidated Sportsman class. He was so strapping, it jarred my innards. He said, 'Heya, Koba.'

Only my oldest comrades dared call me Koba. I was 'Comrade Stalin' to everyone else. I knew then he was already a dead man: he already stank like a cadaver. It is a bad smell – the stench of a corpse who thinks he is alive. But he did not know that because I smiled warmly, slapped him on his back and said, 'Lovely to see you, Crabbie, you old mucker.' I could talk their talk but his insincere ruggerbugger bonhomie made my flesh creep.

By the time Crabbe had arrived, the others were back from foraging for grain and armaments. They all said hello to him in a dangerously friendly way – especially dear Pelham who liked to boast he was 'fair to everyone'. But can you be 'fair' to enemies? I was surrounded on all sides by enemies pretending to be friends. Like Stalin before me, I was alone in my strength and clearsightedness. I saw through them all. Those like Minto and Danby wanted me to fail.

But failure was not in my Five-Year Plan.

Then Crabbe leaned over, turned off the tape recorder and put in another tape.

'This should be our Soviet anthem,' he said. 'It's Queen's new album – *Day at the Races*.'

The song was called 'We are the Champions'. He was right: it was the perfect anthem for our workers' paradise.

'You're a Leninist ideologue, Comrade Crabbe. The Stakanovites can sing it on their way down the Donbass mines. I myself will suggest it to the Central Committee.'

'Right,' he said and then carelessly reached under the secret floor and pulled out a pack of Mars Bars and tossed me one. Didn't he realise that this Grub belonged to the People not to him?

'Crabbe,' I said. 'I want to make you my Deputy as Central Committee Secretary. And I want to promote you to Marshal of the Soviet Union.'

'Strooth! That's really exciting.' He held the Mars between his fingers like a plutocrat's cigar.

'It is a great honour for you, Crabbe. Marshal Crabbe.'

'You bet your bottom dollar,' he said. What a vulgarian!

'But I want to reward you in a more important way than that.'

'What? What!' The greed on his face. He longed for the Grub Cupboard, the holy of holies. He suspected nothing.

I reached into my pocket and tossed him the key.

The school's best fielder in the slips caught it in a flash of steel in the sunlight: he was such a natural that he seemed to draw it into his hand as easily as a magnet attracts metal.

'The Grub Cupboard key: the revolution honours its best.'

Crabbe was so excited that he jumped up and ran out into the sun, like a duplicitous medieval baron shouting 'Saddle my horse!'

'I've got so much to do: the Future,' said the swank proudly.

That vermin.

The next day, the best lesson was given by the English master, Mr Fitzroy-White. He was tall, distrait and ramshackle like Wurzel Gummidge, with Bohemian grey locks that fell onto his face. He wore his trousers pulled halfway up his chest, held up by braces. He liked to teach us idioms by jumping up and down as he said them and then asking us to repeat them.

That day he was teaching us 'The pen is mightier than the sword.' He jumped up and down at every word,

He asked Ogleton the Latchkey Kid to come and write it on the board.

Ogleton, who leaned forward when he walked, dragging his feet, 'like a Gypsy thief' according to Mr Fitzroy-White, slunk up to the board and wrote, 'the PENIS mightier than the sword.'

This made us hoot. Crazy Ogleton laughed like a Transylvanian Tommy gun. Mr Fitzroy-White was such a jolly decent man that he laughed too, but he regretted it because whenever he mentioned it again, we all said the word PENIS as frequently as possible.

On his way back to his desk, Ogre put three drawing pins on Mr Fitzroy-White's chair. When the master sat on them, we held our breath. Nothing happened. When he got up again, the pins seemed to be stuck into his big bottom but he had not noticed. Ogre called this 'One of the Seven Wonders of the World'.

Mr Fitzroy-White, by the way, was an official war hero ('the real McCoy' said dad) because he had been in the SAS during the war. Perhaps he made the enemy laugh so much they gave up the ghost.

That day he revealed something to me about Stalin.

I put my hand up and said, 'Sir, this PENIS' ('Spontaneous applause' is shown in the Central Committee Archives) 'saying is all very well, sir, but it is not true, is it, sir? I mean the sword IS mightier than the pen or the PENIS?'

'Is it right, Conroy, that you worship Stalin, you funny fellow?'

'Yes, sir.' There was applause from the Politburo.

'Quiet, you picaroons.' He liked silly words. 'Go on, Conroy!'

'Stalin had a direct answer to this saying.'

'What was it, Conroy?'

'Stalin said "*How many divisions has the Pope?*"'

'Very true, Conroy. Well done. Collect your Order of Lenin later. Now why do you think Stalin sought power? Nonsuch? Lamb? Ogleton?'

'Money, sir,' said that gumby Money-Banks.

'To have a stately home, sir,' said that wetty Bridgewater, who probably possessed one.

'To be as famous as Freddie Mercury, sir,' suggested Lamb.

'Come on!' shouted Mr Fitzroy-White, jumping up and down so that the floorboards of the whole room jumped. He always taught us in the games room so that even the balls on the billiard table jumped too. 'OK, Conroy, this is how Aristotle answered that question.' He went to the board and wrote, '*Men don't seek to become dictators to keep out the cold.*'

When the fire alarm woke me, I was just dreaming that I was too wet to be Stalin. I must be harsher, crueller, more brutal, even if it was against my bookish, Trotskyish nature.

Crabbe was not a convincing Leon Davidovitch. What if I still WAS Trotsky? It made me homesick. I imagined the hols at home in London with my elder brothers and their girlfriends: a secret cargo of hash-pipes, kaftans and miniskirts. The girls always had funny seventies names like Soukie. I longed to see my dog, Honey, a cocker spaniel with a noble forehead and loving face. I trusted Honey, unlike most of my comrades. I wanted to cry.

Beaconsfield, the dorm prefect, shook me awake. Fire practice. I relished the jostle of drama; the fear of the unknown. The rushing through half-lit corridors to screaming, deafening alarms. It was exciting being up in the middle of the night.

We seized our dressing-gowns from the end of our beds, struggled into our slippers, fighting our sleepiness. The smelly Diggle-Johnson would have died in the flames if Beaconsfield had not kicked his bedframe.

Of course, there were no flames. When we gathered in the big games room, where Mr Fitzroy-White had taught us about penises and swords that very day, Mr Trevelyan, puffing on his pipe, and the vicious Orangeman were quite awake, as if they had never gone to bed. The Orangeman, smelling of whisky, sat on the pingpong table swinging his beefy legs, like a gangster who has just pulled off the Great Train Robbery.

Mr Hester was in his day clothes – he had obviously stayed up for some reason. The others were all in their pyjamas; it was most entertaining seeing what the masters looked like in their dressing-gowns. Mr Blunt wore a nightshirt under his silk blue robe. Mr Trevelyan bulged out of his woolly gown. Miss Snow came in a little late in a turquoise satin dressing-gown like an Ottoman vizier and olive-green pyjamas with leather slippers. Her black hair seemed thicker and more unkempt than ever before, as if it was overflowing her very head. It made her look older.

Petty in his tartan dressing-gown stood beside me with his Lubianka gloves peeking out of the pockets. His eyes flicked towards me. He smiled weakly and then, pretending his hands were a shotgun, he followed an imaginary bird along the ceiling and foolishly said: 'Pow. Pow. Another brace in the bag.'

There was a rollcall. School rollcalls were as funereal and sombre as such occasions in history, always the prelude to some mass-punishment – executions or deportations. The same fear. The same suspense. The same helplessness. Each boy replied, 'Here, sir.'

'Conroy?'

'Here, sir.'

'Petty major?'

'Here, sir.'

'Petty minor?'

I could tell Petty was listening as closely as I to the names.

They missed out Duggan and Crabbe. Ogre raised his eyebrows. Ormonde flicked his yo-yo.

Rollcall complete, Mr Trevelyan said, 'Thank you, everyone. It seemed a good moment for a fire practice because there's been rather a shock that we needed to tell you about. We caught two extremely SENIOR boys raiding the Grub Cupboard tonight. The Cupboard had been raided on a weekly basis since the key was lost at the beginning of term. If any of you think this was clever – yes, Ogleton, shut up or you'll be for the high jump! – these boys are responsible for about £400 of theft. We considered calling in the police. But instead, we have beaten both concerned and then expelled them. This is a hell of a shame, because both of them had passed Common Entrace with flying colours. You'll find out who they are tomorrow.'

'Snubs to you, Comrade Crabbesky!' I thought to myself.

I whispered Stalin's practical saying to Petty, *'One man; one problem. No man; no problem.'*

'The ice pick in Trotsky's skull?' wheezed Petty.

'Almost. When Trotsky was expelled in 1929, Stalin was already the most powerful man in the Soviet Union. But he always regretted letting him out alive. It took the NKVD eleven long years to kill him ...'

'Shut up, Conroy!' Mr Hester pounced off the pingpong table. 'Right, chaps. I'll send you back to bed, dorm by dorm. No talking and go straight to bed. Is that clear? And by the way, since clearly more of you knew about this, there will be NO GRUB for a term! Goodnight!'

Many years later, long after my affair with Stalin, Crabbe, that hideous caveman, joined the British army as an officer in a regiment of Guards. He fought in the Falklands War. Her Majesty Queen

Elizabeth II awarded Captain Crabbe the Victoria Cross for singlehand-edly massacring a trench of twenty-two Argentinians, armed only with a bayonet blade, an ice-hardened Mars Bar – and a cane which he always carried. For luck.

That is the way heroes are made.

19

STALIN THE POET

When a busload of Americans schoolboys visited the school to sing songs with us, I learned that there was disloyalty in the Central Committee. One day I would have to settle scores ...

But I also became even more intrigued with the leonine Miss Snow, who was kinder than Mrs Trevelyan but somehow less wholesome. What was she doing in England? Why had she come to Coverdale of all places? What did she leave behind?

'She's like a witch,' I said to dad.

'What do you call a beautiful witch?' He answered himself: 'Bewitching.'

And she was.

The American visit was Miss Snow's show because she was American.

'America and Britain have what Churchill called the Special Relationship. We are like cousins. Be polite and welcoming to the leaders of the free world,' she said in the gym before they arrived, in her soft accent, educated yet racy. She wore swashbuckling suede boots, leather waistcoat, incarnadine blouse and black jodhpurs just like the girl-dressed-as-a-boy who played Jack (of Beanstalk fame) when my grandmother took me to the Christmas pantomime at the Bournemouth Palladium.

'My father says Britain's the leader of the free world,' interrupted Petty. 'Not those brash Yanks!'

'Well, he is wrong, Petty minor. Show them how much we have in common. But there are great differences too. We call your George III "George the Tyrant"; we call a waistcoat, a 'vest'; and our braces, we call 'suspenders' ...'

We laughed. No one could help giggling at any mention of female underwear.

'So are you more American or English?' asked Nonsuch.

'I am Transatlantic. I straddle the ocean,' she said daringly. Her American accent was more Scott Fitzgerald than John Wayne: it was as light as those feathery dandelions which children blow to tell the time. Her words floated but never seemed to land.

When they arrived, the Yanks, with their cropped GI hair, were far more regimented than us. The gym, filled with wooden chairs, was in an outhouse near Kiev. There, we sang American songs which Mrs Gladwyn-Jones played on the piano: she was a scaly dragon whose eyes looked in different directions. Often in lessons, her glass one slipped out and landed on the piano keyboard, striking a single note. Mrs Gladwyn-Jones would keep playing to the end of the tune and then seize her eye like a harridan wicket keeper and then replace it nonchalantly into the optical abyss at which we stared with a macabre fascination.

While she was playing 'Yankee Doodle', one eye was looking at us on the right and the other at the Americans on the left.

Wielding an eyeliner pencil as baton, Miss Snow conducted us singing 'Marching Through Georgia'. Ormonde sang the solo in 'Star Spangled Banner' beautifully until his voice broke in the middle, which was not surprising since he was ahead of us all in terms of Stalinist Production. Then Ormonde and I had to recite some poems. First I recited my favourite poem, which was most dramatic:

> There's a one-eyed yellow idol to the North of Katmandu
> There's a little marble cross below the town
> There's a broken hearted woman tends the grave of Mad Carew
> And the little god forever gazes down.

I shouted the climax with all my heart:

> An evil knife lay buried in the heart of Mad Carew
> T'was the VENGEANCE of the little yellow god.

The Americans clapped robotically.

Mad Carew sounded as infernal as Ogleton.

Then Ormonde recited his favourite poem, which was 'The Highwayman'. Ormonde was a brilliant actor. Our hair stood on end when 'Bess, the inn keeper's black-eyed daughter' killed herself to save the Highwayman.

Then I stood up again and said, 'This is another poem by a poetic genius,' and I recited:

> And worn out from this hope
> I am joyful and my heart beats high.
> Can the beautiful hope that came to me in that instant
> Really be winnable?
>
> Know this: He who fell like ashes to the ground,
> He who ever oppressed,
> Will rise higher than the great mountains
> On the wings of a bright hope.

The Americans applauded dutifully, though I admit that these poems were not as exciting as the first two.

'Our guests would like to know the name of the poet?' asked Miss Snow.

'Those were two early poems by our FAVOURITE poet, Josef Stalin.'

This was the signal for Danby, Minto and Commissar Archeamboye, who were standing at the back of the gym, to unravel a banner suspended from the gym ladders. We had prepared posters to welcome the Americans in the art classes. They announced banalities like: 'Coverdale School, Dorset, England Welcomes Harriman Lovett School of Brookline, Massachusetts.' Boring as hell.

Ours said: 'Coverdale School says: LONG LIVE STALIN, OUR NOBLE TEACHER!'

When I nodded at Danby and Minto, they pretended not to notice and did nothing. It was precisely as I suspected: Trotsky was exiled but the Party was still riddled with enemies, traitors and saboteurs. Finally, Commissar Archeamboye unravelled our banner.

The American boys did not laugh. But my cadres cheered enthusiastically. The American master became more and more agitated. His spectacles misted up. The second it was over, he jumped up like a jack-in-the-box and advanced stiffly towards Mr Trevelyan. We gathered around to hear the shit hit the fan. So did the American boys.

'Frankly, Headmaster Trevelyan, we are profoundly upset by the references to Stalin in your performance,' said their Headmaster, Dr Calthorpe, in his almost unintelligible Long Island lockjaw. 'I believe that there is or may well be traces of the taint of ...' He hesitated.

Then: 'COMMUNISM amongst your pupils. This is a disease that should be ERADICATED at an early age.'

'It was just a boyish joke, possibly in bad taste,' Mr Trevelyan answered.

'I teach English here, Dr Calthorpe,' said Mr Fitzroy-White, who stood beside the Headmaster. 'Stalin's poetry may not be as consummate as, say, Wordsworth, Blake, Donne or even his contemporary poet, Wilfred Owen. But, by Jove, it's yards better than modern rubbish like Larkin ...'

'It's not Stalin's iambic pentameters I'm talking about, Mr Fitzroy-White. Our last boys are choppering out of Nam fighting the Red Gooks,' shouted the American master, his voice high and strangled. 'And we didn't come to your school to have our boys who died in Nam to fight the good fight, insulted.'

'Just high jinks and horseplay!' said Mr Trevelyan, his halo of hair standing out in a shimmering fuzz.

'What – when Saigon's lost to the most evil Communist regime in the world! They say Britain's ROTTEN, riddled with aristocratic degeneracy and Soviet espionage. I didn't believe a darned word of it! I always stood up for the land of Shakespeare, dreaming spires and the Queen. Now I see the truth!'

Mr Trevelyan and Dr Calthorpe faced each other in arctic silence, like the superpowers surrounded by their satellites, until one of the American boys hissed, 'Communists!'

Unfortunately, he chose to spit this insult (actually an extravagant compliment) into the wolverine face of Ogleton. The Red Ogre simply punched him. The next thing I knew the Americans were standing with their fists raised in a formal boxing posture with sanctimonious expressions on their faces. Ogre, Archeamboye and Ormonde formed a scrummage and simply charged the Yanks out of the way before collapsing onto them as if they were on the rugby field.

Dr Calthorpe and Mr Trevelyan shouted and tried to pull out their ringleaders. The American master frogmarched his outraged minions to their bus.

Mr Trevelyan went to see them off. But before he went, he said, 'Conroy, Archeamboye. The study. Ten minutes.'

For some reason he had forgotten the Ogre, who had actually started the fight.

When I heard this, I realised wearily I might be beaten again.

So I sent Ogleton scampering along to the study where he hid Twanky under the cushions on the sofa.

'I can't help you this time, Koba,' said the low voice that already enveloped me in her mist of scent.

'Miss Snow, I'm sorry. But ...'

'I guess you gave my compatriots a unique glimpse of Stalinist Britain.' Her slim, dry hand with its long fingers bearing too many jewels rested on the back of my neck. I felt slightly dizzy. She narrowed her eyes: 'You ruined the whole damned visit. You deserve whatever comes your way!' Then she broke into a beguiling smile and turned heel, bracelets jingling.

'But Miss Snow ...'

Five minutes later, Mr Trevelyan was saying to us in the study, 'Bend over the sofa together, you pair o' rascals!' If he called us 'rascals', it meant he was not too angry.

Then I heard him feeling around on top of the bookcase for the cane. Five minutes later, Archeamboye and I were still bending over that sofa.

I prayed that Mr Trevelyan would not find Widow Twanky. We could hear him feeling behind the books and then pulling the books out. The suspense was killing me. We waited like that for a few more minutes. I was about to burst out giggling. But bit my lip.

Mr Trevelyan kept looking. He could not find it. He swore under his breath. Finally after a long time, he said, 'OK, you can get up again now. Bloody Yanks take everything far too seriously! Stalin's poetry? Hardly Wordsworth, eh? Get lost, your pair of incorrigible mountebanks.'

20

THE CONGRESS OF VICTORS 1934

At the end of every year there was a feast at Coverdale called Prize-Giving Banquet, at which prizes were given and songs sung. There were crackers and oodles of nosh. The Banquet had one peculiar but splendid tradition: that was when Ancient Mr Blunt's class saluted him in Latin, as if he was the Roman Emperor and they were gladiators about to die. How romantic it was! It was a most sinister tradition if you think about it, as I did. But somehow it had been allowed to survive from 'Tsarist' times.

That year, I was in Emperor Blunt's class, so we had dutifully learned the salute. Imperator Blunt, the Deputy Headmaster, the image of Tiberius's beloved lizard, was the oldest man I had ever seen alive: a grey-green colour as if already in advanced stages of putrefaction. His face was densely wrinkled. He had lots of hair, but it was all white. He walked slowly, teaching in a cracked groan; we fidgeted through his classes.

But Mr Blunt cheered up when he told us stories of the wicked antics of the Roman emperors: his favourite was Caligula, which he told me meant 'Little Boots' or 'Bootkins'. So when he discovered my affair with Stalin, he called me 'Bootkins' ever after, which made me proud. He also told me that Caligula's best saying was, *'Let them hate me so long as they fear me.'*

Then Ogre boorishly asked, 'Did Bootkins FIDDLE like Nero when Rome burned?'

Spontaneous giggles followed.

This was the big joke of Roman history that made dead Latin bearable: the word FIDDLE meant playing the violin to Mr Blunt. But to us, 'fiddling' meant playing with another boy's forbidden machine. Thus, no lesson was complete without discussing Nero and roaring with laughter ... That day was no exception.

Nero was Mr Blunt's second best emperor, who said, '*If only Rome had one neck ...*'

Stalin echoed this gibbet of a joke when he said, '*If only there weren't forty million Ukrainians, I'd deport the lot of them.*'

Mr Eye once told me a secret about Mr Blunt which explained why I was his favourite. (It was not because of my Latin, which was terrible. I came eleventh out of fifteen that term.) Mr Eye preferred to tell other people's secrets. Never his own. Anyway, Mr Eye said that Mr Blunt, 'as a young man, was a British secret agent who penetrated Soviet Central Asia in the 1920s, pretending to be a travelling tradesman of Turkestan.'

Of course, I did not believe this because why would an adventurer like that want to teach Latin to simpering children? But I resolved to ask the forbidding Mr Blunt who, beneath his antiquity, was surprisingly mischievous. At the end of a lesson just before Banquet, I waited behind and said, 'Sir, is it true, that in the 1920s you were a British spy in Central Asia?'

Ancient Mr Blunt was still sitting at his desk. He did not move much. If he had died in a lesson, it would have taken us about twenty minutes to notice. But this time, he turned to look right at me. His neck was so leathery that it actually creaked. He smelled of pipe tobacco. The imperial iguana smiled.

'Avé, Bootkins,' he said. 'If I was a British agent in those parts, I certainly wouldn't tell you.'

'Oh, yes, of course. But do you speak Russian?'

'Yes.'

'Do you speak Turkestan language, sir?'

'Yes, Bootkins.'

'So it could be true, couldn't it?'

'Possibly, Bootkins. There is a book that tells the story of that particular mission, but it doesn't mention my name.'

I was enraptured at the thought of my Latin master having wild affrays in the corners of Stalin's empire.

'But, sir, if it was really you, sir, why did you become a schoolmaster, sir?'

'The preparatory school is where British spies come to die.'

How glorious! I looked up the book, of course. It did mention that heroic spy who did indeed become a schoolmaster. But was it Mr Blunt? He would not say anything more about it. He just said,

'Bootkins, do you and your class know the Gladiators' Salute ready for Banquet?'

'Oh yes, Emperor,' I answered. But I did not tell him my secret plan ...

Stalin called his 1934 Party meeting 'The Congress of Victors'. This was to be our Banquet of Victors. Despite the expulsion of Crabbe and Duggan the week before, it was a time of triumph.

But triumph is meaningless unless the people know about it. Like Stalin, I took propaganda seriously. That was why I went to see a boy called Rafferty about his marvellous, mysterious gadget.

'It is called a ghetto blaster,' said Lasch Rafferty, the only American pupil in the school.

'A what?' I asked again.

'Think about it, dude,' drawled Lasch in his laid-back Californian accent, so different from Miss Snow's Brahmin drawl.

Every term Lasch arrived in his dad's Silver Roller (driven by a chauffeur wearing what appeared to be the uniform of a marshal of the Soviet Union) with a bigger, blacker and louder tape recorder: the latest from LA. That term, he had arrived with a gargantuan black tape recorder that was also a television AND a record player AND a radio. It was bigger than a tuck box but smaller than a trunk. Yet it had a handle so Lasch carried it around.

'The ghetto blaster's straight from the laboratories in Japan, man. My father gave it me. I'm the only kid that's got one of these in the whole world.'

Lasch started rolling a cigarette – openly! He wasn't like anyone else. He scorned school rules and wore his black hair long like a hippy. He wore dark glasses all the time, even at night, for 'medical reasons'. His tie was always half undone. He only wore shoes called Gucci loafers. He put his feet on the desk, did no work. In other words, he was amazingly groovy and splendiferously foreign. The only boy who understood Lasch was Mendoza. 'So what can I do for you?'

'Stalin and the Communists understood the importance of media and propaganda. That's why he was always calling Pasternak in the middle of the night to tell him to rewrite ...'

'I don't care if Stalin did write *Dr Zhivago*; it was an awesome movie.'

'Right, Lasch.' He was the only boy called by his first name. 'Lasch, can I borrow the ghetto blaster for Banquet?' I explained the idea.

'Awesome – no problem. Groovy concept! Stalin was one hell of a star, an international jetsetter and a swinger, bigger even than Warren or Steve.' He meant Warren Beatty or Steve McQueen. He knew them. Warren and Steve.

What was a jetsetter? And a swinger? I did not ask because I was too ashamed to show I did not know. Then he paused. 'My father was a Communist in the fifties. He almost lost everything during the Witchhunt.'

'Gosh.'

'You know the first person I'd like to see SHOT in the revolution, Stalin?'

'Who?'

Lasch got up and walked over and put his face really close to mine, dripping sarcasm. Too close. He smelled of that sickly sweet bubblegum. 'My asshole father!'

'You don't really mean that, Rafferty.'

'I really do,' he said.

'Well, thanks a million! Umm, Lasch? Mendoza says you're the only boy in the school who isn't a virgin.'

'Get out, Conroy. Don't give me that lip. You may be Stalin but you're just a kid. And here, take that asshole's ghetto blaster. Throw it in the Lake if you like.'

Mr Trevelyan closed his eyes and crossed his hands above his crescent stomach. 'For what we are about to receive may the Lord make us truly thankful.' He said grace at every meal. Everyone answered, 'AMEN!'

The dining hall was full. There was a master or a matron at the end of every table. The rest of the masters sat at the top table with the prefects and the captain of the school. Everything was emblazoned with banners and decorations. There were paper hats and crackers on every table.

Mr Trevelyan gave his speech. He used the martial phrase 'with flying colours' a lot, which made his hair bounce. After he had praised everyone for doing everything, from cricket to exams, 'with flying colours', he said, 'Mr Blunt, Deputy Headmaster, would you stand?'

Ancient Mr Blunt rose slowly to his feet, bones cracking. He smiled decayingly and raised one hand in what might be called a Roman imperial greeting, though it was not unlike a Hitler salute.

We knew this was our signal, so we stood up and raised our hands like Romans. Then together, as one voice, we chanted:

> AVE CAESAR! NOS MORITURI TE SALUTAMUS.
> Hail Caesar! we, who are about to die, salute you!

Now was the usual moment for Mr Ancient to read out the order of his class. But I had made special plans. This was my Congress of Victors after all.

Ogleton suddenly proclaimed, 'Now we must salute the Red Caesar!'

'Za Rodinoo! Za Stalina!' shouted Ormonde.

As one body, the class turned to face me. Other boys who were Stalinists stood up too. They raised their arms, not in the imperial Roman salute, but the clenched fist of the Communist hurrah. Then they chanted again, 'Ave Stalinus, Imperator et Princeps, nos morituri te salutamus!'

That was when NKVD General Petty pressed the Play button on the ghetto blaster, hidden under a table. The chorus of 'We are the Champions' by Queen played in loud glory. Everyone joined in to celebrate the achievements of our brave new world.

When the song was over, there was a tense silence.

Comrade Ogre raised his swarthy, over-sized hands and placed them palm to palm. 'Now let us pray,' he said. 'For what we have just eaten, may Stalin make us truly thankful! Amen.'

'Amen.'

Summer was over.

21

THE GREAT PURGES 1936–8:
THE *YEZHOVSCHINA*

'*W*e deem it absolutely necessary and urgent that Comrade Yezhov be nominated to the post of People's Commissar of Internal Affairs (NKVD). Yagoda has definitely proved himself to be incapable of unmasking the Trotskyite-Zinovievite bloc. The OGPU is four years behind in this matter. STALIN.'

At the end of his summer holidays, on 25 September 1936, Stalin sent this telegram from the Black Sea resort, Sochi, in the south, to the Politburo in Moscow in order to accelerate his notorious Purges.

At the end of my summer holidays, on 25 September, just before returning to Coverdale, I sent this same telegram from my granny's local post office at Bournemouth, in the south, to Comrade Petty in Roxburghshire, Scotland, to accelerate my notorious Purges.

Petty was to be my Nicolai Ivanovich Yezhov, that poison dwarf, Lord High Executioner, my dear butcher-in-chief.

Stalin's massacre of his own people, known as the *Yezhovschina* – the time of Yezhov, was about to commence.

On the second day of the Michaelmas Term, Commissar Archeamboye, who played prop in the First Fifteen scrum, thundered up the centre of the field during the practice for the game against Heathfield. The Brobdingnagian was tackled by Minto, Danby and Grimshaw: only three could bring down one good Bolshevik prop. He hit the frozen earth with a crack and could not move. Mr Holly and Mr Selwyn stood at the centre of a huddle of boys who gathered around the leviathan body of this Bolshevik hero.

'Poor chap's leg might be broken!' said the history master.

'That was an assassination attempt,' said Commissar Petty, who was standing beside me. We both wore our greatcoats and had our right hands resting between the buttons 'à la Stalin-Bonaparte'.

'Why would they assassinate HIM? Why not me?' I asked enviously. We strolled onto the pitch to look at poor Archeamboye, waiting for a stretcher and ambulance.

'He's popular in the Party AND amongst Bloods,' said Petty. 'Plus, he would have won the game for Soviet Coverdale against Heathfield. This is sabotage, Comrade Stalin. It is no coincidence that Trotskyites like Spanker, Danby and Minto did it. Koba, this is the assassination of Kirov, which gave Stalin the excuse to begin the bloodbath of his enemies: The Great Purges.'

'Good thinking, Comrade Yezhov,' I said, calling Petty by a name that will live forever in infamy.

Mr Holly was kneeling beside Archeamboye.

'It's OK, Archeamboye,' said the history beak warmly. 'I know it really hurts. But hang on in there, old chap. Diggle-Johnson's run for an ambulance. Lamb – get a blanket from the school and rush back.'

'I'm sorry, Archeamboye,' said Minto.

'Don't apologise you wetty,' hissed Spanker Grimshaw. 'It was a perfectly fair tackle on that black Cyclops!'

'Enough of that,' said Mr Selwyn. 'I want to talk to you about that tackle. Disgraceful.'

Petty could not restrain himself. 'It was a deliberate assassination attempt against Comrade Stalin's Politburo! You'll pay for it, you running dogs, you Trotskyite jackals!'

'Shut up, Petty,' shouted Mr Holly.

Mr Selwyn pointed at us. 'What are you two lunatics doing on the pitch? Get lost!'

'Crabbe's expulsion was someone's revenge,' that pond-life gumby Minto murmured, looking at me as he arranged his teddy bears in our new dorm, Stables 3, named because it was above the old stables. 'Lots of us don't think it was fair.'

'I'm quite a Stalinist,' agreed Pelham, pulling on his Pooh Bear pyjamas. 'But Minto's got a point, Koba. You must admit that Collectivisation of the Gardens wasn't too fair on the gardeners either. Why don't you trust your friends more, Koba?'

'Oh, Pelham. I say to you what Stalin told H. G. Wells in 1934, right at the beginning of the Purges: '*You, Mr Wells, appear to proceed from the assumption that all people are good. But I do not forget that many people are bad.*'

I adored Steady Pelham: even I could not pretend he was bad. But this scale of betrayal could not continue. It was that 'fairness' canard again. What did 'fairness' have to do with the dictatorship of the proletariat? Terror, not fairness, changes History.

Petty was next door in Stables 2; he came in that night to plan policy. He said he had some capital shoots in the holidays and, using his fingers, pretended to shoot pheasants out of the sky with 'pow' noises that rained spit on Nonsuch, who was in the next-door bed but never complained.

Petty whispered that Pahlavi had met those clowns Money-Banks, Grimshaw and Bridgewater in the holidays: their parents lived near each other.

'Those three met Trotskyites Crabbe and Duggan. The Trotskyites and Bukharinites are joining together to unseat Stalin. He heard them grumble about what Collectivisation was doing to the peasants. They said they felt guilty. Deluded weaklings!'

Sitting cross-legged on my tiger bedspread (Stalin's favourite animals were wolves, which he often sketched when bored), I signed a secret Central Committee Order. This gave Petty and his NKVD limitless powers to interrogate and execute Enemies of the People. Petty, who was showing signs of being too keen on this work, had actually copied Stalin's real decree out of my most beloved book, *The Great Terror* by Robert Conquest.

It was clear to anyone who was not naive that there were members of the Politburo and Central Committee who were masked Enemies of the People. Enemies pretending to be friends were worse than open enemies. With war coming, they had to be destroyed.

Stalin decided around 1937 to shoot most of the Old Bolsheviks, who had been Leninist before the Revolution. I faced the same problem with fake Stalinists like Money-Banks and Spencer-Percival. Even trusty Pelham said he was only 'quite a Stalinist'. It was not coincidental that the first two were from old English families because Stalin killed everyone from old Bolshevik families. Our purges were parallel.

All I needed was an excuse. The assassination attempt on Archeamboye would serve. But things were still going far too slowly.

That evening, during the free period before bed, we held an emergency Central Committee plenum in the Black Shoe Room.

It was already tense before the accusations. Money-Banks asked the

Chairman of the Supreme Soviet, Weeping Wharton, permission to speak. But President Wharton just snuffled as usual.

'Granted,' snapped Ormonde, taking the chair, luxuriantly yo-yoing.

'I wish to denounce Diggle-Johnson: his lying, bed-wetting and pooing in his pants is not Leninist-Stalinist behaviour. If he continues to stink of the detritus of Capitalism, I request the OgPOO to take him down to Lubianka and torture him ...'

'Hear, hear!' agreed many comrades. 'What punishment?'

'Death!' suggested Money-Banks. The doomed weasel was accusing others, hoping to prove his loyalty and protect himself.

'Is Diggle-Johnson here?' I asked.

Mumbling. Then: 'No.'

'All right. Let us not be too hard on this Comrade. Let us be merciful,' I said, playing Stalin's game of pretending to be the moderate. 'Comrades, we seem to agree here. Commissar Petty will warn Comrade Diggle-Johnson that his smelly capitalistic habits must cease.'

'I should remind you,' added Ormonde, 'that in our Workers' Paradise, there is neither crime, nor unemployment, nor vagrancy, nor bed-wetting. Comrade Lenin made that clear.'

'Passed,' said Pahlavi. Petty made a note in his secret police notebook. President Wharton sadly stamped this Supreme Soviet decree. The Head of State was nobody in Stalin's day: all power was with the Party, not the state structure.

'Comrade Petty to speak!' said Ormonde. He stopped yo-yoing. The room went icily silent.

'Crabbe has followers still working for him secretly in the apparat,' said Petty in the crowded little room. 'Crabbe was an Enemy of the People – and a Gumby!'

'Not a word Lenin would have used,' I commented. 'Lenin did say, *"A good Communist is a good secret policeman!"'*

'I want to denounce Spencer-Percival!' shouted Money-Banks, pointing maniacally around the Committee.

'I denounce Danby for Trotskyism!' said Grimshaw.

'You'd know!' muttered Ogre.

'I denounce Grimshaw,' replied Danby. 'I call for Death!'

This was the hysteria of fear: the place exploded in denunciations.

'Can I speak?'

It was Steady Pelham. That awkward phlegmatic voice calmed the frantic, scared denunciations.

Ormonde glanced at me. I shrugged. Ormonde beckoned to him.

Steady Pelham stood up, the sturdy spectacled boy with his serious, old man's face. He was never really young.

'I just wanted to say – why is all this beating up necessary? We've won, haven't we? By Jove, you don't have to kill your fallen enemies do you, Koba old chap? You're not Ivan the Terrible, Conroy.'

'Hear, hear, Steady.'

The wavering members of the Committee nodded at Pelham – so like Bukharin. If Steady went on, there would be no Purge. But I had Stalin's 1937 speech to hand:

'Let Comrade Stalin speak!' hissed Petty.

'Comrade Stalin!' called Ormonde.

'*The further we move forward,*' I said, relishing Satan's own words, '*the more success we have, the more embittered will the remnants of the destroyed exploiter classes become, the sooner they will resort to extreme forms of struggle, the more they will blacken the Soviet state, the more they will seize on the desperate means as the last resort of the doomed ... We will smash our enemies in the future, as we do now and we did in the past!*'

'Hurrah! Hurrah!'shouted the Central Committee. 'Hear! Hear!' said the Scallywags and the Politburo members. 'Vigilance! Destroy our enemies! Death to gumbies and Trotskyites!'

Minto and Money-Banks shouted loudest.

Steady Pelham applauded politely but he did not call out like the others.

Then Ormonde chose the Queen song for the day.

It was called 'Death On Two Legs'.

Glam rock and firing squads.

In the gloom of the Kremlin yard, Petty walked up to Minto and softly slapped his right cheek with his leather gloves: medieval gauntlet gently meeting modern totalitarianism.

Minto was arrested by Ogleton and Ormonde, who grabbed his hands. He was the first. I hoped no more would be necessary.

As they led Minto away, Money-Banks ran up to me: 'They denounced me, Stalin. But I'm your best friend and the greatest Stalinist. I'm safe, aren't I? Kill the Enemies the People!'

He was crying. I embraced him and soothed his tears!: 'You're safe.

You're my closest comrade. I'm promoting you to the Orgburo. Don't worry!' I reassured him warmly.

That made him feel safe. But he was still doomed to Stalin's speciality – the gradual liquidation. No wonder Bukharin called Stalin that 'genius of dosage'.

Minto surrendered wearily. They led him out through the archway of the Kremlin into the courtyard that was surrounded by wire to form a sort of concrete football ground.

It was dark now and bitterly cold. It was scary outside. Really frightening. Sometimes we stood on the steps and listened to the darkness: we heard a creature out there which coughed like a devil and made snuffling noises. We called it The Grunter: it was either a vampiric monster or adenoidal Mr Humphries, walking his dog. I never found out which.

I do not know what Petty and his torturers did to the traitor. I did not concern myself with such menial work – not in public anyway, though, like Stalin, I was very keen to know how Enemies of the People took the torture. They tended to shout, 'Long live Stalin!' which showed what idiots they were. Why didn't they go to Mr Trevelyan? Because the Purges became part of schoolboy lore, as much of a pillar of the school as Latin grammar, cricket and playing conkers.

Minto, when he was tied naked to the wire in the freezing night air while the NKVD heroes kicked footballs and threw conkers at him, kept saying, 'If only Comrade Stalin knew what was happening ... If only ...'

I was pleased that he cried.

But it was not enough.

At breakfast, Petty triumphantly slipped the piece of paper onto my plate of Rice Crispies as if it were a holy relic.

'Is it a signed confession?'

'Yesth,' lisped Petty.

It read: 'I, Minto, admit to betraying the Leninist-Stalinist Soviet Union in cahoots with the German Nazi General Staff and the Tsarist masters of Coverdale Prep School. I confess to organising the attempted assassination of Comrade Commissar Archeamboye during rugby practice which was only foiled by the daring work of Commissar Petty. Long live Comrade Stalin. Signed Minto.'

Petty increasingly needed his own glory: was it necessary to mention himself like that?

I stuck it up on the board the next day. The masters thought it funny: 'Most droll,' said Mrs Gladwyn-Jones. But Minto knew how serious it was. He was put 'in Coventry' (the British version of Siberia).

'Tonight, after lights out, I want you to arrest Danby. He's in dorm K. The dorm prefect is one of us and will sign any arrest order.'

'Very good, Comrade Stalin,' whispered Petty proudly.

That night, Danby was awakened by the 'knock on the door at four in the morning' – in fact, it was more like midnight because it was difficult for our virtuous secret policemen to stay awake. They were so tired after rugger.

Danby was interrogated and signed.

At the next day's Central Committee meeting, I sat silently as comrades old and young accused Danby and Minto of being vermin and hyenas. Petty was best: he said they should be shot like 'dogs, dolts and gumbies'. He had also arrested Pelham's little brother: Pelham minor was a Berk – in his second term.

Even Pelham, my brave friend always noble enough to stand up to Stalin on behalf of the innocent, approved his own brother's arrest. 'I support the arrests of traitors,' he said in a voice without expression, sitting alone at the back – though later, when we were grown-ups and met again at some business symposium, he told me he never forgave himself for his weakness.

I then gave Stalin's most hypocritical speech, pretending everyone was happy when in fact there was death and fear all around us. *'Life has become better, comrades,'* I said. *'Life has become gayer!'* Everyone cheered and there was a standing ovation that lasted for ages because no one dared be the first to sit down again.

But they knew what awaited the traitors: Bunsen burners.

This time, Ormonde played 'Staying Alive' by the Bee Gees. Executioners and victims danced together to its high-pitched chorus. Its title gave this Stalinist disco fever a certain macabre magic: they were literally boogeying to stay alive.

At the end of the meeting, Grimshaw was arrested and taken out to the courtyard, where he cried bitterly. When he was back in Lubianka Square, the steamy boiler room, he too came up with a signed confession. This time the confession was much fuller. He confessed that he, together with Minto and Danby, had been: 'Spies, saboteurs,

terrorists, Trotskyites, Zinovievites, Bukharinites, Rightists, Mensheviks, SRs, Anarchists, nationalists, White emigrés, gendarmes, kulaks,
scoundrels, Kolchakites, swine, Dashnaks, Bundists, vipers, vermin,
Traders of the Motherland, Left-wing Infantilists, Petty Bourgeoisie,
Right deviationalists, Fascist degenerates, Constituent Assemblyists,
Petliurists, Musavists, Georgian Mensheviks, national chauvinists or
any other counter-revolutionary outfits.'

Everything, in fact. As you can see, it is not an understatement to
say that he had been pretty active in his evil opposition.

He added, 'Together with this lickspittle, we with certain OTHER
COMRADES planned the wounding of Comrade Commissar Archeamboye and the poisoning of Comrades Stalin, Petty and Ogleton by
putting cyanide in their Grub.'

When Petty handed me this, I could not help but smile.

'What do you think?'

'Very thorough,' I said. 'But find these "other comrades" quickly.'

'Yesth, Comrade.'

'They must be brought to trial. A show trial.'

'Well, that's already Minto, Danby, Grimshaw and there are two
others. Old Bolsheviks all! One may be a terrible surprise.'

'Save them for the trial.'

When Grimshaw's full confession was posted up on the board the
next day, beside the First Fifteen team written in Mr Trevelyan's
generous hand, I also put up this message: *'The glorious Soviet
intelligence service, headed by Stalinist Commissar N.I. Yezhov, has
smashed the vipers' nest of these vermin.'*

Everyone knew of course that Yezhov was Petty minor. The more I
read about Yezhov, who organised the most horrid things for Stalin in
the Great Purges, the more he resembled Petty. Like Stalin, I rewarded
him with Yezhov's title 'Commissar-General of Security'.

Petty and his men worked day and night on these confessions: all
were taken directly to the science lab. One glimpse of the naked
Bunsen flames was usually enough. But if not, they stoned them in
the fives courts, dipped their faces in the chapel's font or hung them
by their feet off the squash court balcony. (In fact, those butter-fingers
dropped Minto. But he survived.)

Soon it was obvious that I had, if anything, UNDERestimated the
scale of betrayal. Petty really seemed to believe the deliberate perfidy
of what *Pravda* called 'The Archeamboye Leg Breakage Trotskyite

Plot'. I was inclined to agree – even when it turned out that Archeamboye's leg was not broken at all, just sprained.

Anyone could be arrested with that knock on the door in the early hours. Stalin ruthlessly arrested many of his oldest friends, men who spent time with his family and who knew him best. No one was safe.

When I read about this in my books, I wondered like everyone else how Stalin could have done it. Until I did it myself. Stalin's daughter Svetlana understood this when she wrote in her brilliant memoir, *Twenty Letters to a Friend*: '*At this point – and this is where his cruel, implacable nature showed itself – the past ceased to exist for him. Years of friendship and fighting side by side in a common cause might as well never have been. "So you've betrayed me," some inner demon would whisper. "I don't even know you anymore."*'

Stalin does not appear to have experienced the slightest conventional guilt. But he did worry about how his God of History would see him after the Great Terror. One day, while signing some of Yezhov's Death Lists with Molotov, he said quietly, '*Who's going to remember this riff-raff in ten or twenty years' time? No one. Who remembers the names now of the boyars Ivan the Terrible got rid of? No one ... The people had to know he was getting rid of all his enemies. In the end they all got what they deserved.*'

Molotov reassured him.

'Anyone else, Comrade Yezhov?' I said to Petty as I signed the death lists sitting in the empty art school that I used as a Kremlin office sometimes.

'Let me arrest that dangerous Ormonde, that bourgeois poet ... he's too independent.'

'*No, leave that cloud-dweller in peace,*' I said, sparing Ormonde as Stalin spared Pasternak.

'St John ...' he suggested, moving down his list.

'He sleeps with his sloppy mouth open.'

'Never trust a boy who sleeps with his mouth open,' said Petty, just as I was about to say precisely the same thing.

'Why, Comrade Yezhov?' I tested him.

'His gaping mouth means he is open to Trotskyite subversion. His vulnerability when asleep suggests lack of vigilance against Enemies of the People. His willingness to sleep in such an unStalinist way means he's a traitor.'

I nodded. 'And Petty? Arrest everyone who sleeps with their mouths open.'

'Done, Comrade Stalin. I have exactly such a list already prepared. Here, will the Central Committee sign?'

I signed. The rest of the Politburo had already signed. I noted the signatures – Ormonde, Nonsuch, Ogre ...

'Commissar-General, why hasn't Steady signed?'

'He hasn't signed any lists,' said Petty. 'Besides, his brother's on that one.'

'Where is he?'

'Downstairs.'

Moments later, Pelham stood before me.

'Sign the death lists please, Steady,' I said. 'Everyone else has signed.'

He walked heavily up – he had such big feet – and took up the pen. But then he laid it down in his stolid way.

'I can't. I won't sign.'

'The Politburo's signed. Please, Steady. If you don't, I won't be able to protect my dear Bukharin any more. Are you against your Party, your friend Stalin?'

'Shall I arrest him?' asked Petty.

'I just can't sign. It's not right. I'd never forgive myself,' said Pelham in his plain, matter-of-fact way. 'I knew it would end in tears.'

'Are you still my friend?' I said.

'Yes, oh, yes, Koba. Your best friend. Your first friend at Coverdale.'

When I had finished signing, I came out of the Kremlin, leaving Petty to check the paperwork.

Pelham was waiting for me in the dark, nervously tapping his big shoes on the concrete; Steady looked touching and sad like an old ox, nearing its trip to town.

'Koba,' said Pelham. 'You don't know what's happening in your name. Petty's NKVD are torturing innocent boys. The evidence is gobbledegook! Bloody bunkum! That's the long and the short of it.'

'I'm grateful,' I replied. 'I had no idea. I'm shocked that the security apparatus is so out of control. Petty hides everything from me. I'll order an enquiry at once. Thank God you told me ...'

'My little brother is quite innocent and is being tortured on the conveyor belt in the toils of Lubianka,' said Pelham. 'Now you want to shoot him.'

'S'truth – I'll have him released at once. Thank Lenin! I love your honesty, Comrade,' and I gave him a Brezhnev bearhug. 'We must stop these criminals. But at least we have arrested true monsters like Minto and Danby.'

'Death isn't good enough for them,' said Pelham dutifully.

'Actually it's too good for them,' I added.

'Thank you, Comrade Stalin. You'll be remembered for your justice.'

'You're the only friend who really tells me the truth these days, dear Steady.' He was walking away when Petty slunk out of the shadows with the death lists.

'Indignatio principis mors est,' said Petty to poor Pelham as he passed him. The anger of the king means death. He had learned it in Emperor Blunt's lessons. Steady Pelham's gallumphing footsteps grew further away.

'Pelham minor is in Lubianka?'

'You just signed his death warrant, Koba.'

'Petty, release him now to keep Pelham happy.'

'But he's confessed ...'

'You can arrest him again after Scottish dancing on Friday.'

'Clever move, Koba.'

'You do understand, Commissar-General, that we must destroy not just those who HAVE betrayed us ...'

'... but also those who MIGHT.'

Commissar-General Petty could even finish my thoughts.

'Shall I begin the executions?' he asked.

'Not yet.'

That dark afternoon, Ogleton called on me at the Kremlin with Archeamboye and Ormonde.

'Why don't you come and play rugger with the Third Fifteen,' suggested the Transylvanian. 'You can play on the wing. Whatever team we are on, we'll protect you. We can nobble our Enemies of the People.'

'There are so many now that we are wasting valuable police time,' said Ormonde seriously.

I hated rugby and did not look good in shorts. But I could not think of a way out of this suggestion.

'Who's taking the game?'

Ogre cackled.

'Young Mr Selwyn,' said Ormonde.

I had to smile.

22

STALIN PLAYS RUGBY

My bodyguards were as good as their word. They never left my side during the game even though Archeamboye and Ormonde were supposed to be on the opposing team. Petty was not much more impressive than me, a wounded bird shivering on the wing.

Mr Selwyn had a lullaby voice and that unformed foetal face. We were not even sure if he could Produce. He looked silly in a grey suit with the trousers tucked into rugby socks and rugby boots. Poor Mr Selwyn just could not keep control. He blew his whistle after about five minutes and said to my bodyguards, 'What are you two doing? You're on the other side.'

But Ormonde answered, 'Yes, sir, but we're marking Stalin, Mr Selwyn. He could break through the line.'

Of course, everyone laughed at the very idea of my doing any such thing. I hoped the ball would never come near me. It was bitingly cold out on the wing. The keenies played while we comrades talked Stalinism.

'How is coal production in the Donbass?' I asked Ormonde.

'Up!' he said.

'Efficiency at the Stalin Tractor Factory?'

'Up! Up! Always UP!'

When the game really got going, it was time to continue our vigilance.

Minto and the other Enemies of the People were playing. As soon as there were piles of bodies around the field, I sent in Ogleton and Ormonde piling on top. Their mission was simple: 'Break the will and kneecaps of the Enemies of the People.'

They did this nobly.

Every time the scrum moved on, there would be Danby or Minto lying on the muddy earth crying and holding their shins.

'No fouling there in the scrum. You hear me, Ogleton! Archeamboye!' Mr Selwyn blew the whistle but the Terror continued.

Mr Selwyn knew he received no respect. Instead of leaving it at that, he made a bad mistake that he would regret. He looked for the weakest person on the field and decided to pick on him. The blunderer.

The weakest person APPEARED to be me. Stalin's withered arm and my semi-blindess without spectacles. Little did he know.

He blew the whistle again and strode over towards me on the wing, surrounded as usual by my comrades.

'Conroy,' he said. 'Did you come out here to play or to hide from the ball? Look! You haven't even got a speck of mud on your knees. While look at Minto, Spencer-Percival or Howell here! They're not afraid, Conroy. Are you a milksop? I suggest you start playing.'

All the boys stood and watched me.

AFRAID? Stalin a milksop? After all I had done in the Revolution?

'Wetty,' said Minto, bumping deliberately into me, almost knocking me flying.

'Milksop,' called Danby.

'Milkie Stalin!' teased Spencer-Percival, still a member of the Central Committee. 'Milkman!'

The Purges were not enough: this was the moment I understood why Stalin insisted on Death – the Highest Measure of Punishment. Torture and fear were inadequate. You cannot teach traitors loyalty.

I blamed Mr Selwyn for this display. Even diehards like Ogre and Archeamboye could be influenced by this sort of black disinformation. They looked at me differently as if I WAS a milksop.

I required an intrepid stroke of Stalinist genius to prove I was a Man of Steel not Man of Milk.

Mr Selwyn left me standing there and ran back to the centre. He blew the whistle. Then he knelt down to tie up his rugby boots. His bottom stuck out, his suit trousers tight over his pert ruggerball buttocks. Without a second's doubt, I ran across the pitch and up behind him. Then I kicked him as hard as I could in the bottom. I then planned to run away and pretend that it was someone else.

But Mr Selwyn did not leap up to catch the culprit. He remained in that position. Then, in terrible slow motion, he put his hands between his legs, collapsed onto his side and rolled around in the mud. He was writhing in what I could see was agony: his face was frozen in a shout. His mouth was wide open but no sound came out.

The game continued for a couple of minutes but then it ground to a halt as the boys noticed something strange was afoot with Mr Selwyn.

Mad Ogleton was by my side and typically thought this was a daring exploit of Stalinist prowess. 'Good shot, comrade!' he said, nodding. 'You Stalinist harum-scarum lion! Down with the Trotsky-ites! Off with their heads!' You never knew what he was talking about half the time. Then, throwing his hammer-head back, he gave his firing-squad laugh.

But the other boys were shocked. Quite naturally, they formed a half-circle around Mr Selwyn, but at a safe distance, as if Mr Selwyn might explode or turn into a sabre-toothed tiger and bite them.

I was worried that he might do something of the sort to me.

'I don't know what I did,' I muttered to no one in particular. 'It was a mistake.'

'God, you're two-faced,' said Bridgewater.

'Two-faced?' I said. 'I've got many more faces than that!'

I found myself in the semicircle with the others about fifteen feet from Mr Selwyn, who was rocking himself from side to side.

I was especially afraid. To attack a master was beyond the pale – even the Russian Pale. If people kicked their superiors, teachers and bosses at work, in the bottom, maybe the whole of Britain would collapse! If someone kicked the Prime Minister in the bottom on the *Nine O'Clock News*, his head would be on a pike by dawn!

'You did it, Conroy,' said Bridgewater, who was still a Central Committee member. 'You better go and see what's wrong.'

Minto pushed my shoulder and said, 'Go on, Conroy.'

'But I only kicked him in the bottom,' I said. 'How could it hurt so much?'

Ogleton shrugged, clearly bemused. But Ormonde knew better. He could Produce.

'You must have kicked him in the Googlies,' he said. 'That's where they are.'

'But I thought the googlies were in the front, not the bottom,' I protested.

'Sort of,' said Ormonde. 'But they join in the middle.'

'I think you got him in the Ammunition Box,' said Petty, pretending to shoot one of his bloody shotguns.

'You'd better say something,' said Ormonde, 'to Selwyn Agonistes.' Milton's *Samson Agonistes* was Ormonde's favourite – even though I thought it was quite impenetrable. Ormonde was a poet too.

'Will you come with me?'

So the two of us left the safety of the semicircle and slowly, watching our steps as if we were in a minefield, we approached the gasping, quivering, rocking Mr Selwyn his suit caked in mud. His mouth was still wide open and nothing still came out of it.

Instinctively Ormonde and I rested our hands on each other's shoulders as we got closer. When we stood over the master, who had silent tears rolling down his pale cheeks and who was curled up into a foetal ball in his torment, I said, 'Mr Selwyn, sir, are you all right?'

He tried to speak but could not.

We glanced back at the semicircle of boys, standing there on this desolate winter's field in their muddy rugby shorts, striped coloured shirts and studded boots. They crept forward like a chorus line, ears cocked, agog to hear what my victim said.

I tried again. 'Mr Selwyn, sir, Mr Selwyn ...'

Ormonde shrugged his shoulders.

'Sir,' I said, 'I'm really sorry, sir. It was me. Conroy, sir. I didn't mean to, sir ...'

Finally, Mr Selwyn managed to answer. 'I'm ... fi-ne. Ju-st ... leave ... me. Al-one. Lea ... ve me! Ga-me's OV-ER! Go ... ba-ck to the Sch ... ur ... ur ... OOL! Don't te-ell a so-ul!'

'I'm really sorry, sir.'

'Le-ave me AL-ONE!'

Poor Mr Selwyn. The pain was obviously overwhelming.

I walked back to where the others waited.

'Go back to the school. Game's over. Don't say anything to anyone about Mr Selwyn's agony. Go!'

For a moment, they hesitated, looking over at the ignoble sight of Selwyn Agonistes. Then we ran and did not look back until we were in the showers. We never told any adults about Selwyn Agonistes.

Petty began the executions at once.

And Mr Selwyn was too ashamed to complain. It was a hard time for everyone, those terrible thirties.

*

After tea, Miss Snow was outside.

'Was it a good game, Conroy?'

'Yes, Miss Snow.'

'Did you play well?'

'I was too cold.'

'What? A fine kid like you! Cold?'

Before bewitching Miss Snow, I could not help but revert to being just an over-sensitive spaniel. She alone could de-Stalinise me.

'Do you think Mr Selwyn enjoyed the game?'

'Yes, very much so.'

She looked at me hard.

I knew that she knew. So I knew that she knew I was lying. I relished our complicity. It was like getting Molotov and Malenkov to co-sign Stalin's death lists.

I wished that moment could last longer. I was flushed, though not out of shame. Perhaps I divined that adult rule – a shared lie is more intimate than a shared caress.

'I want you to do me a favour.' She changed tack again. 'The new boys this year are hunky-dory. But there are one or two missing home terribly. When you arrived you missed your mum grievously, so I wondered if you could keep an eye on them ...'

I did not like this idea at all: Stalin was not a cry-baby. None the less, I had cried bitterly that very term until I was hailed by my Stalinist comrades. SHE had seen me and comforted me.

'Running the Soviet empire is a full-time job ...'

'You'd be MY deputy,' she finished.

'Really?' That made a difference.

'We'd have to work closely together to keep an eye on the less fortunate. Of your subjects.'

Well, put like that, how could I refuse?

'What would my title be?'

'Title?'

'Well, I'm already Secretary-General of the Communist Party of the USSR ...'

'Oh, I see. How about "Homesick Commissar"?'

She had chosen me for this honour – out of everyone. It was only later that I realised that she had chosen to comfort ME because I was the most homesick of the lot.

As soon as she was gone, I called in Pahlavi to the Politburo urinals.

'More betrayal,' I said as we performed beside each other.

'At your service, Comrade Stalin. We have five more Enemies of the People on the Conveyer tonight.'

'Bravo. Miss Snow heard about Selwyn Agonistes by teatime. Find out how.'

I little knew then what pain this order would ultimately cause.

23

THE GREAT SHOW TRIAL 1938

'Silence in court!' yelled Ogre.

When the Transylvanian shouted, they obeyed.

'I hereby declare the Great Trial against the Enemies of the People – open!' bellowed Judge Archeamboye, standing on top of the broad table in the model railway room wearing full cricket whites to symbolise the purity of Leninism. Then he sat down with a thump of his tabular buttocks on his precariously balanced throne. *'The whole world will see,'* he read haltingly from a little notebook, *'that the Accused will have every chance to defend themselves. But be in no doubt: the Soviet People demand that Justice will be done!'*

'Hear! Hear!' shouted the audience: there were probably fifty boys, some in sports gear, crammed into the room. Most were young Twits, Berks and Scallywags, which was good because they were the future of the revolution. They were there to witness one of the greatest acts of political theatre ever performed.

The nervous defendants sat against the facing wall in their little tweedy sports jackets and striped Coverdalian ties: in the model railway room the table went round the edge of the whole room so the judge faced the defendants while the audience sat in between them.

The defendants were Minto, Danby and Grimshaw, but they were notorious old Trotskyites.

After they filed in, there was a pause. Then Money-Banks, whom I had recently promoted, was led to his place, followed by Bridgewater, who had rashly called me 'two-faced'. Another gap.

Suddenly, Pelham was standing between two NKVD guards in the doorway. Then he was led to his place in the dock. The audience gasped: Pelham, like Bukharin, *'the darling of the Party'*. Steady Pelham, the benign and beloved. If HE was a saboteur, then nothing was sacred. The audience gasped – they listened intently. I had loved

Pelham until he became an enemy. In our harsh time, there was no place for his soft heart. Now his popularity was dangerous.

Since no one knew how to turn off the model railway, the *Flying Scotsman* whirled round and round at the feet of the men fighting for their lives. On Archeamboye's left and right stood Petty and Pahlavi, the lawyers, also wearing cricket whites.

'All right,' said the judge. 'Comrade Petty, please begin your examination of defendant Pelham.'

The convenience of the trial was that everything unpopular that had happened in the school in the last year was blamed on these Enemies of the People: cadres hissed and booed every time the Grub ban was mentioned.

Petty pranced up and down the table, just missing the fragile railway line with each turn. He was playing the part of another of Stalin's vilest creatures – Prosecuter-General Vyshinsky – with such odious exuberance that even as he began the first indictment he was wheezing ominously, 'That Pelham, known during the revolution as Steady, did: (1) wreck tractors on the School Farm, poison cattle, spoil the sausages for the whole school last week, burn the toast, break the chip-making machine for a month last term and he also threw nails into the porridge and salt into the butter. But above all, he was surely responsible for having GRUB banned for a whole term!

(2) He also hired a hit squad of Bovverboys, indulged in terroristic attacks on leaders such as Comrade Archeamboye, who almost broke his leg, and Comrade Stalin.

(3) He conspired with enemy powers, rival prep schools, to betray the Soviet Union during cricket and rugby games so that our glorious team would lose.'

The audience of prep school rugby fanatics, who lived only for sports, chips and Grub, seemed to believe all of this. Pelham's popularity soon vanished when the food-wrecking indictments were read – and supporting other schools in rugby: the serpent! When everyone had loved and trusted him so much! Some Scallywags mocked the defendants. One Berk, who was a fanatical rugby player, was so outraged at the thought of any sporting betrayal of Coverdale that he even spat at Pelham.

Pelham let the wad of saliva run off his face: how solid and superb he appeared in the midst of this twisted circus.

'Silence in court,' said Archie.

'Are these accusations true or false, accused Pelham?' asked Petty, pointing at the defendant.

Pelham hesitated, but when he caught Ogre's black gypsy eyes, he replied robotically: 'ALL TRUE! AND THERE'S MORE!'

The audience muttered. The NKVD, led by Petty and assisted by Ogleton, Ormonde and Pahlavi, had achieved amazing, indeed unbelievable, confessions. Pahlavi had got Minto and Danby to confess by blackmail. Nonsuch told him he had witnessed a Fiddling Encounter in the carpentry room with Minto and Danby. This allowed the subtle Persian to force them into admitting even more terrible things by screwing Danby's head into the carpentry room's 'vice anglaise.'

'Did you, Bukharin, really plan to assassinate Comrade Stalin and his entire Politburo during a rugby practice?'

'Yes, not just me but others too ... I blame myself for everything bad that has happened not just in the school but in Britain, America and the world ... The Flood, the Black Death, cancer, WW1. Let me be blamed for it all. Spare the others!'

This was not in the plan. Pelham was cleverly mocking the trial, undermining its ludicrous claims by pleading guilty to everything.

'Calm down, Pelham. Please preserve your dignity,' interrupted the silky voice of Pahlavi. 'Can you name other saboteurs?'

'I CAN NAME THEM!'

'Names! Names!' hissed the audience.

'And did you, Pelham, really wish brave Soviet Coverdale to LOSE against Fascist Sunningdale and capitalist Ludgrove ...?'

'Yes! Yes!'

'Did you sell your soul to the devil, to Trotsky, to Crabbe?' Petty worked himself up, spitting and wheezing like a posh little witch doctor.

'Oh yes. Did I ever?' His calm dignity made him stand out. Yet he went through with the trial.

'Was it at Eaton Square during the hols?' prompted Pahlavi seamlessly.

'Indeed. Trotsky asked me and the others – I'll name them later – to poison the school ... rugger ... assassinate ... cricket ... German General Staff ... Grub ... murder ... English imperialistic spy ... wreck machinery ...'

The sheer evil of this satanic web of treason! The audience leaned forward to listen, titillated by the promiscuous treachery of this criminal gang.

The great show trial, attended by diplomats and journalists across the world, was the climax of Stalin's Purges. At the trial in 1938, intelligent and able Old Bolsheviks, including Russia's most brilliant theorist, Bukharin, as well as fallen NKVD boss Yagoda, confessed to unlikely terrorist acts. Stalin knew the charges were lies. The charges were silly, but in that witch hunt of whipped-up hysteria, most Russians believed them. Even foreign dupes, like the American Ambassador, swallowed the big lie.

Petty stamped his feet for silence. 'I call my next witness: Merke the school cleaner!'

'Merke!' the court officials called outside. 'Bring in witness Merke.'

The white-haired and slightly touched Lett, who had appeared at the school during the war and worked there ever since, inhabited a cottage in the Siberian Outback. In the witness box he wore his overalls; he held his broom.

Merke was a prestigious witness because he was adult and an Easterner, almost a Russian. He had been teased by so many generations of Coverdalians that this seemed to be a good chance to get his own back.

No one understood his testimony but he did seem to agree that he had seen some acts of 'terrorism in the kitchens' that had put the 'strategically vital' toasting machine out of action.

I reproduce here, from the official trial record, a section of cross-examination, as it later appeared in *Pravda*:

Petty: Did you, Comrade Merke, see that lickspittle of Trotsky's excreta, Pelham, put nails in the porridge last week?

Merke: Tovarish! Tovarish!

Petty: Thank you, Comrade, for your patriotic testimony.

The defendants gave evidence against each other. Here is Money-Banks on the stand:

Petty: Did you see Minto, that running dog of Bukharinist slime, try to make the school lose in rugby against Heathfield by tripping up Archeamboye during First Fifteen practice?

Money-Banks: Yes, Chief Prosecuter, but it wasn't only Minto. It was also me, Danby, even Pelham. We were terrorists ...

Petty slipped on his black leather gloves, finger by finger, to give his summing-up. He demanded the Highest Measure of Punishment: what Mr Trevelyan called 'Execution at dawn by firing squad with ice cream'. Petty used Vyshinsky's real words, which actually sound as preposterous as the taunts of prep school boys.

'*The whole country are waiting for, and demanding, one thing: that the traitors and spies who sold out our Motherland to the enemy be shot like vile dogs,*' he began, beating his hands together. But he appeared to be suffocating. Nonsuch ran forward and handed him his asthma puffer. He took a few breaths and calmed down a bit. Then he went on, '*The people demand one thing: that the accursed vermin be squashed.*'

The audience burst into frantic applause at this point, even though Petty's jabbering and spluttering were not a pretty sight.

'Off with Pelham's head!' they called.

'*We our people will, as before,*' finished Petty, '*stride along our path now cleansed of the last trace of the scum and vileness of the past, led by our beloved leader and teacher, the great Stalin.*'

Applause!

But this proved to be one Stalin too far. Merke had sat restlessly, enjoying this odd scene, gaily agreeing to anything he was asked. But the words 'great Stalin' pushed him too far. He jumped up and started screaming in Latvian, whirling his broom perilously around his head, aiming for Petty. He just missed Archeamboye, who had to throw himself off his chair to escape. When the defendants, too, were forced to jump out of his way, the trial broke up in disorder.

Merke ran back to his small house out in the Siberian forests with tears running down his face.

The model railway continued to whir round and round.

Where was Stalin during his theatre?

I found a book in the library called *Eastern Approaches* by a chivalrous Scottish adventurer called Sir Fitzroy Maclean. He was the real basis for Ian Fleming's James Bond 007. He attended the great trial. This caught my imagination:

'*How did the Supreme Puppet Master view the proceedings? At one stage of the trial, a clumsily directed arc-light dramatically revealed to attentive members of the audience the familiar features and heavy drooping moustache peering out from behind the black glass of a small window, high up under the ceiling of the courtroom.'*

So the Supreme Puppet Master hid under the table – and listened.

The sobbing echoed through the shadowy Victorian kitchens with their yellow peeling walls and bare stone floors. In old-fashioned schools, the showers and the kitchens are interchangeable.

It was a Stalinist Scallywag called Kildare.

'What's wrong, Sebastian?' asked Mrs Trevelyan when she found him there. She had heard his crying in her cosy kitchen next door. When she had given him a cup of tea and sat him down for a chat, he confessed that the reason he was crying was that Pelham had sabotaged the toaster – and was planning to kill a 'really nice older boy called Stalin'.

Mrs Trevelyan could have ignored this rubbish – but suppose some of it was true?

'I'm sure it's all nonsense, Sebastian,' she said sensibly.

'There was a real trial. There was evidence. We all thought Pelham was jolly decent until we heard about his Trotskyite wreckerism,' sobbed Kildare. 'There must be SOME truth in it!'

'Koba ... are we still friends? I did all you asked. I played the part. Pax? Come on, old chap, I'm your oldest friend ...'

They led dear, big-hearted Pelham past me. He was dignified and brave throughout: he refused the blindfold.

Steady put out his sturdy hand to shake mine.

The NKVD guards and even Petty watched carefully to see what I would do.

I did not offer my hand.

'Surely, even after that ridiculous performance, we're still friends,' said Pelham, his voice echoing in the courtyard. 'Glad the ordeal's over. Can I go now?'

'It was plain that yesterday we were personal friends,' I said, *'and now we are parting company politically. I don't think all these wailings are worth a brass farthing. We are not a family or a côterie of personal friends. We are the political party of the working class.'* I looked at dear old Steady. 'That's the long and the short of it,' I said mockingly and walked away, bleeding inside. The NKVD tied up his hands.

Bukharin was shot straight after the trial in the cellars of Lubianka.

Our defendants were taken out into the courtyard in the darkness; they were tied to the wire; and shot at dawn by firing squad with ice cream. The bullets were choc ices stolen from the kitchens. These icy missiles were hard, cold and painful.

I watched the whole scene from the shadows.

'Trotsky called Stalin "*Genghis Khan with a telephone*",' said Steady. 'What does that make you?'

'Stalin with a cricket bat,' I snapped back.

The NKVD guards laughed boorishly. 'Well said, Comrade Stalin!'

'Long live Stalin!' said Steady drily as they raised the ice creams.

Yet, even then, I missed his good counsel.

'Fire' ordered the NKVD officer.

24

THE CLIMAX OF THE MASSACRE 1939

Afterwards Pelham, the Purge was no longer fun. It was real. And it had a life of its own. The denunciations and tortures came quicker and quicker. When did it begin to spin out of control? When did the Politburo begin to merge with the life of the school so that the edges became fatally blurred?

Every day after prep, Petty recounted the atrocities committed in my name.

'I shot Lamb last night. The Trotskyite jackal. Tonight, we've pulled in Spencer-Percival. And I've perfected that new torture that really makes them confess ...'

'Surely the Purges are almost finished now,' I suggested.

'No way, José! We're discovering more and more betrayal, Comrade Stalin! Give me a little more time. And a few more heads!'

'A little more time,' I said.

At midnight, the brave commissars of the NKVD, wearing pyjamas and dressing-gowns, rushed Spencer-Percival through the school, past Leningrad through the Kremlin and straight into the science lab.

The door swung open. Inside there were no lights on. But there were three Bunsen burners alight on the top desk. It was silent in there, except for the roar of the burners and the shuffling of the locusts. Watching from the shadows of the storeroom, I stared at this ritual, fascinated.

'What's this?' shivered Spencer-Percival.

'Shut up, you prostitute,' said Petty. None of us knew precisely what 'prostitute' meant. No one would tell us. But Stalin and and his craven sidekick Voroshilov wrote 'scoundrel and prostitute' on the letter of an innocent friend begging for mercy. 'Move it!' He shoved him forward. Ogre and Ormonde and two bloodthirsty Scallywags were

waiting. Ogre's swarthy nutchuck face was particularly Transylvanian, half-lit by the flickering flames.

'What are you going to do to me?' stammered Spencer-Percival.

'We might burn your hair off with the Bunsen burners,' answered
Petty.

'But I have a better idea,' said Ogre.

'What's your especial fear?' asked Ormonde.

'Rats,' said Spencer-Percival stupidly.

'Bring Comrade George Orwell's contraption, Comrade Ogre,'
ordered Petty. 'It's *1984*, traitor!'

'That's not for years,' came the victim's high foolish voice.

'Time flies!'

Ogre walked around the desk, carrying what appeared to be a glass
pipe, and approached the prisoner who was held on both sides by
Bolshevik heroes. I stood up and took a step forward from the
storeroom door.

Ogre placed the pipe on top of the incubator that was lit up so the
chicks could hatch.

There was something alive and wriggling inside the pipe. One end
was sealed but the other was only closed by a piece of paper, with
holes in it.

Spencer-Percival would have screamed but Ormonde put his hands
over his mouth and then tied on the gag.

'You see how it works, Percival. The pipe is against your face.
Richard Nixon, that's the rat's name, can only escape from the pipe by
eating its way out.'

'It starts with the eyes then the lips,' added Petty.

'Petty! Outside! Now!' I snapped, stepping out of the darkness.

Everyone stopped in their tracks. Spencer-Percival's eyes bulged
above his gag.

'What ...?' Petty said. 'Comrade Stalin!'

'I want to talk to you outside.'

It was freezing. Petty looked like a wealthy little hunchback in his
woollen dressing-gown and slippers engraved with his family crest.

'This is horrible,' I said. 'It can't go on. Let him go, Petty. We've
gone too far.'

'He hates you, Conroy,' said Petty, his breath like steam from an old
train. 'They ALL hate you. Really hate you. Without this, who knows
what they'd do to you? They're stronger than us really. It is only

terror that stops them beating us all up. You should hear what they say about you, Conroy: scurvy coward, gumby, pleb, grockle, towny, but cabbage most of all.'

'They still ... Cabbage?'

'Yes, yes and more, Conroy. He'll confess all of it by the time we go to bed.'

'But the rat's too far. My parents would be appalled. Mum would say we were worse than the sporting bullies. This was a revolution against the bullying. Now we're the bullies, Petty!'

'No, we are the masses making sure they never bully again.' He stopped and blew out a cloud of cold breath. 'Scurvy coward. Cabbage and the rest. What are you: Stalin – or Trotsky?'

The games of children are always cruel. But they have their rules of honour. The measures of the Old Bolsheviks were savage. But they too prided themselves on treating each other with the civilised manners of the Spartan heroes of old. Now both were gone. When I signed off on Petty's rodentine torture, I had lurched into Stalin's realm – a wilderness without innocence, beyond conscience.

But I thought nothing of it until that one terrible afternoon when Petty stood there with his rake in one hand and handed me the piece of A4 foolscap paper across the bonfire with the other.

'Nonsuch has betrayed you,' said Petty as we gathered the leaves in Odd Jobs in our coats and wellington boots. The leaves were burning. The smoke was rich and damp and somewhat intoxicating.

'That's a lie, Petty.'

'I don't bloody lie!' He threw down his rake. 'You don't know how hard I work to protect you from enemies! I try to hide the ugliness of my work from you. But good God, man! Petty's working from the moment Mato twills "Rise and Shine" and draws the curtains to Lights Out for you, Conroy! You should be more grateful.'

'Nonsuch would never say a word against me!'

'Really?'

Petty was displaying signs of such nastiness that even I began to get a bit worried. Petty loved me too much. He worshipped me so wildly that I sensed that one day he would hate me even more because his love revealed his own lack of character. But we were still Official Best Friends. We planned everything together and spent every living moment together.

But he was jealous of my other friends and started making accusations against them, waking them up in the middle of the night and shining torches in their eyes. The rat, Nixon, always seemed to be in the pipe and the Bunsen burners raged all night.

· It was not the first time he had mentioned that Nonsuch had spent a lot of time with the 'wreckers and vermin'. He suspected that he was planning 'terroristic acts' and was more involved than he admitted in the Fiddling episode that had incriminated Minto and Danby.

The piece of paper was a list of names.

'They are for "checking" Comrade Stalin,' said Petty, when I looked at it beside that crackling bonfire.

Sweet frail Nonsuch was at the top of the list.

'What's he there for?' I said. 'He's devoted to me – and the Party.'

'I have evidence,' answered Petty. 'I didn't tell you. But he was denounced by Minto.'

Even dogs were secret policemen at the climax of the Terror.

Mr Humphries' mathematics lesson was as incomprehensible as usual that afternoon: fractions and square roots were pure Chechen-Ingush to me. I could not stop thinking about Nonsuch. Was he being framed? Or was he too against me and my revolution? Soon, there would be no one left but Petty and I, Yezhov and Stalin.

As Mr Humphries tried in vain to explain the meaning of a percentage and my dyslexia was making me see something completely different from $\sqrt{}$ or %, his little dog emerged from behind his desk where it usually sat. It was a precious Chihuahua which Mrs Humphries had in all innocence named Lavrenti after Beria.

Lavrenti sat for a second, cocked his nose, whimpered and then trotted out of the room, pushing open the door with his shoulder. He seemed to know precisely where he was going.

Five minutes later, the door swung open again. Lavrenti the secret policedog stood there with his mouth filled with a collection of brown rags that appeared to be far larger than his whole body. Lavrenti was excited, wagging his tail, shaking his head, waving the rags.

Mr Humphries stopped in mid-sentence. 'So the square root of ninety-nine is ...' He glanced at Lavrenti. 'Whatsit? Come here, come here ...'

Lavrenti trotted over. Mr Humphries, pince-nez aglinting, knelt down to look.

'Yuck!' shouted Ogre from the front, peering over his desk. 'Those are underpants! They're covered in ... GROSS! ... that's poo! It stinks!'

'Shut up, Ogleton! Right now!' said Mr Humphries. But Ogre was right. We were all standing up now, staring in horror at the pile of underpants, caked with human detritus.

'Blimey!' said the maths master. 'Dear oh dear. Sit down everyone – Conroy! Petty! Lamb! – sit down NOW!'

'That's disgusting!' shouted Ogre again.

'What a stinker!' said Nonsuch.

'Quiet! Does anyone know who these belong to?' asked the master.

We shook our heads. Gradually, we sat back down in our chairs. Despite the smell, it was really a godsend to an anaesthetic maths lesson. You could almost hear twenty little minds calculating: WHOSE were they?

'Look at the nametapes, sir?' recommended Ogre.

Mr Humphries lifted one foul pair on the end of a ruler like a scientific specimen, held it in the air and strained his eyes to see the name on the little tape sewn onto the waist. When he saw the name, he hrrumphed and then said, 'Right, let's get on with the lesson. Square roots!' He clapped his hands. He put the pants in the black bag in the bin, tied the ends in a knot and put them outside the door. 'OK, Conroy, what is the difference betwixt squaring a number and square rooting it?'

'I'm a bit confused, sir.'

But already, Ogleton had whispered to Petty and he had mouthed it at Ormonde and Nonsuch was about to tell me ...

The name.

Usually I would have defended Nonsuch but it was strange year, 1938. Nazi Germany was rising and it looked as if there would be war soon. Stalin began to think about foreign affairs more than before.

'Well, you better pull Nonsuch in then,' I said wearily. 'Just for "checking".'

Every dictator has a Petty. He guessed things that were really just evil flecks of mischief in my mind. I would probably never have dared mention them. But Petty would guess them and say them aloud. By saying them, he made them acceptable and real. So I said, 'Perhaps we better torture Nonsuch. Perhaps his devotion is just a mask.'

'The Bunsen burner?'

'No, no. Something gentler.'

'Orwell's rat?'

'No.'

'The bed in the wall. Dorm B?'

And Petty would actually do it.

You could kill a boy by stoning him with hairbrushes.

That was what Petty and Ogre appeared to be trying to achieve. But they were not the only ones. They stood there in the modern gym's changing rooms round the labyrinthine honeycomb of pigeon holes, where we kept our hairbrushes.

Mr Humphries kept me back in that boring maths lesson because I was unable to complete the simplest arithmetic. $\sqrt{\ }$, %, + and > all got mixed up in the miasma of my dyslexia. Besides, my mind was elsewhere: Hitler's Germany meant there were enemies everywhere.

When I came out half an hour later, I could hear the rumpus coming all the way across the lawn from the gym: the smashing of solid wood thrown hard at a concrete wall. You did not have to be a doctor to know what one of those things could do to the human body.

I ran straight out to the gym complex through the showers and urinals, to emerge at the hairbrush honeycomb.

It was half dark in there. But I could feel the hairbrushes flying past me and crashing into the far corner of the changing room. Petty, Ogre and a lynch mob of others were systematically taking the hairbrushes and hurling them with all their might, shrieking, 'Long live Stalin! Down with traitors!'

In the shadows of that corner, their target was a quivering boy, curled up like a hedgehog, terrified, trying to protect his head.

Ogre peeled away from the crowd as I came in.

'We got the name! We know whose pants they were! Enemies of the People!'

There were many faces raised to watch my reaction. I walked through them to the centre and they parted. I stopped in the middle of the room so they would have to hit me too. They ceased their barrage, but stood there, breathing heavily, brandishing those heavy wooden hairbrushes that our mothers had bought us.

When I looked behind me, Diggle-Johnson raised his freckled, wall-eyed face. He was crouched down there surrounded by hairbrushes. His face was bleeding on the upper lip and above the eye.

134

'Please, please, stop them, Stalin,' he said. 'I'll never do it again. Never. I know it was wrong ...'

'The NKVD warned him,' barked Petty.

'... But I can't help it. I don't mean any harm by it. Surely it's no threat to Stalin and the Soviet Union?' sobbed the School Liar.

Petty put his hand on my shoulder to regain my attention. 'Diggle-Johnson shat in his pants against the Central Committee's Order 768,' he spat. 'Then he hid them every day under his mattress in Stables, threatening to subvert Soviet society.'

'Stop it now. It is not right,' I said quietly. 'Put the hairbrushes back.'

There was a murmur of discontent. These imbeciles believed in the Purges. The momentum of terror and glamour had converted from rugger players to Stalinists. They were born to follow.

Then Ogre replaced his hairbrush in its cubby hole. Ormonde did the same, then stepped back. He drew out his yo-yo. But Petty did not stop. He raised his arm.

'Permission to apply the Highest Measure of Punishment?'

'Stop it NOW, Petty.'

'I don't think ...' he started.

'Now!' I shouted. 'Do I have to make you myself? Who disobeys Stalin?'

It was touch and go if they would obey me. The secret police were an empire within an empire.

Diggle-Johnson's demented sobbing was the only sound. Fear and pain made his freckles and pimples stand out like archipelagoes on a map. He crawled over and wrapped his arms around my ankles. Then he got to his feet and scampered out, almost on all fours, barely human, ragged as a staring-eyed street beggar. The sight of him gave a sense of foreboding.

Next afternoon, everyone had to go up to the playing fields to watch the First Fifteen play. As I was on my way up, I saw Petty and Ogleton bringing a crying Nonsuch up from the boiler room.

'Confessed anything?' I asked.

'Not yet. He says he worships you.'

'Maybe you should let him go then and come and watch the game.'

But Petty said, 'No, we're going to give him the bed in the wall.'

'Are you sure you should? He's a loyal comrade.'

So I went with them up towards Dorm B, where there was one bed in the corner that did not really fit into the room so the mattress was strapped in and the bed was pushed up into the wall.

Mato was not around.

I was never present for torture. That was the genius of my system – and Stalin's. So I sat just outside on a linen cupboard full of y-fronts and socks, swinging my feet, listening to Nonsuch's cries. Whenever they reached a crescendo, I hummed a wistful Queen lovesong called 'Love of My Life' to stifle the shrieks from my mind. But its words seemed oddly appropriate: 'Love of my life, don't hurt me ...' A gorgeous tune. Every now and then, Petty came out and asked what he should do.

Shrill Nonsuch kept shouting, 'If you're out there, Comrade Stalin, please! Please! Stop it!'

I wanted to stop it. But I had to be strong, stronger than my own soft nature. I was a Bolshevik, not a schoolgirl; Stalin, not Trotsky. And suppose the 'canary' did begin to 'sing'? Sure enough ...

When Petty and Ogre strapped Nonsuch into the bed, he began confessing all manner of naughty things, such as planting dead flies in the soup and saying, 'Conroy is a Cabbage.'

Perhaps he WAS an enemy after all. And an enemy who pretended to be a friend was the blackest blackguard of all. If it was true, Nonsuch should be liquidated.

'You heard him,' said Petty, 'he's an Enemy of the People.'

'Investigate. I'm going up to the game. Meet me up there when you have a confession. *If not, you'll be shorter by a head. Beat, beat and again, beat.*'

I left them up there. I was glad to go down with Ogre, away from Nonsuch's gasps. I'll never forget the sheer hurt and despair of them: it was as if he had been reduced to a mere dog, pinioned in some Mephistophelian trap. God only knows what Petty was doing to him.

We put on our boots and coats and went up to watch the game, singing that Queen song, ''39'. What a coincidence that Freddie Mercury had chosen to sing about that very year in our Stalinist chronology!

Petty came up later in slavering excitement, telling us that Nonsuch had confessed to virtually everything.

'Well done. Where is Nonsuch?'

'Umm,' murmured Petty. 'I've left him in the bed. He's up in the wall.'

'You better go and put him down. Now.'

'After the game,' said Petty.

For a moment, I saw us both objectively – overshadowed by the menace of our own paranoia. But then someone cried out, broke the spell and the shadow lifted.

'The turncoat!' I heard myself say.

After the game, it was tea in the dining hall. We had biscuits and cakes. I was just raising my tea mug to my lips when we heard the sound of a living thing squealing in uninhibited, overwhelming pain. Mr Allcock and Mr Hester, who were taking tea, ran up the stairs towards Dorm B. A saucer spun off top table and shattered. The school hushed.

I looked at Petty. I felt myself sweating.

Some boys were running up the stairs to see what had happened. Petty and I followed. As we got closer, the penetrating screams got louder. I thought it was like a maddened horse, trapped in a burning stable. But there were no horses any more.

I sensed the keen bustle that comes with emergencies. Once my mother and I were walking down Ken High Street when there was a bank robbery on NatWest. We heard shots. There was a man lying outside. Never saw his face. I remember his jeans and leather jacket bunched up so that his white tummy hung out above his belt as if he had gone floppy as a dead fish. My mother hurried me on and said, 'Don't look, darling.'

So I looked. The blood ran in the gutter. Red and flowing.

In Dorm B, Mato and Mr Hester were unstrapping Nonsuch from the bed in the corner.

He was now quieter, but his breathing rattled as if his throat was made of corrugated iron gone rusty. His lips were coated in the sort of foam that floats on the Lake near the drain. His whole body was wriggling, almost vibrating.

Mr Hester frantically loosened the straps. There was a moment's calm. Then suddenly Nonsuch threw himself through the outstretched arms of Mato and Mr Hester, just missing the steel frame of the neighbouring bed. When he hit the lino floor, he began shaking in electric spasms so violently that Mato and Mr Hester did not know what to do.

That was when Mr Allcock ran in with two men in uniform, who must have come in the ambulance.

'Out! Out! all of you,' snapped Mr Hester. We traipsed downstairs. In silence.

'That was an accident,' whispered Petty. 'But come on, Stalin. If Nonsuch had actually died, NO ONE would ever cross you again. You really would be Stalin. Remember you said it yourself about Crabbe: we're going to have to actually kill someone one of these days. Or else, in the end, they'll call us Cabbage again. Who should it be? Let's make a list. A real one, this time.'

The Great Terror ended that afternoon.

We thought Nonsuch might die.

I had never seen anything so terrifying as Nonsuch shaking all over and foaming and had never heard such a sound as Nonsuch screaming. No one knew he was epileptic.

If I could imagine hell, that was the sight and sound of it. It was the first time I imagined, as I went to sleep that night, what it was really like in Lubianka Square, where men and women must have screamed like Nonsuch all night.

Nonsuch survived. But there had to be an investigation. He would not sneak on me at all. He just said it was a game that had gone wrong. But in the end, he admitted it was Petty who had left him there. Petty was beaten hard by The Orangeman.

Nonsuch remained one of my best friends and closest comrades; in fact, since his father was Admiral Nonsuch, I appointed him Admiral of the whole Soviet fleet, rafts which we were hurriedly building on the Lake. We knew the war against Hitler would come in the end.

You might wonder how Nonsuch forgave me after the NKVD tortured him until he foamed at the mouth. I wondered myself. But the answer is to be found in his devotion to the Party.

But someone still had to pay for the 'excesses' of the Purges: rats, locusts and Bunsen burners.

25

THE BATTLE OF BRITAIN 1940

Europe was at war. The dormitory lights were blacked out. Far from Russia, the RAF fought its honourable tournament with the fascist Luftwaffe.

One night, at the height of our vulgar version of the Battle of Britain, an explosion of anger blew the dorm door open, blinding us with a flood of light from the corridor outside: it was the Orangeman on patrol.

The engine droning, the soundtrack to our dogfights, stopped dead like a Doodle Bug about to drop.

The shining light from the corridor revealed to Major Hester's piggish eyes what we called The Finest Hour. Every boy was holding his penis in one hand and a torch in the other.

Mr Hester looked at the ceiling of the dorm. There, silhouetted in the torchlight of five separate hand-held torches, were the erect penile 'Spitfires' of all the boys in the dorm.

Mr Hester switched on the light. In single movement, every boy pulled up his pyjama bottoms and blankets.

Mr Hester clicked his tongue. 'What the devil's going on in here? What the hell was that noise? Dormitory prefect Mendoza, what's going on?'

Mendoza pretended to be fast asleep. So Mr Hester rounded on me.

'Right, Conroy, what's the game?'

'Sir, it's called "Spitfires on the Roof". It's our version of the Battle of Britain.'

'And why, Conroy, does THAT involve getting your private parts out?'

'Umm, well, sir, we don't call them "private parts", sir. We call

139

them Spitfires, sir. And Spitfires fought the Battle of Britain. And using our torches after lights out, we project our Spitfires in silhouette on the ceiling.'

'And that terrible noise?'

'It's the Blitz, sir. That's the engines of the Spitfires.'

'I see, Conroy.'

Mr Hester tapped the metal tips of his shoes on the floor, stroked his moustache. Then he clicked his tongue again; the clicking was like the rattle of the snake.

'Mendoza. Conroy. The pair of you better come downstairs. Now! Sick to the back teeth of Conroy thinking he's above the rules. You're for the HIGH JUMP!'

Ormonde was always getting his thing out, even in Politburo meetings. When we were discussing Comrade Yezhov's death lists or Ukrainian grain appropriations in Lenin's hallowed old office, out it came in all its glory.

As a good Leninist, Stalin referred to Lenin's writings to show he was doing the right thing. As a good Stalinist, I did the same. But it was hard to find any reference in Stalin's works to Molotov or Beria getting their things out, especially during Party Plenums. Then finally I found a letter from Lenin to Stalin on 7 July 1918 in the middle of the Civil War, ordering the Georgian to be yet more ruthless. Stalin replied, '*Your communication received. Be assured that* OUR HAND WILL NOT TREMBLE.'

As a Stalinist theorist, it was clear that this meant that Ormonde was behaving within Leninist-Stalinist orthodoxy. So one evening, Ormonde got his thing out, turned on his torch, placed it behind his thing and there, out of the gloom, it loomed like an aeroplane on the roof. The moment I saw it, I said, 'It's a Spitfire! Spitfires on the roof!'

The name stuck. The historical reference to our favourite battle inspired every member of the dorm to get out his Spitfire and play the game. We fought 'Spitfires on the roof' every night.

While Stalin hoped that his Molotov–Ribbentrop Pact with Hitler would give him time to prepare his armies, Russia was not at all ready. Most of the general staff had been shot. Three of the original five marshals of the Soviet Union had been liquidated.

So only brave Britain with her squadrons of thrusting young Spitfires stood defiantly against Hitler's Germany.

*

*

Mendoza and I miserably put on our dressing-gowns and walked slowly behind a strutting Mr Hester down to the study that smelled of old leather.

Mendoza never played the Battle of Britain, but he did not mind what we did. He was not there most nights. Mendoza was an insouciant dorm prefect. Often after lights out, when he thought we were asleep, he got up, put on his silk Chinese dressing-gown and disappeared. We did not know where he went. I did not find out until the next year.

The Orangeman made us bend over the sofa. His Eau Sauvage made my eyes water. Then he clicked his tongue and beat us six of the best hard with Widow Twanky. Very hard. The blows sounded like rifle shots. Crack! Crack! Crack! Ouch! Then click! Click! went his serpentine tongue, always flicking over his red moustache, cleaning the hairs as a dog licks its belly.

I think even Mendoza cried afterwards, though I did not look at him because I respected him and did not want to see him cry.

When Mr Hester beat us, he took a run-up of two steps and he gasped as the cane hit our bottoms.

'Hooo-ah!' he went, like the obscene grunt of a Wimbledon tennis player serving.

When he had finished, he was out of breath. And his eyes had the bleary, bloodshot look that sated vampires have in horror films.

History only records one joke by Molotov.

While the Battle of Britain raged between the RAF and the Luftwaffe, Stalin sent Comrade Molotov, Soviet Foreign Minister, to Berlin to see Adolf Hitler and his Foreign Minister, Ribbentrop. During their discussions, the British started an air raid. So Ribbentrop served champagne to Molotov in his air raid shelter.

'*The British are defeated,*' said Ribbentrop, raising his glass.

'*In that case,*' replied Molotov whom Lenin nick-named Stone-Arse. '*why are we in this shelter?*'

When we observed the forbidden, Pahlavi was so clandestine that he seemed to breathe through the slits of his eyes. He barely moved.

As ordered, he had stepped up his NKVD surveillance of the grown-ups. Now his surveillance was to lead me down new paths. It was to change the Soviet Union. After prep, he had called me urgently to hear his secret report on the results of his investigations.

'Miss Snow heard about Selwyn Agonistes from Selwyn himself. He's leaving the school. He's too ashamed to continue.'

I shrugged. 'No room for the weak. We Bolsheviks.'

'Selwyn Agonistes and Mr Allcock are often with Miss Snow. But Mr Allcock has been having tea and drinks with Miss Deirdre every day,' he reported without emotion. When he was not arranging NKVD surveillance, Pahlavi spent his free time painstakingly constructing and painting little aircraft models that he hung from string. They were always flawless.

'Is he still trying to steal her ring?'

'No. You've seen them kissing?'

'Yes. More. Far more. You'll have to see it yourself ...'

'When?'

'Now, Comrade Stalin. Strike while the iron is hot.'

We crouched outside Mr Allcock's cottage near Kiev.

We could see Mr Allcock with Miss Deirdre, the Under-Matron with frizzy blonde hair, sitting on his knee. They could not see us because they were kissing so ravenously that their faces were shining with sap. The under-matron wore a short blue skirt. Mr Allcock's hand was creeping up under it at more than a creeping pace, exposing what Khrushchev called Virgin Lands.

'I think we should go,' said Pahlavi.

'No. Wait.'

Suddenly Mr Allcock crawled over her on all fours, then raised himself melodramatically on his haunches with his hands in the air, fingers open as if they were a big cat's paws. Then he growled at her like a leopard. 'Grrraaaa ra-ra-ra!'

Miss Deirdre liked this. 'Oh, Geoffrey, you sound like a LION!'

We burst into hysterics. Even ascetic Pahlavi could barely control himself. Adults were so ridiculous. We held our noses to be quiet. But we could not staunch our convulsions. A strangled gurgle escaped.

'WHO'S THERE?' shouted Mr Allcock. 'I heard it. Someone said it. All cock and no balls. Someone said it ...'

'You're imagining it, Geoffrey,' said the under-matron.

'I heard it. I'll catch the blighters!'

When we stopped running, we were beyond the Gardens.

'Was he trying to do IT?' I asked Pahlavi breathlessly, still laughing.

He considered this gloomily. 'Do what?'

'Press-ups? My brothers say sex is like press-ups. What am I going to do? I can only do three press-ups. That's how we all got made by our parents? It looks so ... untidy.'

'And unscientific,' said Pahlavi.

'Maybe Mr Allcock isn't doing it properly. Anyway, it looked horrible to me.'

'Ditto,' said Pahlavi.

'I wasn't made that way,' I decided. 'Were you?'

'Never. Not like that.'

'Ever been tiger-hunting, Stalin?' Mr Eye asked me.

That afternoon, I was in the squash court gallery, examining the stuffed animals and fishes up there, not watching the squash, which was a boring game even by the standards of sports.

There was a bear rug, and a stuffed tiger in a glass case. Its svelte savage beauty fascinated me: I spent hours admiring its 'fearful symmetry' – 'what dread hands and what dread feet!'

I was looking at it when that voice said, 'How's Petty?'

It was Mr Eye, now wearing his winter black suit and broad-brimmed hat. He knew about Nonsuch's fit and Petty's thrashing. He took off the hat: I admired the dazzling spurt of birdshit spattered on the brown dome of his cranial mosque.

'Devoted comrade,' I answered carefully.

'Wouldn't want to go tiger-hunting with him,' said Mr Eye.

I did not understand. But I was beginning to see that Petty's admiration was a decidedly mixed blessing.

So Mr Eye explained. 'While involved in the dangerous pastime of tiger-hunting, in the olden days of the British Empire, it was wise to be accompanied only by the brave, the honest and the loyal. No one else.'

The imminent Great Patriotic War was a most risky tiger hunt.

Mr Eye was smiling in a hungry way that set off his white tombstone teeth against the angry yellow of his skin and eyes as molten black as a Magnitogorsk blast furnace.

'What happened if you went tiger-hunting with someone who you found wasn't necessarily brave, honest and loyal?' I asked.

'In that case,' said Mr Eye, 'you had to kill him ... before he killed you.'

Then he replaced his hat and walked away.

At the end of the Purges, Stalin knew that the evil dwarf Yezhov had gone too far. Yezhov had only obeyed his orders. None the less, Yezhov had to take the blame.

Yezhov was appointed People's Commissar of Water Transport (whatever that meant). Then he was removed from the NKVD, replaced by Beria and, finally, arrested. Yezhov was said to have gone insane. And he was found hanging from the prison rafters with a placard around his neck.

I was secure enough to move against the hated Petty. He was no longer safe to take tiger-hunting. I had him arrested by his last victims Spencer-Percival and Nonsuch: that's Soviet justice for you. But I wished Steady was still with me: would things have gone so far with Pelham around? I often tried to think – what would Pelham have done in the same situation?

I ordered Petty to wear a placard in front of the Central Committee. The placard was identical to the one Yezhov wore. It read simply:

'I AM CARRION.'

26

THE GREAT PATRIOTIC WAR 1941

I did not cry when mum dropped me back at the end of half-term. Crying was not Bolshevik behaviour. I was accustomed to power and respect.

When I heard the crunch of the gravel as my parents drove away, I waited confidently for the Politburo to welcome me back.

But, for some reason, they were not there.

I saw two Enemies of the People, Minto and Money-Banks, both once Central Committee members. When I approached them, they did not salute nor wait for orders. They just laughed and ran off down the corridor. I could not find Ogre or Ormonde or anyone I trusted. Ominous.

There was no one else around. I was back early.

Spanker Grimshaw was leaning against the wall beside the back door, sporting a flashy grin. My hair rose on my neck: he was waiting for me. When I got close, he drew out the riding crop that had won him his name and swished it right in front of my face.

'Blimey, Grimshaw! You could have blinded me,' I shouted.

'Hard cheese, Cabbage: I might just do that.'

He did it again: it passed so close to my face that it stung my nose.

'Why do you always have those pathetic little books stuffed in your pockets, Cabbage? Makes you look a real weed,' he sneered.

I was speechless. No one had dared speak to me like that since Lenin died.

Before I could do a thing, he raised the crop and did it again and this time he flipped my glasses off my face. I instinctively tried to catch them. But they spun away into the blur of my short sight, then dropped with a clatter somewhere beyond.

'You pig! You creepo!' I shrieked and threw myself at his blurred profile. It was foolish. But my glasses were my Achilles Heel: anyone who touched them filled me with a fearless, frantic rage. I darted behind him, put my forearm across his neck and my knee into the small of his back so that he collapsed. But he pulled me with him. I could smell his sweat: it was stronger than mine, bitter like vinegar. His breath tasted of sickly milk. He put one hand over my face, as if to gouge out my eyes. Then, with one twist, he tugged me down beside him. The next thing I knew, he was just sitting astride me as if I were an old nag. He was laughing and I was crying.

'I dunno why you're wasting your time on me, Conroy. If I were you, I'd check Stalingrad, Kiev, Kharkov, Moscow!'

He released me. I was just glad no one had seen the blind Stalin. We both stood up, staring at one another like breathless wrestlers.

'Pick up your specs then, Cabbage,' he said.

'Where are they?'

He just jeered. So I kneeled humbly on the parquet floor and felt my way through the dust until I found them.

I drew myself up to my full height and tried to walk past him with Stalin's dignity, pretending I was reviewing the troops from the top of Lenin's Mausoleum. But, as if I wasn't already humiliated enough, he put his perfidious foot out to trip me.

I flew through the air and landed, winded, on the concrete floor of the lobby.

Spanker leaped over me and sprinted up towards the Camps.

I lay for a moment. My knees were grazed; blood oozed through my greyers. I did not think about what it all meant. It was happening so fast. But I began to run towards Stalingrad, old Dugganoes' Camp, to see if my comrades were there.

When I arrived, it was full of boys who weren't even Bolsheviks: Enemies of the People Money-Banks, Minto, Grimshaw, Danby, Trotskyites and Rightists! They would not let me enter.

'Let me in,' I shouted. 'What the hell's going on?'

A barrage of pine cones landed around me. One hit me point blank in the face and it burned like a wasp sting. It was an ink bomb. I saw a blue panorama as ink filled my eyes, wedged behind my glasses. I staggered backwards. They shouted 'Schnell!', 'Slav Schweinhund' and 'Achtung, Ruski!' which they had learned from their inane comics.

The gate opened. Petty stepped out from behind the curtain made of tent canvas. He stood erect for a second and then marched towards

146

me before stopping. He wore a little black moustache, like a second-rate conjuror

'Hiya, Petty, welcome back,' I said. For the first time ever, I was afraid of him. His eyes did not blink – he just peered fixedly, ogled me almost, with his pupils vibrating with the thrill of supreme power.

He said nothing.

He carefully and slowly raised his right arm so that it was pointed towards the sky at a sixty-degree angle. For a second I did not understand. But he was smiling.

I was amazed to see that the boys keeping guard replied with Nazi salutes.

'What's going on?' I asked, my voice close to breaking.

'I am Hitler now,' he said. 'It is 22 June 1941. Operation Barbarossa. Hitler was far better than Stalin and I know as much about him as you do about Stalin. More probably. Anyway, Conroy, everyone's joined my side. Your Politburo are now my Gauleiters and SS. Get out, Comrade Gumby, or we'll pelt you with pine cones. It's over. Stalin is finished, you fairground huckster. Nobody's going to believe any of your wet bunkum any more.' He stopped. Then, '*I know history will remember Stalin.*' Petty used Hitler's own words. '*But it will also remember me.* Besides, the Nazis had far better uniforms than the Reds. The SS was magnifico!'

'Hear! Hear!' said his Gauleiters.

'Your Slavs are only good enough to be slaves,' he added. 'And Jews ...' He whistled.

'The Soviet people already are slaves,' I joshed grimly, thinking of my slave labour Gulags.

'Now they'll be a German empire of slaves ruled by the master race. Try reading this,' and he threw a book right into my face as hard as he could. 'It's *Mein Kampf*! Every word of it is GOSPEL! Auf Wiederschen, Conroy. Buzz off! All you Bolsheviks are Jewish swine!'

Hitler's book lay open in the dirt. I left it there. Petty clicked the heels of his black brogues, raised his hand in a Nazi salute, shouted 'Heil Hitler' in a shower of saliva and marched back into the old Dugganoes.

On the sign that read 'Stalingrad', he had written 'Wolf's Lair'.

'But, Petty,' I shouted as if I were suffocating. 'Petty, you're my best friend! You've even been to stay with my parents. Petty! Petty! Why? Answer me – why?'

'Stalingrad's as good as ours; Leningrad's surrounded; and we'll be in the Kremlin by Lights Out, if not Prep!' shrieked Spanker Grimshaw, swishing the riding crop that, with his straw-like hair, blue eyes and axe-like chin, made him Hitler's Heydrich.

The pine cones had begun landing again. I did not even notice when a couple hit me. I was hurt far more than any pine bombs could hurt. Then a conker crashed into my mouth. My lip swelled up like a prize vegetable.

'I should have killed you all,' I shouted at them. I was not joking. I was heartbroken: '*If only Rome had one neck*! Petty, you dwarf, you'd be LOST without me. LOST! I should have liquidated every last one of you!'

'If you'd been Stalin, you would have,' answered Money-Banks as he fired more missiles at me. Backing away, I tripped over a tree root. The cones hit me all over and I just lay there sobbing like a baby, not even caring as the Nazis taunted me.

A hand rested on my shoulder. Then the hands took hold of my arms and pulled me slowly but surely out of range, into safety.

My saviour was Diggle-Johnson.

27

SCORCHED EARTH

Alone again, I limped out to the Snake Path, stumbling and crying. Not so much because my Stalin empire had fallen, but because all my friends had turned against me.

My best friends. Betrayal! There is no one on earth more alone than the dictator facing his nemesis.

Stalin was so shocked by the invasion of the Soviet Union by Hitler's Wehrmacht that for about ten days he was in a state of collapse. He did nothing. Perhaps he was drunk. Certainly he was depressed.

'*Did we deserve this?*' Molotov pathetically asked the German Ambassador.

Meanwhile, the German forces pushed forward, surrounding and capturing literally millions of Russian soldiers.

My Great Patriotic War would be a terrible struggle. More terrible than anything that had gone before – even the Purges. I was bereft. Petty's Operation Barbarossa betrayed me. I was crushed on the wheel. I could not stop crying. It was my first broken heart. I did not cry so much again until a girl Barbarossaed me many years later.

So I went into the school, sat at my desk and wrote a letter to Mum that said, 'My friends are fading into the darkness. My enemies are flourishing on me like ants.'

I stuck a stamp on it and left it with the other post in the Inner Sanctum. Then, feeling desperate, I sprinted towards the door and collided into three adults – Mrs Trevelyan, the bewitching Miss Snow and Mr Eye-Russian Spy. Mrs Trevelyan caught me in her arms. 'You are in a hurry, dear,' she said.

'The war's started. Hitler's invaded. My friends hate me.'

'Ha! Ha!' boomed Mr Eye. 'If you play dictator games, you've got to take the rough with the smooth.'

I ran out of the front door.

'Come back,' Mrs Trevelyan called after me, her soft little hands beckoning. As I fled, I heard Miss Snow say, 'Oh dear, Salvador, look what you've done!'

Down at the Lake, as it got dark, I sat on Mendoza's tree and cried until I was tired. A twig snapped.

It was Mendoza, my tiger-Lenin-Clint with a fag hanging raffishly from the corner of his crooked Bogart mouth.

He was not alone: in the shadows just behind him stood Catalina, the Portuguese girl who worked in the kitchens; D'Artagnan's daughter. The Bovvers stood around them like a Praetorian guard, smoking, their fag ends orange eyes in the dusk.

I could not really tell how old girls were. They were so different. Catalina was perhaps a year older than Mendoza, now thirteen and a prefect. I did not even look at her. I saw Mendoza's thick-set sensual face with the glossy skin, the aquiline nose. He put his paw on my shoulder. I started crying all over again. The girl came up and started mopping up my tears with a tissue. I did not really notice her. I was a bit ashamed that she should see me like this. But she was a stranger. So what did it matter? Then she reached for her bag. She drew out a white paper package and pulled out a cake – the juiciest slice of carrot cake with white icing on top. She handed it to me. 'I make the cakes,' she said simply. It was the only thing she said. She distributed slices to the others. When I had eaten the cake, I felt better.

'Calm down,' said Mendoza. 'Tell me all.' He listened. The Bovvers and Catalina awaited his Solomonic judgement. Then he asked sensible questions like, 'How do you know ALL your friends have left you?'

I could not answer that. But if Petty said that, why shouldn't it be true?

Then he laughed. 'Hitler's the enemy,' he told me. 'You are Stalin. So you must fight the fascist invader. Like World War Two, it is now just a plain battle to the death between good and evil. Even Stalin is good, now. Has Petty forgotten that Stalin WON?'

I had not thought of that.

When I arrived at supper that night, I dared not look towards the Politburo: had they really turned against me?

The next day at breakfast, Mrs Trevelyan entered the dining hall and

150

started looking for someone, bustling from table to table like a little old bird with dowdy feathers.

She soon found me.

'Ah, William Conroy. Come with me for a cup of tea.' When I was sitting in her cosy private kitchen, she went on: 'Your mother's just been on the phone. She's very worried about you. She says you sent her a poem that claimed all your friends had abandoned you.'

'That was yesterday, Mrs Trevelyan.'

'Well, you were sitting with Ormonde and Ogleton and all your usual friends and everyone was laughing.'

'Petty told me all my friends had left the Politburo.'

'The Politburo?'

'You know, Mrs Trevelyan, the highest body of the Communist Party ...'

'Oh of course.' Her frown broke into an endearing smile. She was that unusual combination of warmth and briskness. 'But then what happened?'

'Well, at supper last night, I discovered that the Politburo supported me against Hitler and it is war. In fact last night, Ormonde delivered Molotov's famous speech: *Our cause is just. Victory will be ours.*'

'Your poor mother is terribly worried. You mustn't send such awful messages to her. She was all ready to drive over and take you away from Coverdale. Do you want that?'

Away from my Soviet empire, my Politburo and possible victory?

'No way, José!'

'Then why don't you phone your mum now from the Sanctum and tell her how you are.'

'Yes, Mrs Trevelyan.'

She gave me the phone and left me with it.

Before she left, she said, 'Don't forget that Admiral Nonsuch is taking you and Henry Nonsuch to the Royal Tournament this afternoon. Make sure you both look EXCEEDINGLY smart: brush your hair! Oh William, you look a complete scruff!'

'I'm at war. War's an untidy business.'

'You don't know what war means.'

Admiral Sir Julian Nonsuch had an elegant, fine-boned face, iron-grey hair and the most lovely uniform. He enjoyed the Royal Tournament as much as Nonsuch and I. He was the Governor of a British island in the Caribbean. The Twinkling Admiral, as mum called him, was always smiling. Mum said he was the handsomest man she knew (except dad and the Shah in that order) and I believed her. He looked to me like a real hero.

The soldiers and sailors fired howitzers. They jumped over walls and climbed up ropes at the Tournament. Admiral Nonsuch squeezed our arms and said, 'There's no spectacle since the Charge of the Light Brigade to beat the Royal Tournament.'

I had to agree, though I had not seen the Charge of the Light Brigade.

Afterwards, as a special treat, the Admiral said we could go to tea with mum and dad while he did a little chore. Afterwards, he would pick us up again and drive us back to Coverdale.

So the Admiral said hello to mum at our house in Pimlico. He kissed her on both cheeks and went off in his car to run his errand. He said he would be back in half an hour – tops.

Mum made us scones and crumpets. We sat in the drawing room at home and told her our news. We did not see dad because he was in his surgery, which was in our basement.

Soon it was six o'clock. The Admiral had said he would take us back at five-thirty. Mum began to wonder where he was.

Nonsuch and I chatted away about the Great Patriotic War, planning our first counter-offensive in the Battle of Moscow.

At about six-thirty, the telephone rang. Mum came in. She moved towards us in an inhuman, clockwork way as if her limbs had gone rusty. She did not seem to know what to say to Nonsuch. She hesitated for a long time. Then she said to him, 'Henry, I have to tell you that there's been a terrible accident. Your dad is very badly hurt. Your mum is coming round to fetch you.'

I could not imagine what this terrible accident could be. It seemed impossible because we had only just seen the Twinkling Admiral in his navy blue and gold braid.

A few minutes later, Mrs Nonsuch arrived to the wailing of sirens. A young policeman came with her. My mum kissed her hello. Mrs Nonsuch looked similar to my mother, except mum was blonde; Mrs Nonsuch was brunette. They both dressed the same sensible way, ever wearing silk scarves that seemed to perform no useful task. Mrs Nonsuch burst into tears in front of us and, kneeling down beside the sofa, she told Nonsuch, 'Darling, Harry, Daddy is dead. He was killed an hour ago. We've got to go in a minute and do everything.'

Mum gave her a glass of brandy and sat her down in my father's own chair. Usually only he was allowed to sit in it. But in the circumstances, I did not point this out.

'Have a sip of that stiff drink, dear Valerie. The evil of men staggers me,' said mum and she burst into tears too. Then she stopped herself because her job at that moment was NOT to cry like everybody else. Even the policeman, who was as young as Mr Selwyn, was almost crying. He stood by the door, cleaning his shoes on the back of his trousers.

'He won't be able to drive the boys back to Coverdale now,' said Mrs Nonsuch through sobs that sounded like drowning. It was a funny thing to say. Though undeniably true.

'Don't worry about anything now,' said Mum. 'Alexander [my father] will take William back.'

Nonsuch was crying bitterly but I did not blame him. I wanted to cry too and soon I was. But then, strangely, Nonsuch stopped. He said he was fine. He did not really understand what had happened. Nor did I. He thought death was just a temporary absence like another tour of duty at sea, from which the Admiral was sure to return.

Then mum took me out of the room and said, 'Darling, I know it's an awful shock. The IRA planted a bomb right under his car just round the corner and blew him up. It's too ghastly to contemplate. Poor Henry and poor Valerie: what are we going to do with them?'

I did not know the answer to that question. I was crying too much to say anything. But Mum said, 'We're so lucky that you and Henry weren't with him. Thank God! Thank God!' She hugged me so that my face was lost in her hair that smelled of orchards, looking over her shoulder. Then she pulled herself together. 'Now, you must go and phone Dad downstairs. Tell him what's happened and that he has to take you back to school in a minute.'

Mum went back to the drawing room. I phoned downstairs. Dad was not pleased to be interrupted in surgery. He did not even know I was at home.

'What are you doing here?' he asked. 'You're supposed to be at school. Can't talk. I'm seeing a patient.'

'Dad, you've got to drive me back to school.'

'Admiral Nonsuch is taking you back.'

'He's been blown up by the IRA. He can't drive me back to school. Mrs Nonsuch is in the drawing room and we're all crying.'

'I'll be right up,' said Dad.

Dad was sublime in a crisis. He always said, 'Nothing matters but your health. Nothing matters much and very little matters at all.' But even dad could not say that about Admiral Nonsuch.

I did not love him as much as my own dad. But almost as much.

'Lenin built all this and now we've gone and fucked it up,' I said to myself, just as Stalin said on that dark day, 28 June 1941.

I sat alone in the Kremlin. The lights were off. I did not want anyone to see me. This was the scene of some of my triumphs. But now Admiral Nonsuch was dead. The Germans were advancing on every front: I could not really tell if Stalingrad had fallen or whether Leningrad would last the day. Yesterday, I ruled an empire. Today, there are German tanks not thirty metres from the model railway room.

'Comrade Stalin! We're so sorry about the Admiral.'

I jumped. There were three of them, standing in the doorway.

'Have you come to arrest me?' I asked pathetically.

The three men looked at one another timidly.

'Far from it, Comrade Stalin,' said Ogleton.

'May we turn on the light?' asked Ormonde gently.

I nodded.

They looked at me sorrowfully, peering up at them like a hopeful rabbit, blinded by the light.

'Do you want me to resign?'

'No. Only you can lead us,' said Ormonde.

Then, like Stalin that day, I heard myself say, *'Can I live up to the people's hopes any more, can I lead the country to final victory? There may be more deserving candidates.'*

'You know very well there is no one else. We have not come to discuss your leadership. We have come for our orders,' said Ormonde as stiffly as old Stone-Arse Molotov himself.

'All right.' I saw then that they were more terrified of me than they were of the Germans. That was the way I wanted it to be. That was the reason for the Purges. The Politburo was sound. 'Summon the Politburo in an hour to the old air raid shelter beneath the pottery.'

'Oh – and Ogre?' Ogleton stopped in the doorway. 'Is Pelham a Nazi?'

'No. Steady refused to join either side. He said, "It'll all end in tears."'

'Thank God.'

'This is real war,' I told the Politburo. 'We will fight Petty and his Hitlerites to the death, in the school, in the Camps, in the cornfields of Ukraine, the grousemoors of Scotland, the plains of Kursk and the Borough of Kensington & Chelsea.'

We were gathered solemnly in the partly flooded and dilapidated old war air raid shelter (which Mendoza told us about). At the front, our villages were burning, our camps were despoiled, our armies were surrounded, our traitors rewarded. The Nazis advanced across our rich Russian Motherland.

I no longer spoke of Communism. No, like Stalin, I simply evoked old Russian heroes – Kutuzov who defeated Napoleon; Suvorov who was Catherine the Great's Generalissimo; Alexander Nevsky. Their portraits now hung in Stalin's office.

'We would use and welcome ANYBODY we could attract to our just cause.'

'What? Even Sportsmen and Scallywags who don't understand Stalinism?' asked Ogleton quite angrily. It was cold down there. We tried not to shiver. But at least we were safe from air raids.

'Yes, Mad Ogre,' answered Ormonde earnestly, playing yo-yo. 'We'll take swats like Buchanan, Bloods like St John, goody-goodies like Lamb, non-Communists, Bundists, nationalists – and even bed-wetters like Diggle-Johnson.'

'Even bed-wetters?' repeated Ogre, crestfallen.

'Yes. I nominate Comrade Diggle-Johnson to the Central Committee,' said Pahlavi, fastidiously examining a perfectly constructed aircraft model – a Lancaster bomber.

'Seconded,' I said.

Scallywag Kildare put up his hand. Ormonde nodded.

'Marshal Stalin,' asked Kildare.

'Speak, young fellow patriot,' said Marshal Stalin.

'Can we really win, Marshal Stalin, with so many divisions of sporting Bloods against us, with Leningrad and Moscow besieged? Are the Germans invincible, Comrade Marshal?'

I considered of course whether to have him executed for defeatism. But instead I put my hand on his shoulder and used Stalin's broadcast of 3 July 1941. *'Are the German fascist troops really invincible? Of course not! History shows that there are no invincible armies and there never have been.'*

Everyone clapped. Chairman of the Supreme Soviet Weeping Wharton wept. And Ogleton, unhinged as ever, put his long, swarthy head back, shook his black ringlets and laughed rapid-fire.

At the end of the meeting, we, all of us, marshals, generals, Politburo members, Central Committee members, secret policemen, stood with our fists clenched and bowed our heads as we chanted, 'Ave, Stalin, nos morituri te salutamus.'

A couple of days later, Nonsuch was back at school.

Mrs Trevelyan had to hide the newspapers.

By day, I fought the hardest struggle of my life with streaming blood and scorched earth. But each night, I could not help but cry under my bedclothes for the best of men, the Twinkling Admiral.

28

STALIN'S PORNOGRAPHIC COLLECTION

'Stalin will remain in Moscow. Whatever happens.'

Petty's panzers were probing the outskirts of Moscow by the next afternoon. We retreated down into Lubianka's boiler room: a stink bomb was tossed down the stairwell and shattered at our feet.

'Surrender! You've lost,' shouted the high voices of young fascist stormtroopers, led by Spanker Heydrich.

'You better evacuate the Kremlin,' suggested my new NKVD boss Ogleton, holding his nose against the disgusting bad eggs stench. We could hear their cries of 'Heil Hilter' and 'Hang Stalin!' and the patter of their feet. 'We're moving the Government behind the Urals to the back of the squash courts. You must leave, Koba.'

'No,' I said. 'Stalin stays. Moscow's not going to fall.'

Footsteps on the stairs. We threw ourselves to the ground, squeezing into the awkward oily corners behind the boilers, where there were cockroaches, scraps of newspaper ('Nixon resigns' said one), soiled tissues. We gripped our boiled conkers, pine cones and catapults so hard that our hands sweated.

'It's me!' called the visitor. 'It's Marshal Diggle-Johnson!'

The Marshal was covered in exploded ink bombs and there were pine needles in his hair.

'I just broke through,' he said. 'Timoshenko's just holding them off. The rumours of German paratroopers landing near the Bolshoi are nonsense. Permission to report to Stavka (the Russian Supreme Headquarters), Supreme Commander-in-Chief ... Marshal Stalin?'

'Hang on a second, I've found something rather fascinating. Comrades, look!' I climbed down from behind the boilers. I had found a single page of a remarkable magazine. I showed Stavka. None of us had ever seen anything quite like it.

'What is it, Conroy?' asked Diggle, who was actually blushing.

'THAT is a pornographic magazine. It's ILLEGAL! We're UNDER AGE!' exulted Ogre, our expert on any vulgarity.

I laid it out on top of the boiler. It was badly crumpled. It smelled of lavatories, hand cream and damp paper. It was so old and damp that parts had faded away. But from amongst the patches of mildew on that torn half-page shone a glimpse of something that it was difficult to identify. I turned it this way and that until we saw that it was a pair of legs splayed in a fashion that reminded me of Tower Bridge opening. In the midst of this was a flash of pink flesh which mystically draw our attention. But there was no top half of this vision – no face, head or torso. Underneath, it read: 'MARY MILLINGTON.'

Who was this decapitated Mary Millington?

The whole of Stavka was speechless, unsure of our feelings, barely able to breathe, forgetting the crashing sound of Hitler's artillery tearing the outskirts of Moscow to smithereens. Shrapnel and fascism were nothing compared to this startling maw that smacked its lips at us, beckoning as Lenin-Stalin had never done, hinting at secrets that even Lubianka could not tell.

'That's Nazi propaganda!' said plain-spoken school liar Marshal Diggle. 'It's unLeninist. It's unproletarian! It must be destroyed. My mummy says that is the most disgusting, only read by dirty little old men in raincoats. She says they always wear raincoats.'

'Why raincoats?' I asked.

'I suppose it's their uniform.'

Ormonde and Wharton hesitated to see what I would say, but Ogle's black-lipped mouth was hanging open. The other side of the page advertised an arsenal of gadgets, presumably to use in sex, though how was a mystery even to Ogleton.

'What do you do with that?' Ormonde pointed to a colossal model of an organ with two identical ends.

None of us could work it out.

'This could be a secret weapon to use against the Hitlerites.'

'Stalin's Organ,' muttered Ormonde.

'Stalin's Organ was a missile launcher. Marshal Diggle, Commissar General of Security Ogle, Foreign Commissar Ormonde, before the invasion, I would have burned this bourgeois balderdash. But now I want to preserve it, show it to the troops. They'll fight harder.'

'They'll BE harder,' giggled Ogle.

'What about my offensive?' asked Diggle.

'Offensive! What are you going to achieve, you bed-wetting school liar?' snarled Ogle. 'Let me arrest him.' During the war, the secret police, led by Beria, were continually trying to subvert Zhukov and the generals.

'Save it for real enemies, Ogre,' I ordered. 'The counter-offensive will hit them on a broad front, Marshal: on the athletics grounds, in the fives courts, behind Leningrad and before Moscow. Throw in the reserve Siberian Bovverboy penal divisions. Proceed!'

The Marshal scampered up the steps out into the light. At the top, silhouetted against the Moscow sky, with the battlements of the Kremlin behind him, he called, 'Any message for the troops?'

'Yes,' replied Ogle. 'Rats and Bunsen burners if they lose; Mary Millington if they win!'

And he was gone.

The State Defence Committee, now the highest political body in the land, turned back to stare at the dim remnants of the pornography.

I could only think of Mato's Order of the Red Banner. Miss Deirdre sitting on Mr Allcock's knee, his climbing hand – and his growling like a lion. Was this where playing lion led?

'Does every woman have one of these?' I asked finally.

'Oh yes, Koba. Every one of them.'

'Even our mothers?'

Ogleton's brow crumpled: 'All except mothers,' he said magisterially.

That news was as much of a relief as the relief of Moscow.

29

LAST STAND AT MOSCOW 1941–2

Marshal Stalin and General Winter saved Moscow.

The next morning, we all awoke early before Matron called 'Rise and Shine.' The air was cool but muffled and soft, as if the entire world had suddenly been padded with cotton wool.

I vaulted out of bed and parted the curtains. Coverdale was covered in thick snow. It had never looked more beautiful, as if, overnight, God had simply recreated the woods and pastures to a new design.

'Moscow is safe!' I shouted, waking up the dormitory. 'The Germans don't know how to fight in snow! Hurrah for Lenin!'

At lunch, Mr Trevelyan clapped his hands as usual and announced, 'Good news, chaps. The Lake is frozen. The ice is thick. So after lunch, skating! If you behave, at two-thirty, the whole school can play ice hockey together. Now, if there is any yahoo buffoonery, the culprits will face the high jump!'

By two-thirty, my weapons factory had been working flat out for an hour, creating snowballs with pine cones and conkers inside. We had at least a hundred of these shells; Twits and Berks were kept working by Ogre's thugs in the arms factories safely behind the Urals.

The surface of the Lake was covered by the figures of over a hundred schoolboys. Bovvers watched from the edge. Not far away, I saw Mendoza, who was not playing, accompanied by Catalina, who watched everything impassively, without blinking.

I imagined the skaters to be armies before Moscow: some were regiments of tanks; others were cavalry. Everyone was dressed in plus-fours with trousers tucked into rugger socks. Mr Allcock issued the skates and hockey sticks.

Mr Trevelyan, Mr Hester and Miss Snow were on duty on the ice. Miss Snow wore a full-length fur coat and a towering Astrakhan hat. But the boys were so exhilarated by the white trees and glistening ice and bracing air, which almost burned our lungs, that it would have taken a troop of mounted Cossacks to control us. And fortunately, the mounted Cossacks were on my side.

'All right, Zhukov, take Ogre, Kildare and everyone else and BREAK Hitler's Army Group Central.'

The Headmaster stood in the centre with a flag: we were actually spread between the two huge teams but that made no difference.

The moment the flag fell, we were skating across the ice, picking off the startled Germans one by one. The troops went into action, singing along to Bony M's 'Ra-ra-Rasputin' which was played on Rafferty's ghetto blaster.

I went with them, naturally a little behind the frontline. Ogre and Kildare turned out to be skilled skaters: leading our last reserve armies, they threw themselves against Feldmarshals Minto, Money-Banks and SS General Heydrich Grimshaw, smacking their hockey sticks against their shins. Petty was hit in the ear with an ice bomb. The other Nazis were felled brutally; they were surprised, dizzy, confused. Bare hands and soft cheeks collided with the burning ice, cutting them, scouring them.

Almost mad with triumph, I yelled, 'Long live the brave Russian people,' watching my elite Guards regiments win as Minto skidded face down across the ice. 'Long live Lenin! Long live Kutuzov and Survorov! Long live St—'

That was the last I remember for a few minutes.

I felt as if I had hit a padded wall with irresistible force. There was just darkness. Then the ice was burning my face and hands and there were voices calling, 'Sir, sir, Conroy's hurt! Miss Snow, Conroy's come a cropper!'

I opened my eyes and saw Miss Snow's face close to mine. She cradled my head in her arms so that I could feel her shape inside her furs and her polo neck sweater. As she leaned over me, her hat fell off onto my face, smelling of her suffocating perfumes. Her thick black hair followed it. It tickled my face and I wanted to catch it in my teeth. Clouds of her breath enveloped me and I breathed it in as if it were opium.

'Are you all right, Conroy?' she asked in a low voice. She was always narrowing her eyes as if she were short-sighted.

'What happened?' I asked.

'It's OK, Marshal Stalin,' whispered Diggle-Johnson so that everyone could hear. 'Zhukov reporting to Stavka: Leningrad and Stalingrad are still under pressure. But Moscow is out of danger.'

'This'll serve you right for fighting on the ice,' rasped Major Hester, whose brick-red face was now the same colour as his whiskers. 'Mark my words: we're cracking down on these faction fights. If you don't grow up, we'll ban Camps altogether.'

'Was it the Nazis?' I asking haltingly.

'Did someone hit him?' asked Mr Hester. 'If they did, I want to know who. Now!'

'No, sir,' replied Diggle-Johnson, unhelpfully. 'Marshal Stalin was so jolly, sir, he skated into a tree.'

Evil is so rarely a matter of black and white. Usually, you just have to grade it in shades of grey. Until the war, everyone thought Stalin the most evil creature that had ever lived. But when faced with Hitler, Britain and America decided the Nazis were worse. They were right. But only just. Now Hilter was the very manifestation of pure evil on earth, Stalin was regarded as more of a rogue than a monster: the boys began to call me Uncle Joe. Even the masters were appalled by Petty and his fellow fascists making Nazi salutes; when Petty ordered his men to wear Hitler moustaches from magic shops as their badge of honour, even the beneficent Mr Trevelyan began to worry.

Suppose the newspapers wrote about it?

Or the parents ...?

30

THE BATTLE OF STALINGRAD 1942–3

Mr Trevelyan shepherded the parents round the school with his old-fashioned manners and his round face shining with genial pride.

'And here's where the chaps change for rugger,' he said as he showed them the changing rooms. We went silent as soon as we spotted the adult outsiders. 'Cave! Visiting Parents.' Then the moment they left us, heading for the library, we followed them at a safe distance, laughing as we imagined antics we could perform to shock them.

'The boys love the library, Mrs Patton. We try and keep it stocked with the best literature and history books. There are hordes of chaps who love history, so we have stacks of World War Two books,' Mr Trevelyan was saying to the earnest young parents who were deciding whether to send their little boy to Coverdale.

'What a charming little room,' said Mrs Patton, the wide-eyed, eager wife in her tartan suit as she looked at the books in the white shelves.

'Very impressive,' said the dapper Mr Patton, who looked business-like in a black suit.

Visiting parents came in species. There were the noisy vulgarians who bellowed approvingly, 'Very posh, Mr Headmaster, very posh indeed'; the patricians who did not care if the school was good or not because they had been there themselves; the fashionables who were more interested in the other parents than the facilities; and then there were young and responsible parents who were cautiously worried about the facilities, teaching and, of course, the fees. The Pattons appeared to be of the latter ilk.

'May I see some of the books?' asked Mrs Patton shyly.

'She's a great reader,' explained the husband.

'Please do, Mrs Patton,' said Mr Trevelyan, thick blond-grey hair glinting in the lights above his old face.

She reached into the nearest shelf. The book was called *Enid Blyton's Famous Five*. She took it out and showed it to her husband, who perused it gravely and whispered to her, 'Very nice,' as if he wished to confirm to her that it was indeed ... a book and not a trolley or a hat.

'This is an old favourite,' said Mr Patton.

'Oh yes, a classic,' said the Headmaster. 'Adored it as a boy. Still do actually,' and the two men laughed heartily. The Pattons felt safe with rotund septugenarian Mr Trevelyan despite his eccentric head of hair.

Mrs Patton opened the book and a large Nazi swastika fell out.

The Pattons stared at the Enid Blyton and then looked down at the black swastika drawn in a firm hand with a marker pen on red blotting paper and then up to where their eyes met Mr Trevelyan's embarrassed expression.

'You don't expect to find the Third Reich in the *Famous Five!*' said Mr Patton.

'Certainly don't, by Jove!' agreed Mr Trevelyan, hair starting to rise.

'Well, what IS that?' asked Mrs Patton.

'A swastika,' said her husband grimly.

'I know what a swastika is, you fool!' she replied. 'What was it doing there?'

'I should think it's just a schoolboy's prank. Bit of harmless horseplay. High jinks,' replied the Headmaster. Then he rashly added, 'I'm sure there aren't any others.'

Mr Patton agreed. But Mrs Patton was transformed from the mousey housewife of minutes earlier.

'What's THIS book?' She reached out at random to find another. It was C. S. Lewis' *The Lion, the Witch and the Wardrobe*. She opened it.

Another swastika fell out.

She seized a third. This time, it was John Buchan's *Greenmantle*. Another swastika.

She started pulling out books and opening them frantically, grabbing at them. Mrs Patton opened every book in the library. Each contained a swastika. By the time she finished, a crowd of boys, including most of the Politburo and several of Hitler's Headquarters, OKW, were staring at a heap of swastikas on the library floor. Mr

Trevelyan's hair, needless to say, now appeared to be carrying a good proportion of the national voltage.

'This is not a prep school,' said Mrs Patton, now stunned by her disappointment into hysterical accusation. 'This is the Hitler Youth.'

As he guided the Pattons back towards the Inner Sanctum, Mr Trevelyan caught Adolf Petty's eye with a look that must have reminded the Führer of the Night of the Long Knives.

'All ready to go, Comrade Stalin,' crackled the voice on my walkie-talkie as the State Defence Committee sat in the pottery school.

The Coverdale Soviet Union owned four walkie-talkies which were the latest technological gimmick from Japan, via Los Angeles. Lasch Rafferty donated them to the cause because he hated anything his father gave him. Now Secretary-General of the Party, Chairman of Council of Ministers, Chairman of the State Defence Committee, Supreme Commander-in-Chief, Homesick Commissar and Marshal of the Soviet Union, I used the walkie-talkies to impose Stalin's concentration of power.

'Is everyone in position, Marshal Zhukov?'

'Roger,' came Diggle's wavering voice. 'Bovverboy Penal Battalions at the ready.'

'Are the Nazis still unaware of the plan?'

'Roger, Stalin! We can hear them singing "The Horst Wessel Song" and Gary Glitter's "Leader of the Gang" in the camp.'

Just as we Bolsheviks used the music of Queen, the Coverdale Nazis believed that Gary Glitter's 'Leader of the Gang' best encapsulated the *Führerprincip*.

'Our intelligence from Pahlavi, chief of SMERSH, is that all is well, Zhukov,' said Ormonde down the walkie-talkie.

'Then, advance, Zhukov!' I commanded.

Marshal Georgi Zhukov, the tough and ruthless freckled general, who only days before had been regarded as a bed-wetter, liar and purveyor of excreta-soiled y-fronts, was my most gifted soldier: indeed, in 1942, I appointed Diggle Deputy Supreme Commander.

Zhukov raised his walkie-talkie again to address his commanders on either side of Hitler's Stalingrad front. We in the pottery listened to the course of the battle.

'Tora! Tora! Tora!' ordered Zhukov, using the name of a war film about Pearl Harbor that we had seen last week. We heard the troops singing Bony M's 'Rasputin' as they went in. We sang along.

Petty and his armies had thought they had conquered Stalingrad. Now, as that 1942 Easter term afternoon darkened, the holly bushes were crowded with troops, fresh reinforcements who had rested since Moscow the term before.

Stalingrad, the decisive battle of the war, was where the massive egos of Stalin and Hitler collided in the ruins of a city, for which their men fought street by street, factory by factory.

The city was more than just the doorway to the south for me, because it bore my name. In the Civil War, when it was still called Tsaritsyn, Lenin sent me there to save it. I shot many and drowned more in prison boats on the Volga. But in spite of Trotsky and the others who wanted me to fail, I saved the city. That was why they called it Stalingrad – Stalin's city – in 1925.

The radio went silent.

The State Defence Committee sat there tensely, clutching our mugs of tea, chewing Mum's delicious coffee cake and every now and then, staring at Mary Millington's headless but lubricious genitals on the scruffy scrap of pornography that was stuck with a drawing pin onto Stavka's wall. Who WAS Mary Millington? Someone's mother?

'Ogre, get up to Stalingrad and make sure Zhukov's in control. Report in at once. Ormonde. Stay here with me. We'll come if you call.'

'If Diggle's made a pickle, shall I torture him?'

'Just kill Germans for the moment, Ogre.'

As the surrounded German Sixth Army, under Field Marshal von Paulus, surrendered at Stalingrad, Adolf Hitler was not with OKW in the Wolf's Lair.

He was standing with a black moustache glued onto his upper lip before an irate Mr Trevelyan in his study.

'Right,' said Mr Trevelyan in an unusually aggressive way. 'Yesterday, as you doubtless considered most amusing, those parents discovered swastikas inserted into every book in the library. Even Churchill's *My Early Life!*'

'But, sir ...'

'Shut up, boy, or you're in the soup, Petty! This was not the first time. The day before I was showing the American Ambassador round the science labs. We were standing outside when someone dropped a Nazi flag, which landed on the head of the Ambassador's wife. When Mrs Trevelyan helped at the village fête two nights ago, she opened the cake tins to discover scores of swastikas.' He was shouting now: 'THERE WAS AN IRON CROSS IN MY COTTAGE PIE LAST NIGHT, GOD DAMN IT! This is your doing, Petty minor.'

The Headmaster turned to look out of the window, but luckily did not spot General Pahlavi, boss of SMERSH, listening in the freezing air just under the window ledge.

'It's not, sir. My gang's not doing it at all! It's Conroy setting us up, sir! One of Stalin's ...'

'One of Stalin's satanic tricks, is it? Conroy again? You're the one who prances around sporting Hitler's moustache.'

'Not true, sir.' Poor Petty – telling the truth and no one believed him. Give a dog a bad name.

'Take that bloody thing off now' – and the master ripped it off the boy's face. 'It is NOT funny playing Hitler, boy. Hitler was not a joke. It is bad taste. I dont want VILE boys in my school. Hitler was plain evil, Petty. He murdered six million Jews in gas chambers, the first time a man had actually used manufacturing techniques to deliberately burn a whole nation.'

'But Stalin killed just as many. Maybe more. It was HIM that said, "One death is a tragedy; a million is a statistic," and it was him that ...'

'Pipe down, Petty minor.'

There was a silence now. Trevelyan and Hitler stood looking at each other. Hitler knew what he had to do ...

As 1942 turned into 1943 in that study, Hitler saw as clearly as a diving Stuka that the democratic Allies, personified by Roosevelt, Churchill and Mr Trevelyan, were about to open a Second Front to help Stalin. In 1943, they despatched Operation Torch into North Africa, then Italy; in 1944, D-Day.

Germany's one chance was to break up the alliance and persuade them to join him in fighting the REAL villains, the Communists.

'Sir, Father says the Commies are the real danger. Our enemy! We're still fighting them. And Father says that we could very easily lose. HE says there are Commies everywhere – even in MI5, Parliament, Cambridge! So come on, sir, why don't you and me join forces and thrash Stalin?'

It was not a bad speech. But the standard of Hitler's soliloquies, usually now only heard by his tired and bored staff in the subterranean East Prussian bunker, had declined into rants since the Nuremburg Rallies. But he had one threat to deliver.

'Father says there could even be Fellow Travellers in a prep school like Coverdale!'

Pahlavi reports that Hitler was bent over the sofa receiving a DOZEN of the best before he had time to draw breath again.

His intelligence report, as ever elegantly phrased and spelled, written in the exquisite italic hand of an Oriental princeling, concludes, 'Trevelyan then stormed from the room into Mrs Trevelyan's kitchen to declare: "God, darling, these dictators really are proving a fly in the ointment."'

31

STALIN'S TRIUMPH 1944–5

'**I** want Hitler captured, ALIVE. I want him brought to Moscow to stand trial.'

So we were back in the old Dugganoes, Stalingrad Redux. The camp was ruined by fighting. But our brave comrades were cheerfully rebuilding in the warm weather of the summer term. Comrade Kildare's factories churned out new pine cones, conkers, Stalin's Organs and T-34 tanks with the help of slave labour from Comrade Ogleton's prison camps. Stalin remained in the Kremlin. But it was in Stalingrad that we held the last planning meeting of the war.

'Right-y-o, Stalin,' Marshal Zhukov nodded. Pahlavi stood up.

'Pahlavi,' I said. 'Congratulations on the success of your swastika campaign. Now, what do we know?'

'Mr Trevelyan has already stated that he and the Western allies will find the last Nazi stronghold, Berlin, in the woods and destroy it. Over the weekend.'

'Fine. We cannot allow them to capture Berlin. They're about to ban Camps again.'

'Wouldn't it be better to let the English capture it and face the terrible casualties?' asked Comrade Kildare, the Politburo's best manager.

I simply quoted Stalin on Churchill. '*Churchill is the kind who, if you don't watch him, will slip a kopeck out of your pocket! Yes, a kopeck out of your pocket.*'

'I see they can't be trusted,' agreed Kildare.

What useless fools they all were: traitors and puppies.

'We MUST capture it. Marshal Zhukov!'

'Yes, Marshal Stalin.'

'You will be one of the three marshals deputed to capture Berlin ...'

'But I want to command the attack myself ...'

'I think not.'

'You heard what Comrade Stalin said,' Ogleton growled in Zhukov's face. 'Only Stalin has the military genius to take Berlin.'

'Of course,' said Diggle-Johnson, who had rescued me so many times since 22 June 1941, but now regarded himself as almost my equal.

'Marshals Diggle, Archeamboye and St John will command the three-pronged attack on Berlin. Don't delay. Who will be first into Berlin? We attack tomorrow, Saturday.'

'But I think I might be on Exeat this weekend,' whined Diggle.

'No one goes home this weekend, Marshal Zhukov. What will it be: Mummy or Berlin?'

'Berlin!' they all shouted in unison. 'BERLIN!'

When they were gone, I walked back down the Flower Walk.

Steady Pelham was standing in the flowerbeds. I looked behind me but no one was there.

'Better not get caught talking to me,' he said gruffly. 'I'm a Non-Person. Never existed.'

'I miss you terribly, Steady. How have you been?'

'Keeping out of the war, mainly. Playing a lot of chess. I'm draughts champion. But I have to give you a bit of advice, Stalin. You're about to win. Things almost went pear-shaped in the Purges. It'll be worse next time.' Steady turned and set off stolidly back through the flowerbeds. Then he stopped to say, 'Capture Berlin. Then give up while you're ahead. That's the long and the short of it.'

'I wish I could.'

But Mr Trevelyan cancelled the Battle of Berlin.

The three armies were poised for the last push. The ghetto blaster was playing Abba's hit song to celebrate Hitler's imminent defeat: 'Waterloo! Waterloo!'

Then suddenly, those spoil sports, the Headmaster, Mr Hester and the decrepit Emperor Blunt strode straight through the Outback towards Berlin, the fortified ring of holly bushes, where Petty was dutifully making his last stand.

Mr Trevelyan clapped his hands. 'Right! I want all of you here now.'

Miserably I led the marshals and their troops towards Mr

Trevelyan. The Nazis emerged from Hitler's Bunker, rather relieved not to have to face the final onslaught. The Orangeman and Ancient Blunt made sure we all came in. But I did not see Petty.

'Now! No more Hitler. No more Stalin,' said Mr Trevelyan. 'Hear that? Conroy? Camps are now banned again thanks to you lot. And Ogleton and the rest of you, I've found something extremely serious in your camp. If anyone finds anything like THIS' – and he held up a piece of coloured paper.

The boys peered at it. The crowd collectively gulped.

'Mary Millington!' said Ogre, pointing shamelessly at Miss Millington's jewel.

'And Stalin's Organ on the other side,' I said. We were overcome by a fit of giggles.

'Silence, chaps! It doesn't surprise me YOU recognise it, Ogleton. It is exactly your level. This is absolutely disgusting. It is a cane-able offence from now on. But if there's any more of this rubbish, this is your last chance to hand it over. What the hell did you think you were doing with it. Conroy?'

'*Imagine a man who has fought all the way from Stalingrad to Belgrade across the dead bodies of his comrades,*' I said, as Stalin defended the rapacity of his Red Army. '*What is so awful in his having fun with a woman after such horrors?*'

'Where's Petty, Conroy?'

'Am I my brother's keeper?'

'You'd expect Stalin to know where Hitler was,' said Emperor Blunt.

'Hitler's meant to have committed suicide in the Bunker. But you've spoiled it all, sir.'

'Does that mean,' asked that simpleton Archie, 'that Petty's actually topped himself?'

Inconveniently, he had not. History does not always repeat itself. Indeed, it never repeats itself precisely, even when everyone tries very hard to make it.

Just at that moment, Marshal Zhukov said, 'Sir, look! There he is ...'

Everyone craned round. There, walking sadly through the woods, came our little Hitler.

'Buck up!' shouted Mr Hester.

Petty broke into a run. When he finally arrived breathlessly, Mr Trevelyan said, 'What the hell have you got to say for yourself, Petty?'

'Nothing,' he said. 'Except, I surrender.'

171

'Shut up,' said Mr Trevelyan. 'Get back to the school. You're all in detention for the next two hours.'

PRAVDA NEWSPAPER
May 1945
special victory issue
by Pravda's Coverdale correspondent, Comrade Ormonde
(pinned on the school noticeboard)

After Detention this very afternoon, Marshal Stalin, accompanied by Comrades Molotov, Malenkov, Beria, Khrushchev etc and Marshals Zhukov, Koniev, Rokossovky, etc. reviewed his victorious forces from the top of Lenin's Mausoleum (actually, the athletics horse) in the gym after chapel.

As the assembled military bands of the Red Army played the classic wartime hits of Queen's 'Bohemian Rhapsody' and Abba's 'Waterloo', twenty-five Red Army heroes marched past, entering the gym from the back door and exiting towards the squash courts. Each hero carried a hockey stick as a rifle, draped with the despised insignia of the fascist invaders in the form of rugby shirts.

As our heroes marched past Marshal Stalin, they threw the fascist banners at his feet like the legionaries in a Roman Triumph, as advised by Emperor Blunt.

Seventeen German prisoners trudged past the reviewing stand on their way to Siberia, while Marshal Stalin danced to 'Saturday Night Fever'.

In the midst of this Roman Triumph, walking in his underwear with a swastika glued to his forehead, dragging a ball and chain, constructed from a gym medicine ball and some climbing rope, staggered the vanquished German Führer, Adolf Hitler Petty, who was mocked and pelted with stale fruit (from the kitchens) by the long-suffering workers of Moscow.

The flypass of the Red Airforce was delayed due to mechanical problems.

I usually feel sorry for bores who say their schooldays were the happiest time of their lives.

But I had created an industrialised USSR, won the Second World War, conquered a bigger empire than the Tsars: how could my life after Coverdale ever beat that?

When I woke the next morning, I felt strangely depressed. Like Stalin after Berlin fell, my happiness was overshadowed by a sense of anticlimax as I went down to breakfast on Victory in Europe Day.

'Come on, Comrade Stalin, make a toast to victory ...' said Ogre, munching on his cereal.

'Yes, while we eat our toast and marmalade,' joked Nonsuch.

I tried to brighten myself up by giving some Stalinist toasts, drunk in hot sweet tea. But I could not help but be bitter: they obeyed me but they hated me.

'Let us drink to Kaganovich, a brave man. He knows if the trains don't arrive on time ... we shall shoot him. Air Marshal Novikov, a good marshal, let's drink to him. And if he doesn't do his job properly, we shall hang him. People call me a monster but as you see I make a joke of it. Maybe I am not so horrible after all.'

There was an embarrassed silence at Stalin's idea of a joke.

'Comrade Stalin, no one regards you as a monster,' said Ormonde after a moment. 'You're the most beloved man in the world. Indeed, Marshal Zhukov has something to say on behalf of the Red Army.'

'Well, Zhukov?' I said gruffly, crunching on my Rice Crispies.

Diggle-Johnson, who was getting too big for his boots, said, 'On behalf of the marshals of the Red Army and the Central Committee, we hereby announce the promotion of Marshal of the Soviet Union Joseph Vissarionovich Stalin to a new rank specially created to reflect the unique contribution of this genius of battle and statesmanship ...'

'What the hell have you lot cooked up?' I muttered, reflecting Stalin's mixture of false modesty and genuine disdain. Still, even Molotov admits he began to enjoy his deification. When you are Stalin, everyone else does your swanking for you.

Diggle and Ormonde squirmed: they both knew they should have passed it by me first. But it was too late now; what the hell.

'Go on, you pair of blunderers!'

It was Kildare, now promoted to the Politburo as chief economic adviser, who stepped round the two of them and announced, 'Generalissimo of the Soviet Union J. V. Stalin!'

The crowds clapped, even the boys up collecting their baked beans and bacon from D'Artagnan and Catalina, cheering 'Hear! Hear!' Ogre shouted to the troops, 'Three cheers for our Jolly Good Chap STALIN! Hip, hip hurrah!' I inclined my head, modestly.

They expected Stalin to say a few words. Instead he was angry.

Baubles diminish statesmen – something that primitive Brezhnev never understood. This is what Stalin really said.

'*What need has Comrade Stalin of that? Generalissimus? Some title you've thought up! Chiang Kai-shek is a generalissimo. Franco is a generalissimo. Fine company I find myself in!*'

The truth was I had discovered another force, greater even than all Stalin's victories.

32

STALIN IN LOVE

Miss Snow's walk changed everything. I can safely say it altered the course of history. If you believe in the Cleopatra's Nose theory of history, then you will understand the effect of Miss Snow's Ankle.

There was nothing unusual about Miss Snow leading a promenade. She liked to walk in the woods. This was because she was an American, 'a race,' according to Emperor Blunt 'obsessed with hygiene and exercise.' We called these walks 'route marches' but she being a Yank called them 'hikes'. Our conductress walked vigorously up hills and through bowers; nothing could stop her.

So after Stalin's Victory Parade, I noticed she was standing beside Mr Trevelyan as he announced the week's events at lunch.

'And lastly, Miss Snow has very kindly agreed to take a Route March this afternoon beyond the Outback. Anyone who wants to go, report to Miss Snow afterwards.'

'The Politburo will attend,' I said at our table.

'Delighted to, Generalissimo,' they replied.

'Stalin loved to walk,' said Ormonde, who had been doing his homework. 'He walked briskly and changed direction so fast that his lieutenants were either left behind or bumped into him. It was the only exercise he did.'

But the true reason was to be with Miss Snow. She wore brown boots with a green suede knee-length skirt and a long serge navy blue coat with gold buttons.

As soon as we were dressed in our wellington boots and anoraks, we assembled outside my Hero-City, Stalingrad. There were about twenty of us.

When Miss Snow arrived, she did not slow down. She just kept going and we could follow if we liked. That was the deal with her walks. If we could not equal her stride, we had to return to the school before we left the Outback to penetrate the Corinthian Woods.

We Politburo members almost ran to catch up and, once we had, we sweated to keep up. We asked her questions with which we hoped to embarrass her. But we usually only managed to embarrass ourselves.

'Miss Snow, have you ever snogged a man?' I asked.

'Yes,' she replied. 'I once snogged an Eskimo and it was so cold that he froze to me and we had to undergo surgery to be parted.'

We walked in silence for a while, trying to absorb this piece of information. I had learned Stalinist cynicism. But I always believed Miss Snow.

'Was it a painful operation?'

'She's teasing you, Stalin, aren't you Miss Snow?' said Ormonde.

'I wouldn't dare tease Generalissimo Stalin,' replied Miss Snow.

We walked further.

'Isn't it rather unhealthy, snogging? Couldn't it cause a flu epidemic?'

'Yes, Conroy. But it's worth it.'

Her replies usually made me blush.

'Miss Snow, have you ever posed for ... a pornographic magazine?'

'Like Mary Millington?' added Ogre.

'That's not a smart question, Conroy. How do you know about such a thing?'

'We found one in the boiler room,' said Nonsuch earnestly. 'But Mr Trevelyan confiscated it.'

'Well, mam, have you ever posed ... starkers?'

'No, but when I was young, I once posed naked for an artist.'

'Totally naked, Miss Snow?'

'Not even a figleaf.'

'Gosh. What was the artist like?'

'A dirty old man.'

'Was he malodorous, mam?'

'No but dangerously lecherous.'

'What does "lecherous" mean?'

'He had a one-track mind.'

Pause.

'Like a railway, Miss Snow?'

'Sort of, Conroy.'

We tramped on. Miss Snow turned around but did not stop walking. There was really only the Politburo left.

'Many have fallen by the wayside,' she said.

'Like the bad seed in Jesus' Parable,' added Ogre who, despite using gypsy curses, was first in divinity.

'But I'm very glad to have my diehards with me: my real hikers,' she said.

As she spoke, she put her arm around my shoulders and squeezed me. She did not put her arm around Ormonde, Ogre, Pahlavi or the rest of them. Just mine.

I experienced a pang of pride – and something else too. I could not quite place it but I do remember that I could not really stop looking at her. I wanted to walk alone upfront with her always, asking her questions and hearing her funny answers. That squeeze was a secret message that she wanted to be with only me.

I remembered how hurt she was when I fell in love with Stalin. It fell into place.

'Do women really enjoy snogging men?' Ormonde was asking. 'Or are they just being polite?'

'That's a really yucky question!' said Nonsuch.

'How do you know the men aren't just being polite?' she replied.

'Does Mr Allcock have girlfriends?' I asked.

'His private life is his own affair, Conroy. He'll settle down in the end. But he's certainly had an eye for the ladies. What they call "a roving eye".'

'Just ONE eye?' reflected Nonsuch.

'Like Miss Gladwyn-Jones?' asked Ogre.

'Which eye is it?' I wanted to know.

She chuckled at me: whatever an eye did when it roved, I did not like the tone of her admiration for Mr Allcock.

It was a close day with the clouds as awkward and swollen as the udders of Merke's cows. The air was moist before rain had even arrived. Yet the glare from the sky was so bright you could not really look at it. Miss Snow sometimes put on big sunglasses like Jackie Onassis. The light showed up her face: it was a frightening witch's face – until she laughed.

But she laughed often enough for us to know she enjoyed life but rarely enough to make it boundlessly rewarding.

'Are you looking at my wrinkles?' she said.

'Yes, I was admiring them,' I replied. It was the most chivalrous answer I could imagine.

But she scowled at me. We did not know what to say. Since she had not liked that chivalrous compliment, I tried another.

'I like your hair too, Miss Snow, especially the grey at the front.'

'Save it, Conroy.'

'No really, it's lovely. Just like one of my favourite animals.'

'What animal?' she asked warily.

'The badger,' I replied.

'Shut up, Conroy. One day, kid, you'll learn how to talk to a woman,' she said crushingly. She was vain, you see. She was quite angry.

Even the Politburo said nothing. I wanted to cry. I had offended Miss Snow not once, but twice. I could not speak. We just listened to the clump and squidge of our boots on the peaty earth. Miss Snow's face was sweating.

'You shouldn't have said THAT, Stalin,' whispered Kildare, falling back a few steps. 'My mother has wrinkles and if you mention them, she cries. And she'd really blub if I told her she looked like a badger.'

'Comrades Ogre and Archeamboye, I think Comrade Kildare needs a lesson in Communist Party hiking discipline.'

'I didn't mean any harm, Comrade Generalissimo.'

'Hard cheese,' I said.

I nodded and the three of them fell behind, the secret policemen holding onto Kildare's elbows. When I looked back, they were lowering Kildare into the nettles, face first. Crabbe once did it to me. I began to feel better about Miss Snow. But Kildare's insubordination niggled me.

'After the war, people are too relaxed about our enemies. We need to tighten things up again ...'

'You're right, Koba,' said Ormonde, the last who dared to call me that.

'See to it.'

We caught up with Miss Snow again as we entered the Corinthian Woods.

They were magical: firs planted closely together like sentries. Summer or winter, they were cool customers, those firs, cold-hearted trees, bred through tundra snows. We believed the Corinthian Woods were haunted.

The forbidding forest seemed to cleanse me of my blunders.

I caught up with Miss Snow again, trying to think of a way to win back her attention, if not her favour. We were stepping in single file along the edge of a little canyon, filled with leaves. We had to grip onto the pine trees to avoid falling.

'Miss Snow,' I began. 'Why are women who sell their bodies called "horses"?'

'You mean "prostitutes"?'

We listened agog.

'No, my big brother Jonathan uses another word for it: horses.'

'Whores?'

'That's it, Miss Snow, horses. Why do they call them horses? Why not donkeys?'

'Or even zebras?' added Ogre.

Miss Snow's laugh was surprisingly high-pitched considering her huskiness. And she looked back at me indulgently: I was back in favour after the wrinkles and badgers. But as she turned again, she lost her footing and slipped down the slope all the way to the bottom. It seemed a long way to us but it was probably only twenty feet. As soon as she arrived at the bottom with her back to us, she grabbed her leg and began moving back and forth like a worshipping Moslem facing Mecca, whispering to herself and breathing heavily.

As ever, in such circumstances, our first instinct was to giggle nervously.

Our second was look at our leader for guidance.

But I was the leader. I was Stalin. So they looked at me.

And I did not know what to do. Kildare's nettle-stung face was a warning against anyone suggesting anything. This only goes to show why dictators never get good advice.

Normally I would have barked orders like Stalin at wartime Stavka. But I was worried about Miss Snow. Her pain hurt me too. It may sound absurdly sentimental. It was. I wanted to cry again.

'Shall we go down?' I asked.

'Could do,' said the Politburo carefully, noticing Kildare's swelling rash. 'Should we?'

'We could ALL go down and see her.'

'Why don't YOU go down? You're Stalin.' Ormonde always said the right thing. He swung his yo-yo emphatically.

We were naturally suspicious of adults in pain: it was not their job to be indisposed. It might be dangerous for us. They existed to guide us, not the other way round. We were afraid to witness their indignity.

'But we'll come if you want,' added fearless Ogleton. 'It's just ...'

'Stop! I'll go down.' I could not bear to think of sharing Miss Snow in agony with anyone else. I was sure she did not want any of these sycophantic apparatchiks near her. 'Sit up here and wait.' They obeyed.

I sat on my bum and used my feet like brakes as I skidded down the slope to where she crouched.

'Are you all right, Miss Snow?'

She did not reply but kept holding her ankle. Her bad leg was stretched out straight and her good one was bent at the knee so that she could rest her arm on it. Her face kept contorting into ugliness and then relaxing again. When she was relaxed, I tried to ask her things. When she was grimacing, I did not dare. But I placed my hand on her shoulder.

'Damn, it hurts. Fuck!'

Golly! I had never a woman swear before so I knew it hurt.

Then she looked at me and I could tell she was pleased it was me and not anyone else.

'Ah, it's you, William. It's only a sprain. But it sure hurts.'

I can still hear her voice saying, 'Ah, it's you.' That was pregnant with meaning. She used 'William', my first name, not Conroy, not Stalin, but 'William', making me feel needed. No, essential! An equal.

'William, will you pull my boot off?'

So I scuttled keenly around to her feet and looked up at her. But I never got to her eyes. The line of her legs was wonderfully straight. I scanned up her outstretched leg, past her knee. Her skirt was torn and raised. I saw the stockings and barely dared allow my eyes to glance at the brown skin above it – and the unthinkable, unimaginable beyond. Her other thigh, which was bent at the knee, bulged, but only slightly and most curvaceously. The thighs at the top seemed to glow to me out of the shadows under her skirt. I froze. They looked so soft. I simply could not think what I thought, except I thought of little else.

Miss Snow pulled her skirt down briskly.

'Oh, I'm sorry, Conroy, to put you through THAT,' she joked through clenched teeth, as if she had subjected me to an atrocity. In retrospect, she probably felt she would appear old and unappealing to young eyes. She blushed. But I only noticed that she was distancing me again with my surname. 'How awful for you, Conroy.' She forced a smile.

'Don't worry, mam, I'm a doctor's son,' I said, trying to be chivalrous, adding what my father once told me: 'It is impossible to shock a doctor.'

I remembered how important I felt when I first reviewed the May Day Parade from Lenin's Mausoleum! But now I was convinced I was even more important!

'That's all right then,' she said. 'Try not to look and pull my boot off.'

'Geronimo!' shouted one of the boys at the top. 'Miss Snow's favourite! Miss Snow and Stalin!' They guffawed. They could not see what I could see, because she was facing the wrong way, but they could see that there was something to see even though they could not see it. One of them, doubtless Ogre, wolf-whistled.

'Cut it!' she snapped, suddenly very Bette Davis.

They did.

I put my hands around the ankle and heel of the boot and began to tug. I tried not to look of course, but I had every opportunity because pulling down her skirt had not achieved much. Those bare thighs sang such songs to me that I kept staring at them, then desperately looking up into her eyes. But they always drew me back. I can see them now ...

When the boot gave, I was pulling so hard I fell over backwards. The leather was warm. As I held it, I could smell her, not just the perfumes that she probably applied excessively, but her. The body underneath. It was a strong exercised smell, but not grubby. I never knew women could smell like that, like everyone else, like normal people.

As soon as the boot was off, she tried to reach for her stockinged ankle but it was hard without bending her leg, which she could not do.

So I reverently placed my hands around her ankle, feeling the solidity of muscle and the sweat.

'That's better! Christ! That's better! That's better.'

So I pressed a bit more and she said, 'Ahhhhh! That's better, keep doing that, Stalin ... I mean William. Thank you. What a touch! Go on ... again ...'

She did not mean to call me Stalin. But Stalin, Conroy or William, she just said the first thing that came into her mind because I was singlehandedly curing her.

So I stroked her ankle, working hard at it, pressing my thumbs onto the swollen bit, relieving the pressure, as she sighed. Her breath was on my face. I was overheating. Sweating. Perhaps because no one had ever thanked me so much.

She placed a hand on my head, ruffling it a little, as if to guide my massaging hands better. But that hand made me so happy because she needed me; I was helping her; she was grateful. I was so close to her bareness that I swear her thighs actually radiated heat, as if I were near the Earth's core.

Even when I met Churchill and Roosevelt at Yalta, even when I succeeded Lenin, even when I got the H-bomb, I had never knew such tender power.

And I was a megalomaniac.

'Comrade Stalin, are you going to your office to decide about Hitler?' asked Ogre after I had organised the rescue of Miss Snow and we were back outside the Kremlin.

'I'll decide later. Crikey, I don't know what to do ...'

'Yes, Comrade Stalin. Very wise.'

The war had aged me. I was no longer just an eleven-year-old. I was almost thirteen. My voice was breaking embarrassingly; it switched between high and low. Not having a single voice is like not having a name. Even before the Walk, I was having difficulty concentrating on Leninist-Stalinist dialectical materialism. My body was sprouting foliage in all manner of secret places. I myself could now Produce on an industrial Stakhanovite scale. My entourage were bound to notice that I was older. Would they start to talk about nominating a successor? What would happen when I 'rejoined Lenin'?

If history had a Lonely Leaders' Club, I would be a member along with Stalin, Tamurlane, Genghis Khan, Napoleon and Hitler. And I was so lonely because my best 'friends' were terrified of me.

Even Ogre.

'Crumbs. I can't think about Hitler now. Ogleton, should I retire?'

'God, no, oh Great Teacher Stalin! What would become of us without you?'

'You're right. We haven't done a bad job, eh?'

'You've done a brilliant job, Comrade Stalin. Genius!'

'*What's the point in talking to you? Whatever I say, you reply: "Yes Comrade Stalin, of course Comrade Stalin, you have taken a wise decision, Comrade Stalin."*'

'Sorry, Comrade Stalin!'

'Never mind. I have some secret work for you. Order Pahlavi and all your other agents to watch Miss Snow. Day and night.'

'Just Miss Snow?'

'Cancel all other surveillance of grown-ups.'

'Why?'

'There's not to reason why. But she needs my protection. She expects it after I helped her on the Walk. Oh, yes, and watch Mr Allcock too. Find out which of his eyes rove. He's a potential enemy.'

'Of course, Comrade Stalin. Good evening.'

He disappeared towards the Pottery.

I did not want to hear about my responsibilities that afternoon.

I could only think about Miss Snow's ankle, how helpful I had been. Our shared secret made me look upon her in a new light.

33

THE COLD WAR AND THE HOT
WAR 1946–51

'**M**endoza, do you think Miss Snow has ever had sex?' I whispered as I sat on Lenin's bed in the dormitory.

'Surely *Stalin's Collected Works* might grant us a clue?'

'I'm hollow-eyed with reading them but even they have no answer. Besides, Stalin wasn't good with women: his second wife shot herself ...'

'So there ARE things that Stalin does not know about?'

'No, Koba had the answer for everything!'

'Yes, in the USSR. But maybe THIS is another country. Why do you ask about Miss Snow?' added Mendoza.

'Never mind.'

I just could not tell him.

For us, the Cold War was the beginning of a period when our world changed dramatically. Suddenly, for the first time in our lives, we learned that the human race was divided into armed camps with opposing ideologies and methods, each ready to stop at nothing to impose their wills on the other.

The two camps were called Men and Women.

Even in my Union of Stalinist Soviet Republics of Coverdale, the ideological debate was shifting from pure Leninism to sex: we now spent as much time discussing that mystery as we did Stalin's paper 'On the Nationalities Question'. We passed afternoons discussing the lost Mary Millington. Sitting in constant session, the Politburo debated for weeks. 'Essay Question – is Mary Millington normal or is she a freak of nature?' It tormented me how this spread-eagle could be the same species as, say, Miss Snow. I was certain that Miss Snow would NEVER look like that. Both were women. But SHE must be a different and altogether superior species of the gender.

When I asked Mendoza about sex, he just laughed in his tigerish way. At night he just disappeared and no one knew where he went. He returned some time before dawn. That Christmas term was his last; he and Rafferty stayed an extra one for some reason, probably because, as my mother said, 'Their parents did not want them a moment earlier than necessary.'

The others of Mendoza's generation were already gone, so he walked among us boys like a man-creature from a future age. Ormonde was Captain of the School, even though he was younger than Mendoza. Even I was a prefect. We prefects had one special privilege. We were allowed to stay up to watch the tv detectives *Starsky and Hutch* on Saturdays at nine p.m. But Mendoza needed no titles: my Lenin had natural authority.

So Mendoza just chuckled at my questions. 'I don't have to worry about you, my little Koba,' he said, languishing on his bed in his silk dressing-gown and velvet slippers. There was a miners' strike as usual – so the whole school was in candlelight again. The sense of crisis led to an unnatural blossoming of all kinds of mischief – talking, fiddling, pillow fights and memories of Mary Millington. 'With you, Conroy, something will suddenly happen with girls.'

'Really? When?' My heart flew.

'In the next ten years.'

My face fell.

'Hard cheese,' he said.

Only Mendoza could have suggested Stalin did not understand sex without facing the rats, the Bunsen burners in Lubianka and then exile to Siberia.

'But I wouldn't have the darndest idea what to do,' I grumbled.

'It's instinct; you know without knowing ...'

That made me think.

Just then, Miss Deirdre appeared at the doorway. 'Lights out, chaps,' she barked like a good-natured sergeant-major. Her father was in the army. She came over and took the candle from the mantelpiece. It was waxed onto a saucer.

'Can't be already,' I grumbled. 'What time is it?'

'Past your bedtime, Conroy. Get into bed at once, you poltroon. That goes for you too, Mendoza. You have no discipline in this dorm at all ... Night, me darlings!'

'You look very smart tonight, Miss Deirdre,' said Mendoza suddenly.

'Flattery will get you everywhere. Perhaps the candlelight does me justice. Now into bed the lot of you!' said Miss Deirdre.

'Can't we just talk for five more minutes?' asked Mendoza, who had not moved an inch.

'Get into bed, you cheeky monkeys, or else I'll get Mr Trevelyan! I'll get into terrible trouble if you don't. Then I won't be able to turn your lights out again. It'll be Mr Hester or Mr Eye!'

God forbid! We scrammed into bed swiftly at the spectre of the Orangeman or the Russian Spy.

'How's Mr Allcock?' I blurted, recalling Mr Allcock's roaring lion act. I was glad they had not really done press-ups together.

'I don't know what you mean.'

'Miss Deirdre,' said Mendoza. 'I've heard that if the boys in dorm B are in bed on time, you kiss them.'

'What sort of kiss?' I asked.

Mendoza collected himself for this coup. 'A snog!' he said deliberately, enjoying every letter of it.

Miss Deirdre turned a fiery red, which stood out even more against her blonde curls. I sat up and looked at her then. Her face was plump and her nose retroussé. She had spots. But when she blushed, they mercifully disappeared into an incarnadine sea. Her eyes were blue buttons. Her mouth was too big for her face. She wore wrap-around skirts that floated around her ankles and white blouses with red cardigans. She was always smiling. She was only seventeen, scared of getting into trouble with Mr Trevelyan, but she seemed quite old to us.

Miss Deirdre was so busy blushing that she seemed incapable of coherent expression.

'Well ... Mendoza ... well ... it's not true at all. It's a lie!'

Everyone sat up a little then, because schoolboys can always divine when they've probed somewhere sensitive. We narrowed our eyes ... Of course it was not true. But Ogleton, Prefect of Dormitory B, had indeed offered this solution to Miss Deirdre, who was sufficently keen to get their Lights Out that she had almost agreed. 'If you give me a snog,' said Mendoza. 'I promise that we'll all be in bed every night on time and you won't even have to ask.'

'Cheeky monkey!' said Miss Deirdre. 'But you're already in bed ...'

'Get out of bed everyone,' I ordered.

'Aye, aye, Comrade Stalin,' said Kildare, who slept next to me. The whole dorm jumped out of their beds in their pyjamas.

'Right!' shouted the under-matron. 'Right! Get back into bed or else the high jump!'

The dormitory giggled at her confusion.

'Puss, puss, puss ... Temper, temper,' hissed Kildare sadistically.

'Miss Deirdre, come on. One kiss,' drawled Mendoza, raising an eyebrow. 'And they'll slumber in seconds.'

She should have just called Mr Trevelyan but, for whatever reason, she considered it.

'If everyone gets into bed ...'

'You'll give me a kiss,' said Mendoza.

'If everyone gets into bed and everyone promises not to breathe a word to ANYONE!'

We swore our discretion in every oath known to human civilisation.

We got into bed and pretended to be ready to sleep.

'I've delivered my half of the bargain,' said Mendoza, smiling so that his big white teeth shone against his laminated skin.

The school was deadly silent then. We were the last dormitory to have our lights turned out. Miss Deirdre looked at our hungry eyes and then at Mendoza. She could not really believe he would collect his debt. But he WAS Mendoza.

She stepped outside the doorway with the candle and peered down the corridor in both directions. The dorm went dark. We all sat up. The light returned with its mistress.

'Good to see you're all ready for bed,' she snapped.

Then she walked over to Mendoza – Florence Nightingale with her lamp – in the aching silence. Our eyes strained hard. Our eyelids creaked as we tried not to blink, keen not to miss a micro-second. I can still remember the clip of her heels on the linoleum floor. Mendoza stared up at her. She darted towards him like a scared mouse and landed a glancing kiss on his cheek. It was over before it had begun and she was darting back again, saying, 'There you are, Mendoza. Good night you dormitory of cheeky monkeys ...'

Mendoza reached up with his tiger paws, placed them around her blonde curls and pulled her back to kiss her again.

We expected to see her stand up in a second. But they just went on kissing. Her left hand still tried to balance the candle, but it tilted until the liquid wax was running over the brim. We could hear the moisture of the kiss. We could barely breathe. My heart palpitated with fascinated confusion. The silhouette of their joined heads was huge and unforgettable on the wall behind his bed.

I never realised that a kiss could go on for minutes. Kissing did not look very safe. How did they breathe? I was sure that if I tried a similar trick, I'd suffocate.

When she finally disentangled herself, she was blushing again and laughing gaily as she wiped her lips. She did not look the slightest bit short of oxygen. Quite the contrary!

'Right! Lights Out! Not a word to anyone.' She seemed sharper, as if the blood had gone to her brain and oiled its sluggish mechanics. 'Agreed? Not a word! Good night!'

I thought fast about Mendoza's earlier advice.

'Hold it right there!' I said.

'What is it now?' she drawled.

'Out of bed, fellow workers and soldiers of our brave, victorious Soviet Union!'

'You heard Comrade Stalin! Out unless you want a visit from Comrade Beria and his secret police!' echoed Kildare.

The dormitory obeyed like clockwork; not one of the boys was remotely sleepy. It was a night to remember.

'Now look here!' whispered Miss Deirdre wearily, as if she were suddenly bored of the joke. 'I'm warning you, Conroy: I'm going to get angry in a moment. I thought we had a deal, Mendoza!' She sounded as if she might burst into tears.

Mendoza was laughing too much to speak.

'We did,' I replied. 'But this is a people's soviet. We demand equality. The deal is that you have to kiss us ALL before we go to bed.'

'Don't be silly. There'll be big trouble! THE HIGH JUMP! Get straight back into bed. Or else I'll go and wake up Mr Trevelyan and see what he has to say!'

'No. If you DON'T give us a kiss, WE'll go and get Mr Trevelyan and tell him that you snogged Mendoza for more than five minutes without stopping to breathe!'

'Hear! hear! Hurrah for Comrade Stalin!'

Miss Deirdre could barely conceive of the terrible position she found herself in. She had to obey or lose her job.

'You'd sneak on ME to Mr Trevelyan?'

'I'd dynamite the Kremlin for a you-know-what from you!' I replied. (I wouldn't have blown it up, though.)

'We're all witnesses, Miss Deirdre. We all saw you kiss Mendoza,' Kildare reminded her.

Miss Deirdre sighed and shook her head. She popped out of the door and looked around and then came back.

'OK, you can each have a very quick kiss.'

'You start with Stalin!' I said. 'Into bed everyone!' The dorm jumped back into bed.

She came over, shame-faced.

'Stalin ...' she mused. 'Your Commie talk is Greek to me!'

I had never been so nervous. I became more and more afraid as her dancing candle came towards me. Yet I knew she had to do it. Stalin teaches: fear is the best persuader.

She sat on the bed and pressed her lips against mine. Then she jumped up and moved on to Kildare. I was not sure if it was nice or not. Her soft lips left a warmth that I felt cooling in the night air. But that was the truly dangerous moment, when we Stalinists began to dabble in the games of grown-ups. Stalin seemed a most useful adviser in understanding adults. But actually, this was to be the road to disaster.

She marched to the door and switched the light off.

'Not a word! Or I'll be on the next train back to Lincolnshire!'

'There is a precept which says we should forgive our enemies. But there is no precept about forgiving our former friends,' Stalin liked to say.

'Let me come back, Koba,' Petty said. 'It would be jolly d. of you. Jolly jolly d. I made mistakes ...'

'MISTAKES! To call Hitler, Operation Barbarossa and World War Two "a mistake" is a slight understatement ...'

'I only joined the fascists because you made me play Yezhov and then sacrificed me.'

'If you wanted to play Yezhov, you should have read your history. Yezhov was shot; Hitler killed himself. History's vampires never rise again.'

'I created the Great Purges on your orders. I so wanted to please Stalin, I'd have done anything for you. Don't you know gratitude, Koba?'

'Yes, I do, it's a dog's disease.' Stalin's real reply to that question at a 1920s Politburo meeting was not without wit.

'Let me come back as someone else ...'

We stood alone in the cold darkness in the private gardens beside the smoking bonfire. We prefects still did Odd Jobs rather than face rugby. I missed Petty. Now, after he had faced another interrogation by Ogre and the Bunsen burners, he had wandered outside, still smelling of the science lab's sulphur, Bunsen gas and his own burned hair. I followed him here.

'Come back. I miss you. Join the Politburo again. Who do you want to be, Comrade?'

'Zhdanov.' He had lost neither his ambition nor his evil: Zhdanov was Stalin's chosen successor. Just as Yezhov gave his name to the Yezhovschina (Time of Yezhov) so Zhdanov gave his to the Zhdanov-schina after the war.

'What is my mission, Comrade Stalin?'

'People became freer during the war. We needed all sorts of scum to win – Sportsmen, bed-wetters and Scottish reelers. They must all be brought to heel. Destroy them. And ban any punk music. We only want Communists now. No, not Commmunists: STALINISTS.'

'Thank you, Koba. Thank you. I'll close down the Scottish reels at once.'

'Stalin would never have let you back. Still, Stalin is old. Perhaps I'm losing it ...'

'Of course not, Comrade Stalin. You will rule for a long while yet. For ever!'

'The sixties didn't traditionally begin until '68,' Mr Allcock was telling Miss Snow, as she limped along the corridor outside the Latin classroom. 'But I personally date the sixties later – to '69, the Altmont Festival. I was at the Isle of Wight, you know ...'

It was still impossible to tell which of Mr Allcock's eyes roved and which did not. It was the first chance I had to speak to Miss Snow since the Walk.

'Oh, Miss Snow,' I interrupted keenly. 'How's your ankle?'

'Look,' she said and pointed at the bandage under her tights. 'Still swollen, thank you.'

Mr Allcock said, 'She's feeling much better and I hear you were rather a hero, like Sir Francis Drake laying his cloak on the puddle for Good Queen Bess.'

I ignored him and said to her, 'Glad to be of service, Miss Snow.' I looked at him, raised my hand confidentially and whispered to her, 'Don't worry, mam, he'll go soon.'

'I've a lesson at four,' said Mr Allcock on cue. 'Toodle-loo!'

'Bye, Geoffrey,' she said.

'Hard cheese, Mr Allcock.'

'Don't be insolent, Conroy,' he said. 'See you later, Cynthia.'

I did not answer his impertinent farewell. He obviously did not really know how helpful I had been! How she hobbled back leaning on me and Archie. How she said to me, 'Can't thank you enough. I shan't forget, Conroy.' But why would she confide in a grown man idiotic enough to think Clapton was God?

He trotted off with his bouncing step.

'Good riddance to bad rubbish,' I confided to Miss Snow. I could not stop looking at her face.

Her face changed.

'I suggest you respect Mr Allcock. Don't be rude, Conroy.'

'WE don't believe all his sixties stories.'

'Whatever, Mr Allcock's a true life enhancer,' she said coldly. Her smile had turned autumnal, then warmed slightly. 'Just like you, Conroy.' The bell rang for lessons. 'I must rush.'

I watched her limp away. She did not say goodbye. Had she forgotten the Walk?

I did not know what to expect of our first chat since. But I was disappointed because whatever it was I had expected ... did not happen.

34

STALIN'S H-BOMB

'Is Miss Deirdre turning out our lights?' asked Kildare from the bed next door, even though he had been shot a week earlier in the new purge as an Enemy of the People. Abba's song 'Fernando' played on his radio.

'No, I hope not,' I said.

'Don't you want another kiss?' asked Mendoza lazily.

'No, not really. I ... I ... hope Miss Snow turns our lights out tonight.'

It is always a fatal mistake for someone to reveal what he really wants. The other boys instinctively clicked.

'It happens she is on duty tonight: Say "amo" Miss Snow,' teased Mendoza.

'Of course, I don't amo her,' I answered. 'How could I?'

'Look who's mentioned lurrve!' said Kildare.

We should have finished him off. But I could not execute him or anyone else. It occurred to me for the first time that there was no point in dreaming of Stalin if you did not have the power to kill. Death was the only power worth having, after all. The death penalty did not have a use for me any more. But now, with Miss Snow to watch, the surveillance powers of the secret police were indispensable.

'I said I did NOT love her ...'

'But you did help her with her ankle ...' said another voice.

'And you did follow her on the walk ...'

'Calm down, chaps,' said Mendoza.

'I know what,' said Kildare. 'Let's play Dare.'

This seemed a good way to change the subject, though, as it happened, it was not a change of subject at all.

Kildare collected each of our Dares, written on pieces of paper.

I wrote, 'Streak from Mr Trevelyan's Inner Sanctum to the chapel' as my contribution.

Kildare shuffled the papers in his cardboard box.

Dare was a frightening game. If you played – and you had little choice in the matter – you were obliged to carry out its orders. Of course, if the card said 'Murder Mr Eye', you would not be expected to do that. So the Dares were usually tasks that were feasible, but only just.

Kildare drew out a pack of cards to decide who picked first.

The rules were that Dares had to be executed straight after the task was assigned.

So as that little swot shuffled and reshuffled the cards, all of us were praying that we would not be first. It was almost Lights Out, so probably most of us would be saved by twilight.

'Call your cards!' said Kildare. 'Dorm Captain?'

'Ace of Hearts.'

'Josef Stalin?'

'Jack of Spades.'

'I call Five of Hearts ...' called Kildare.

When all six of us in the Dorm had called, Kildare portentously picked a card. Whoever's call was closest to the card was the victim.

'Nine of Spades!' he announced triumphantly, showing everyone the card.

I was the victim. The others gathered around. Even Mendoza wandered over languidly to watch.

'Pick!'

I put on my dressing-gown and sat on the edge of my bed. Kildare held out the flat open box.

I reached in and took a piece of paper.

Kildare seized it out of my hand and slowly opened it.

He laughed as he read it silently and showed it to a couple of others. They laughed too.

'Read it out, you venomous Trotskyite!' I said.

'Read it out,' ordered Mendoza.

'All right,' said Kildare. 'Ready?'

I nodded with as much enthusiasm as I could muster.

'FLASH AT MISS SNOW!' he announced.

I threw myself at him and got my hands round his throat. I knew he had fixed it. Kildare could not stop himself chortling. The whole dormitory joined in.

Finally Mendoza said, 'Leave Kildare, Conroy.' Then, 'You'll have to do it.' The rest of them hopped into bed.

'Do it,' hissed Kildare. 'Do it, Stalin!'

I had no choice; it was schoolboy lore. To break a Dare would be beyond the Pale, like sneaking or falsifying a cricket score. You could NEVER break a Dare.

Besides, it began to appeal to me.

I told myself that this was the moment that Stalin finally got the Bomb: Stalin's scientists had worked frantically to create our own Soviet atomic bomb to equal the Americans'.

So now I was about to test the nuclear flash of my own H-Bomb.

'Everyone in bed?' said Miss Snow, wearing brown suede trousers, bootkins and a blue denim shirt. 'Dorm Captain?'

'All present and correct, Miss Snow,' replied Mendoza.

'Conroy! Bed!'

I walked towards her along the aisle between the beds.

'Conroy, where are you going? INTO BED or report yourself to Mr Trevelyan.'

I was facing her now. I could hardly breathe. The physical effort of opening my dressing-gown now seemed immense, as if its cord was made of iron chains. I was not sure if I could raise the strength to do it.

'Miss Snow, I'm sorry but I have to do this. It's a Dare. Stalin's got the Bomb: here it is!'

I opened my dressing-gown wide to flash and then closed it and ran back to my bed.

The dormitory gasped.

'He DID it?! S'TRUTH!!'

My face was buried in my pillow.

I finally looked up. The boys were laughing; her face was theatrically severe.

'That's charming, Conroy,' she said.

The age of the nuclear arms race had commenced.

She would never be able to forget me after that.

Mercifully, it was half-term the next day.

*

'You're having Miss Snow and Mr Allcock watched by Beria's secret police,' said Steady Pelham quietly while we waited for our parents next morning in the Inner Sanctum. 'You're mad.'

'Schools will one day use Stalin to teach pupils how to manage people,' I said, 'how to win, how to succeed in business.'

'*Stalin is a small, vicious man*,' Steady recalled the long-dead Bukharin, '*no, not a man, but a* DEVIL!'

'So?' I laughed. 'Adults can be Enemies of the people too.'

'Stop it while you can,' said Steady. 'Never involve the adults. You'll find out things you're not supposed to know.'

'Knowledge is power, Steady.'

'No, it's not. It's poison.'

'Your son flashed at me!' said Miss Snow.

When my parents arrived at the Inner Sanctum to pick me up, Miss Snow went straight up to them. I tried to cut her off. I stood between her and my parents, telling my mother, 'Wait by the car. I'll see you out there!'

'I think not, William,' said Miss Snow. 'I think your parents and I should have a bit of chat, don't you?'

'Please, Miss Snow!' I begged. I did not want my parents to hear about it. They would only wonder if I was abnormal. They would worry.

'Hello, Cynthia,' said mum to Miss Snow. 'Lovely to see you. Is he behaving himself?'

That was when she came right out and said it. Gosh, I almost died.

'Oh dear, Miss Snow, I'm so sorry! Aren't we, darling?'

'Yes,' said dad, who did not look remotely sorry.

'Isn't William appalling?' mum added mildly.

'Monstrous!' laughed Miss Snow. 'But perfectly natural.'

So she was not angry. Not even remotely. I was so relieved because her friendship meant more to me than a million hydrogen bombs.

'I hope you punished him!' added mum.

'Not really,' said my friend. 'I've seen it all before. Besides it was very daring and something to do with Stalin. So we just left it that it wouldn't happen again.'

'Miss Snow, you've always been so sweet to him. He doesn't deserve it. You've really made him feel at home at Coverdale.'

'Well, Mrs Conroy, he's such fun you can't be cross with him for long.'

'Have you learned your lesson from Miss Snow?' mum asked me.

'Oh yes,' I replied. I could not help staring at her. 'Oh yes.'

'It's time you grew up, William. You can do a lot better than being Stalin,' snapped my mother to me.

'*You'd have done better to become a priest,*' said Stalin's mother to Stalin.

As we walked across the gravel towards the car, mum whispered to dad, 'Cynthia Snow's such a giver, Alexander! So kind to William.' Then in an even quieter voice, 'Isn't it a shame she isn't married with children of her own?'

'Someone'll snap her up,' replied my father tersely.

As Stalin entered the 1950s, his mind, like mine, was wandering. Suffering from arteriosclerosis, he worked less and became more suspicious until his paranoia demanded another Great Purge. He wanted to shoot his old comrades, Molotov and Beria, Ormonde and Ogleton, linking them to another fabricated case, built around the Jewish doctors in the Kremlin: the '*murderers in white coats.*' He planned to whip up hatred against Soviet Jews, to massacre them in his new purge – and deport the rest. The Doctors' Plot was to be the spark of a terrible conflagration.

But when I returned from the Exeat, I had to face a Doctor's Plot of my own.

35

THE DOCTOR'S PLOT 1952–3

The Leper, Petty's elder brother Petty major, had to see the school doctor every day. The school doctor was incapable of curing common colds. He only seemed to be interested in examining the downwards voyage of testicles. That was why Coverdalians regarded the lazy school doctor with suspicion, if not dread.

People often follow the professions for which they are least qualified. Dr Figes, the school medic, was ill-qualified because he was always ill himself. Even his name, 'Figes', sounded like a disease.

When the gangly Petty major entered the day we got back from half-term, he caught Doctor Figes looking at his tongue in the mirror. Petty major sat down. Dr Figes finally replaced his tongue and sat down, sighing, 'Normal again. Probably shouldn't be working. Well, there it is. Now how are your dear parents? How is Roxburghshire? Trust the shooting's good.'

Dr Figes was handsome despite a completely bald head that always shone. His only hair were plumages of grey that whirled out of his ears; the boys called these the 'bird nests'. He was a retired army doctor.

Fixing his eyes onto the bird nests, the Leper mused as if he were miles away. 'I wonder if I should speak to my parents ...'

'What about?'

'Well,' said the Leper. 'I'm not sure if I should. But I'm really awfully worried, Dr Figes.'

'Horace,' said Dr Figes. 'Tell me. Though I hate to bother your Lady-mother, I will if I have to.'

The Leper was regarded by the boys as a sickly hulk of bad luck because he was so oddly big and his hair so weirdly almost white. Like Russian peasants, schoolboys are suspicious of illness, superstitiously believing it implies some sort of divine disfavour. But they ignored his face, which was feral, too small in proportion to his body but vigilant and manipulative. In the summer holidays, the Pettys had invited the school doctor up to Scotland to thank him for his care of the Leper. Dr Figes was grateful, despite the fact that the Pettys themselves were in London at the time: they had got the measure of the man.

'Papa is very worried about Communism.'

'Quite rightfully so. Communism is a disease like any other. I know. Wasn't in the army for nought!'

'Do you think he would be at all worried if he knew that Wombat – my little bro' – had been INFECTED with Marxism by Conroy?'

Dr Figes understood slowly. 'Ohhhhh. Conroy. Stalin ... I see. Is he infected?'

'Converted more like. He's become a Stalinist, Dr Figes.'

'Ohhhhh, yes of course, Horace. A Stalinist is far worse than just a common-or-garden Communist. Of course. Lord Petty feels very strongly ... Yes, I happen to be writing a report on your treatment anyway, so I might have to mention this.'

'Won't it worry them GRIEVOUSLY? Won't my father want to come and confront it at Coverdale? Pick us up at the end of term. Like a bull in a china shop?' The Leper knew that Dr Figes would love nothing better than a rare visit by Lord and Lady Petty. As for Petty major, the brothers usually had to get a train home. This way he would get far more attention from his distant parents as well as punish his little brother for his lip.

'I hope that your dear parents won't feel the need to come straight down. But leave it to me, Horace. I feel I have to expose this. They put a certain amount of trust in me, Horace.'

'They certainly do, Dr Figes. But it's probably nothing,' said the Leper. 'I'm perfectly well today. The rash has cleared up. Don't bother to examine me.' The Leper jumped up, opened the door and was just leaving.

'Thanks for coming in,' said Dr Figes with rare enthusiasm. 'Horace?'

'Yes,' he replied, from outside the door.

'Er, don't take any notice if I seem a touch peaky?'

But Pahlavi, as usual hiding in the bushes, was already watching the self-satisfied Leper, skipping back to school, pleased with his own Doctor's Plot.

For once, Dr Figes felt marvellous. He reached swiftly for his writing paper, headed

Dr John Figes – MBBS
School Doctor

and put pen to paper.

'And there's one other thing,' said Pahlavi, briefing me in the classroom after the fives match. 'Ogre's agents and mine both agree on it.'

'Well, what is it?'

'It concerns Miss Snow and—'

Mr Trevelyan bounced into the room.

'William, old boy,' said Mr Trevelyan affably. 'A word in your ear.'

He invited me to his study – invited, not ordered. I had to go, but it was a subtle difference. He needed me.

He was friendly, but appeared worried. I was not afraid that I was going to be beaten: I was a prefect, a member of the Politburo and a Generalissimo.

'Sit down, old boy,' said Mr Trevelyan expansively, waving at the leather sofa in the study. He sat on the stuffed leather chair. 'Nothing to worry about. But I need your help with something.'

'Fire away, sir.'

'I'm not really sure where to start, Conroy.' He paused, ran his hands through his hair and then rested them on the comfortable crescent of his ample belly.

'Look here, Conroy, have you ever heard of the ... the Third Man?'

'One of our great espionage triumphs.'

Mr Trevelyan nodded understandingly. His halo rose and fell.

'Well, yes, of course. One of Stalin's ... best agents. But, old chap, we are actually in England. And it was not very good for US!'

'I sympathise, sir.'

'It was a very serious matter, Conroy. It showed many people that the British Establishment COULD be filled with Communist spies. Now, have you heard of McCarthyism?'

'Oh yes, America's Red witch hunt by a drunk called Senator McCarthy ...'

'Against Communists. He was right of course: the Commies pose a pretty deadly threat to us, you know that.'

'Oh yes, sir, with knobs on.'

'Your Stalinist state seemed fine and dandy a couple of terms ago. But it wasn't really funny then. And it is a rather serious subject outside. Come on, buck up, old chap, buck up! Stop playing the fool for a moment!' He suddenly stood up and started pacing the room. 'You don't seem to realise that the fall of Saigon and the war in Angola are not so very far away. This bloody country's in a terrible fix. The unions run the place and they're COMMIES. Real ones, Conroy. Not play acting. There's not a parent here who is not suffering: we've NEVER had fewer pupils here. Soon no one will be able to afford to come to Coverdale. They'll all be tax exiles or labouring in salt mines in the Brecon Beacons! England looks as if it might be going under. Wouldn't surprise me, wouldn't surprise me at all, Conroy. We're on the edge of chaos.'

I was gobsmacked by this speech. I adored Mr Trevelyan: if he was upset, we should all be.

'Term ends tomorrow, Conroy. Your mater and pater are coming down to collect you. Lord and Lady Petty are coming to pick up the Pettys. Lord Petty is ... alarmed by your Communist activities. He would like to ask you a few questions. Otherwise ...'

'This is the School Doctor's Plot. Petty major got Dr Figes ...'

'Too late. Whoever alerted him, we must try to put Buller Petty's mind to rest. Otherwise, he's going to take the matter further.'

'I don't quite understand.'

'He's convinced himself he's happened upon a threat to the realm. He thinks there's a Communist cell here, Conroy.'

'You have to see this for yourself, Stalin. The real thing this time. Strike while the iron is hot.'

On the last day of term, Security Minister Pahlavi waited for me outside the chapel. There was no one around. We had bunked off the Easter term's school hymns. But we could hear the organ reverberating and the sound of boys voices singing, 'Praise him! Praise him! Praise the everlasting King ...'

Pahlavi, the gloomiest and most discreet of my comrades, said nothing at first.

He just turned and walked up past the gym building and round the back towards Kiev and Russia's granary – the Ukraine of pastures. I followed. The singing died away gradually.

The Persian's hooded eyes peered up ahead of us. There was no one around. It was only eight-thirty in the morning. There was still mist over much of Coverdale. The fields were coated in dew.

At the front, parents were already driving up to collect their children after Hymns. The boys had risen early. Everyone was packing and moving things. The masters were happy too: they had a month of holidays ahead.

Pahlavi stopped at the gateway to the cowfields. Coverdale's pastures were even more beautiful in winter than in summer: only an Englishman could think that. But the air was always moist, as if you were standing in a cloud that rested on the earth. Droplets cooled my face. The seamless mist, curling over the greenness, was broken only by the awkward bodies of the serene cattle. Their soft pink noses lazily puffed their own little clouds into the air.

But Pahlavi's face sharpens into the hawkish profile on the coins of those early Persian emperors – Xerxes or Darius: he has seen something. I sense in the second before he points it out to me that it is more important than just treason. It is graver than just another plot, contrived by my Soviet secret police – the centrepiece of a mystifying web of lies and secrets that we could not understand. This term, the atom bomb has made the world more dangerous, more complicated. At Coverdale, we do not really know what makes it tick. But we know it is something only grown-ups can comprehend with any certainty. The bomb is already inside us but only fragments of it. We feel different. It has changed us.

So I know that Pahlavi is about to show me something that will change me. Already I cannot speak. I hope it isn't ...

'There! There they are ...'

He points at the two figures at the top of the fields where the mist almost swallows them.

I see the two little silhouettes. They hold hands.

But as I stare through my spectacles, they pass over the top onto the cricket fields that we never visit in the winter.

'Do you want to follow them?'

'I have to,' I reply.

Pahlavi regards me carefully. He knows too much: does he judge me? I never doubt that behind his Persian obscurity, he burns with opinions and prejudices. Now he just shrugs.

I follow him up the path. He strides up there and I hurry him, almost running.

My sweat dries until it feels like a cool finger at my throat. But then the cool turns to heat as it starts to burn my skin like Deep Heat.

We are outside the Old Pavilion, where the Founder of Coverdale's son died in the age of emperors and kings ...

Pahlavi puts a tallow candle finger to his lips. Then he opens the door noiselessly. I can only recall the old rafters draped in the cheerless gloom of winter mornings.

Pahlavi beckons me towards the room where the bloodied stretcher lies.

But the door is closed and he waves his finger at it: don't open it.

He guides me like an invisible dancing partner around to the internal window, with its dusty glass.

The glowing skin of their scrummage illuminates the morning dusk, a contrast to the stained shadows of the stretcher where the boy died. I imagine waves of light radiating from them like the halo of a Greek god. I could not really see much.

All I can remember is that her legs, the bare legs, were crossed at the neat ankles, high across his naked bare back. They were crossed as simply as a bow on a beautifully wrapped birthday present.

'What are they doing? Is it?'

'Press-ups,' said Pahlavi. 'Real press-ups.'

'How vile!'

I turned and ran out of the Old Pavilion, not caring about the noise.

I did not stop until I was in the Kremlin, where no one could see me. What would Steady Pelham have thought? I wished I could ask him.

After a long time, an hour even, I heard light steps. It was Catalina, the cook's daughter.

I tried to dry my cheeks but I could not really help myself.

The betrayal by Petty, Hitler's invasion, even Crabbe's atrocities, were nothing compared to this. I was bleeding inside. I did not like what I had seen. It was different from the kisses and caresses I had seen before. This went far further. I knew that it outranked anything I could feel. Adults had an arsenal of weapons I could not use. How could I compete with Mr Allcock and his passionate roving eye?

Catalina stood before me and put a paper package on my knee.

'Open it,' she said. Her accent was cockney with a twist of the americanised accent of her Filipino father. 'I made it myself. I make the cakes. It's my job.' But with her, it was not just a job: it was a vocation.

It was a chocolate eclair. Profiteroles were my chosen cake.

I wolfed it down without looking up. Its creamy filling always made me tingle: the sheer enjoyment of the taste was my medicine.

'It's even better than my mother's.'

'William,' she said. 'Your parents are waiting. Mendoza's leaving for good: he wants to say goodbye to you. He sent me to find you. Term's over.'

I ran past her, sprinted up the stairs and rushed down the Long Corridor to say adieu to my hero, my dear Lenin.

It was only when I reached the Inner Sanctum that I recalled that Catalina had been crying too.

36

THE LAST TRIAL

Mr Trevelyan met me outside the Inner Sanctum's drawing room. 'Aha, dear boy, now listen, William, a word of warning ...'

'Darling!' My mother appeared in the doorway and kissed me. 'Come and sit with us!' So Mr Trevelyan never gave me his warning. But what warning did I need? I was far from being Communism's youngest martyr. It was only a joke trial – not like my show trials in the model railway room, which were for the highest stakes: death, for one.

My father got up. He was not smiling, but there was the speck of devilry in his eyes. I was relieved he was not angry. But mum was pale and eager. So I whispered to her, 'It's OK, mum. Stalin's handled more serious matters than this!'

But she put her arm around me and said quietly, 'Darling, now listen ...'

I think she was just about to give me a pep talk, like a team captain before the game, when Lord Petty erupted through the door like a riled wild boar.

'What would you like to drink, Buller?' Mr Trevelyan asked Lord Petty. Buller was his first name, which explains a lot.

'Your usual whisky and sour, Buller?' suggested Lady Petty from behind him.

'G and T? Sherry?' said Mr Trevelyan assiduously.

'A Molotov Cocktail?' I interjected, sotto-voce.

It came out almost in spite of myself, but Lord Petty's veined boozer's cheeks went livid. 'Look here, boy,' he said. 'This is NO laughing matter. We've just come down here to ask you one question and we – I think I speak for both of us, Audrey—'

'One hundred and ten per cent, Buller—' said Audrey Petty.

'When I say I want an honest answer.'

'I hardly think you should speak to William like THAT!' mumbled my father quietly. 'He IS a child.'

'What's he say?' asked Lord Petty, cocking his ear.

'Let's all sit down and try to sort this out amicably,' said Mr Trevelyan. 'Buller, why don't you and Audrey sit on that sofa on the left there, and Dr Conroy, Alexander and ... yes ... and William, why don't you sit over there?'

The two families obediently trooped to their positions. Mr Trevelyan sat on the fireside seat between us, his bottom roasting before the fire like Tom Brown on Flashman's spit.

'Are you the judge, sir?' I asked.

'Judge? I hardly think ...' began Mr Trevelyan.

'It's not a court,' said my mother, as if it was the silliest idea. 'Is it, Oliver?'

'Yes, it damn well is,' said Lord Petty before the Headmaster could answer. 'First question, boy—'

'I'm not having William spoken to like that,' said Mum.

'Don't worry, Mum. I'm quite used to the gruff manners of the underground before the revolution,' I said coolly.

'What are you going to do if you don't like the answer to your question?' asked Dad.

'Right! I'll answer that, sir,' said Lord Petty, pleased to be taken seriously. 'Let me show you something. Look out there. What do you see?'

We peered out of the window at the garden.

'A lawn,' said my mother.

'Look again,' said Lord Petty.

'Rhododendron bushes ...'

'I'll tell you what I see,' spat Buller Petty, eyes fixed. 'Forgive me if I speak in army terms, but I was a Guardsman for fifteen years and I know what I'm talking about. Gentlemen, the tanks are on the lawn.'

'Whose tanks?' I asked.

'I think you know the answer to that question better than any of us,' said Lord Petty blisteringly. 'That's why we're here.'

'To identify the tanks?' asked Dad.

Lord Petty nodded vigorously. 'If you want to look at it like that, yes. To identify the tanks.'

'But there aren't any tanks!' interjected Mum. 'Or am I missing something and being terribly stupid? Alexander?'

My father gently put his hand on mum's knee – they were always touching in one place or another. 'Not at all stupid, darling.'

'Are "the tanks" the name of a new rose they've created? Oh – or septic tanks under the grass?'

'I think men understand politics better than women,' said Lord Petty.

'Hear, hear,' said Lady Petty. 'I hardly know the difference between ...' Everyone waited patiently. '... between ...' But she could not think of anyone at all.

'Let me help, Lady Petty,' I interrupted. 'Can you tell the difference between Idi Amin and the Queen?'

'Well, they're different colours ...'

'Ten points. And anything else ...'

'Impertinence!' exclaimed Lord Petty. 'Enough of your lip, young man. If one of my boys behaved like that, I'd take off my belt to him.'

'William!' said dad.

There was a silence and then Mr Trevelyan said, 'Well, we're here to talk about William's views. If William could restrain his exuberance ...'

'It's his exuberance that worries me,' said Lord Petty thoughtfully. 'It shows there are more tanks on the lawn than we previously thought.'

I saw dad smile quickly at mum as if he did not want anyone to see. But no one did see, including Mum. So Dad winked. But this time, everyone saw and Lord Petty was annoyed.

'I don't find this at all humorous, Alexander, or a particularly amusing way to spend my time. I saw you wink at your wife ...'

'I did not wink,' lied dad. Not that winking was a crime, though Stalin shot babooshkas for less.

'Oh, so I was imagining it!' retorted Lady Petty sourly.

'Like the tanks,' said mum innocently.

'Oliver, what right have they to ask William questions?' Dad was enjoying a new spurt of confidence. 'I thought this was just a chat ...'

'Yes,' said Buller Petty. 'A chat to formulate the TACTICS of attack and the STRATEGY of what we military fellows call containment.'

'Well,' said Mr Trevelyan, hair rising like fresh bread. 'You're right, Alexander. This isn't a court, Buller, and we're just here to ...'

'This is a court and I'm the prosecution,' pontificated Lord Petty. The veined smudges of red in his cheeks were becoming so vivid that I feared one might explode in a fountain of blood. 'If necessary, I will take this to the highest level. I know fellas in intelligence. Won't say any more than that. But how would you like THEM asking the questions? They don't muck around, I can tell you!'

'This is farcical,' said my father.

'Is it? Is it? We're involved in a life-and-death struggle with these chaps. Life and death.'

'But William's a schoolboy,' said Dad. 'Not quite thirteen.'

'I'm no Pavel Morozov,' I said modestly. 'He was the boy Stalin made a Hero of the Soviet Union for denouncing both his parents.'

'The boy's being modest. A chap William's age could cause HAVOC with a cell in the midst of the Establishment,' growled Petty. 'I've heard from my eldest son what HE's been up to and it's DISGUSTING that it's been going on here. You've got an epidemic here, Headmaster – call it Scarlet Fever if you like. But your school's in deep water. This IS a court. Of sorts. And my first question is as follows: William Conroy ...'

'Yes, Lord Petty ...'

'I'm going to ask you a simple question. It worked for my father's generation and it's going to work for ours. I want you to think hard about it and answer it truthfully.'

'Of course.'

'Right,' said Lord Petty. 'Are you or have you ever been a member of the Communist Party?'

Pahlavi was outside. His long fingers pulled me aside into one of the Inner Sanctum's alcoves. The parents were still inside. When Mr Treveylan finally sent me out of the room, Lord Petty was persistently cross-examining my parents: 'Has your boy EVER received any strange letters, or apparently innocent toys, from so-called "pen-pals in Moscow"? They could be KGB communications, Mrs Conroy! They're clever all right, cunning as a fox: traitor Philby once bought me a whisky 'n' soda at the Cavalry and Guards. Seemed a decent fella, but too stacked up top: dammit Dr Conroy, too much grey matter in a man is a dangerous thing; like a red rag to a bull, if you'll excuse the pun.'

After that, it was a relief to talk to my calm Commissar:

'Why did you run off from the Pavillion?' asked Pahlavi.

'I don't know. It was yucky. I didn't know who it was.'

'Mr Allcock's been doing press-ups with her every morning during chapel for a week. More press-ups than gym.'

'I suppose there was the canoodling episode. For a moment, I don't know why, but I thought it was Miss Snow ... Silly of me really!'

'But there's something else far more important to tell you. You won't believe it! My information is flawless. I've seen it with my own eyes. Something terrible. It's about Miss Snow. She's ...'

'Can it wait until next term, Mohammed?' said Mr Trevelyan, bustling out with the kangaroo court following stiffly in his wake. The parents were not speaking.

'Not really,' said the Commissar. 'Miss Snow is ...'

I heard my mother whispering to Dad, 'Darling, if he DOES go to the CIA, it could ruin William's career, couldn't it?'

'It might make it,' said Dad.

'You did well, darling,' said Mum as she saw me standing there. 'Hello, Mohammed. Are you going back to Iran for the holidays? I do love your Shah ...'

'Thank you, Mrs Conroy. I'm off to Teheran this afternoon, so I won't be able to speak to William until ...' We were all walking towards the car.

'Quick, quick,' said my mother. 'William, Alexander, get in the car. I can't face bumping into those Pettys again. Chop, chop!'

'But, Stalin! Our Soviet Union will never be the same again. Miss Snow and ...'

We were in the car. Pahlavi was running alongside, desperate to tell me. I was glad I had had Miss Snow under surveillance: it was for her own good. But after the shock of seeing Mr Allcock and Miss Deirdre the under-matron, I could not imagine how he could have anything worse on my special friend. How terrible could it be?

The car was speeding up, sending the gravel flying.

Then Pahlavi was pointing at his finger, saying, 'The ring. The ring.'

My mother thought he was pointing at her and she waved back. 'That lovely Persian's such a friendly boy,' she said fruitily.

37

STALIN THE CUCKOLD

'**D**o you like my ring?'
    I said nothing.
    'I need to have someone too,' said Miss Snow in her
cottage. When we got back for the summer term, I went around to see
her. I wanted to tell her all about my thirteenth birthday party,
attended by the Politburo. She always gave me tea on the first day of
term: it was one of our little traditions. She handed me the cup of tea
on a saucer. Just as I liked it: sweet with honey. She played with the
dry flowers arranged on her desk. But it was not the same this time.
She had spoiled it.

'I thought WE were friends.' I was sitting at the little table: it was a
tiny cottage filled with pairs of boots. She always wore boots. There
were boots in every corner. 'We ARE friends.'

'Dear William. Of course we are. You've always been my favourite
kid. But ...' She appeared to strain to cross the next threshold. 'I've
been alone a long time. I wasn't at all happy when my marriage
ended. I've never really told you about it but I'm a fragile person. I
was so unhappy, I couldn't even work. I became ill. I had an old friend
in England, and he suggested that I get away from Philadelphia and
come here. And over time we became more than friends.'

'More than friends? What can be more than friends?' Why did not
grown-ups EVER say what they really meant? They used more double-
talk than Stalin.

'There is something more than friends ...'

'Really?' I said. Of course – the press-ups. But they were for dirty
people like Mr Allcock and Miss Deirdre. How could press-ups
compare to our friendship?

'When people are in love, it's really the most beautiful thing in all
existence ...'

'IN LOVE?' I spat, disgusted.

'That's why Geoffrey Allcock and I are going to spend the rest of our lives together.'

'How do you know?'

'William, we're getting engaged.'

'So it's true?' Pahlavi and the ring.

'You heard about it already?'

'My MVD agents hear everything ...'

'How?'

'I had you watched by the secret police, Miss Snow,' I said more in sorrow than pride.

'I don't much like the sound of that,' she said quietly.

'Sorry. But it was for your own protection against saboteurs. You're not the only one I had watched.'

Yet the worst part of it was that Stalin, me and all our secret policemen, were impotent compared to whatever Mr Allcock shared with Miss Snow. '*Political power*,' wrote Mao, '*comes from the barrel of a gun.*' But I saw then that the heart, the trivial heart, overpowers even that. Their horrible partnership had turned all my achievements into dust.

But the mention of the secret police reminded me of something I knew I should not mention.

'Well, it is true. I wanted you to hear first from me. We're having an engagement party next week. So sweet of the Trevelyans ... And we're going to get married really quickly. In the summer holidays. No point in wasting time at our age. And we've both been married before ...'

I regarded her coolly, with something approaching hatred.

'You don't want children, do you?'

'Of course, all women want children,' she enthused. He was already making her into a different person.

'Is it wise?' I asked, trying to be helpful.

She became serious. I could tell I should not have said it.

'Why not? We've got time.'

Silence. Outside I could hear the sound of cricket boot-studs on the gravel, and voices echoing on Coverdale's courtyards. What would Pelham do?

'If you're ... more than friends' – I could not bring myself to say Love – 'do you trust the other person?'

'Oh yes,' she said. Her smile lit up her severe face, with its sheer cliffs beneath high cheeks, more than ever before. Her low voice lightened. 'Of course.' She looked jubilant. 'You must trust to love. You MUST, William. I trust Geoffrey absolutely.'

She thought she was teaching me an absolutely positive rule for the rest of my life. Yet she sensed something amiss too. 'Why do you ask?'

'You said one of Mr Allcock's eyes was a rover. You said he had an eye for the ladies.'

'Did I? When?'

'On THE walk.'

A cold anger passed through me: she had forgotten my walk.

'Oh yes, but that's all over now.'

'No, it isn't.'

'Stop this now, William ...' But I had to tell, I had to.

'His eye's still roving, Miss Snow. Roving and roving.'

She stood up, her leather boots creaking. Her face had aged in that second. Like Ayesha, it was awful to behold. I was only being helpful.

'You'd better go now.'

She said it so venomously that I stood up, ready to scram. But few have the strength to resist proffered knowledge ...

'Wait. What do you know, Conroy?'

'My secret police have been watching Mr Allcock for some time. Only to protect you. I suspected him of being a capitalist Trotskyite spy and ...'

'Cut it out! What did they see?'

'Mr Allcock's been kissing Miss Deirdre every afternoon all last term. Then they started ... well, we call it press-ups.'

'Don't be disingenuous. What do you mean? Tell me now! You must!'

'If you really want to know, Miss Snow, they were having it off.'

'I don't believe you. How do you know?' I could tell she was interested.

'I've seen it myself. In the Old Pavilion on the last day of last term. I ran off. How could Mr Allcock do it? He's dirty.'

Adults think children know nothing. In fact, we divine most things. And my secret police saw everything.

I knew Miss Snow would be grateful for this information. I would have to give Pahlavi his seventh Order of Lenin for this fine Stalinist heroism. Maybe even a marshalship of the Soviet Union. I was smiling smugly when she hit me on my cheek so hard that I fell back in the chair. I put my hand to my face, dazed with surprise. The engagement ring's diamond grazed my cheek.

'You little creep. How dare you? How DARE you interfere in my life. I ... I just don't know ... The fucking cheek of it. After the kindness I had shown you. I treated you like an adult. I was your friend. When you cried as a new boy, I spent hours with you. You visit my home. I gave you extra tutorials. And THIS is how you repay me. This is your THANK YOU is it? You're a destroyer! When I'd rebuilt everything, when I'd put myself back together. You really ARE a little Stalin ... Christ, Christ, you don't know what you've done ...'

I listened to this frantic outpouring with mounting amazement: this was not at all the reaction I expected. Miss Snow was crying and crying with hatred for me! ME! – her only loyal and useful friend. She was still sobbing and shouting. I knew adults could experience physical pain, like Mr Selwyn, but I thought only children could be so sad.

'I'm only telling you to help. I love helping you. I'm only telling you as a special fav. I only want to be helpful, Miss ...'

These were the last words I ever said to her.

She just held her front door open and slammed it behind me.

I ran blindly along the path from Miss Snow's cottage, past the cowsheds. That was the moment my whole world began to whirl and turn so fast that all I could do was hold on to survive. I am trying to recall everything important during the next few days. But I felt as giddy as I did when my parents took me to a fairground and I got stuck on a maverick merry-go-round that no one could stop. I just held on but it went quicker and quicker until everyone and everything familiar to me was just a sickening blur ...

I knew I had done something unspeakable but I was not quite sure what. I had pains in my chest and my head was throbbing. I staggered into the school, found some paper beside the postbox and managed to scribble a letter to my parents. 'I have lost my friend. For ever. I hate it here. I must leave. Take me away or else ... William.'

I posted it, wishing I were dead, wondering if I should die.

I found myself down beside the Lake, which was lush and exotic in the spring. The undergrowth was a delicate carpet of bluebells. They only survived a month and then they died.

I fell to my knees amongst them and began to cry: it was a different species of crying from schoolboy tears. I cried because I had hurt: that was what made them my first true tears.

After that, I could only become crueller, more suspicious, more loveless.

'She was the only creature who softened my stony heart. She is dead and with her have died any feelings of tenderness I had for humanity,' Stalin said on the death of his first wife in 1907. That was how I felt.

I did not deserve a second chance, but I got one. I did not hear her approach me, though she knew the Lake well. It was her private garden.

She put her hand on my shoulder and, once again, she handed me a cake. I swallowed all its chocolate and pastry before I looked up at her. For the first time, she did not seem as old as she had before. She was still older but not too old to be my friend. She left her hand on my neck, so I could feel the heat of her skin. She could feel mine. This made me look at her for the first time.

Her blue denim played off her wholesome brown skin. She had a saddle of freckles across her nose. I could have sworn she smelled of warm loaves, maybe the sponge of her cakes. After her tawniness, what had I seen in Stalin's bristly moustache, his stench of tobacco, his pot-belly and pockmarked skin? What was his tyranny compared to this? She examined me carelessly with amused yet lazy, green eyes, set obliquely and narrowly on her heart-shaped face. Those eyes were the only clue to her Filipino half. I trusted her unexpectedly and laid my head on her hand so that she could weigh my guilt and judge me.

'What have you done?' she asked me.

Like God in Eden.

That was how it started. That afternoon, on a carpet under a blanket down by the Lake. She kept a carpet there, rolled up like the one Cleopatra used to visit Caesar.

I won't recount the details. I was privileged to begin early and to have such a patient teacher. But all our questions about press-ups and Mary Millington were answered so suddenly; what can I say? Gosh, as Lenin be my witness, it was both simpler and far more shocking than any of us had ever imagined.

After his wife's suicide, Stalin's mistress was HIS cook, Valechka Istomina, a peasant girl who was only thirty-eight when the old man died. No one knew their exact relationship, just as no one knew ours.

She kept house for him at his Kuntsevo dacha, outside Moscow, as Catalina did for me down at the Lake, in the countryside near my Moscow. *'Whether or not Istomina was Stalin's wife is nobody else's business,'* said the octogenarian Molotov decades later. Anyway, she too was devoted to him: Coverdale's cook; Stalin's cook. But Catalina preferred recipes to history books.

Afterwards, when we lay there, both of us naked, amongst the bluebells, I noticed the carpet was a Persian. My father loved carpets and he had taken me shopping. Then I guessed it.

'This is Mendoza's carpet. He must have taken it from his Dad's house.'

'Maybe,' she said.

'So ... did you do it with Mendoza too?'

'Maybe.'

That was what Mendoza was always doing down at the Lake, why he was never in his bed at night ...

'Gosh ... I'm not sure what to say.'

'Do you mind? Are you a jealous boy?' she asked indolently with one side of her mouth twisting into a crooning smile. I knew then that she was kind and pleasure-loving, but she did not really care one way or the other.

'Coming after Mendoza?' I reflected. 'No, I follow Mendoza like Stalin followed Lenin. That's dialectical materialism for you. But Mendoza left his dad's carpet. To you.'

'Not to me,' she said carefully. 'To us.'

I could not really talk about Miss Snow.

I can scarcely bear to write about it now.

38

THE DEATH OF STALIN 5 MARCH 1953

At Coverdale, they say Stalin died of a broken heart. In Russia, his death is still a mystery. Was he murdered by Beria to save his skin? This is how it really happened.

'Comrade Stalin, are you quite well?' asked Ogleton at the Politburo in the Black Shoe Room. 'Generalissimo?'

'Fine.' But of course, I was not really well at all. In those two or three days after Miss Snow, I tried to lose myself with Catalina. What a discovery that was. But I could not forget what I had done and what I had lost. I was always on the verge of tears. Yet the machinery of the Stalinist USSR kept going: Central Committees met; Orgburos met; apparatchiks formulated inane Five-Year Plans. 'Carry on,' I said. 'Get on with it.'

Then secret police chief Ogre, dropped a clanger. 'Comrade Stalin, why is Miss Snow leaving?'

'Yes, why is she leaving?' Pahlavi joined in. 'Do you know, Comrade Stalin?'

'No.'

'I saw her running towards Mr Allcock's in floods of tears,' Pahlavi continued, 'Desperate she was!'

'It's none of our business. Leave it.'

'By Jove, she was screaming at him and he was in a terrible state too. You could hear them all the way to the tennis courts!' said Ormonde. He left his yo-yo in his pocket.

'Don't you listen to me! You gumbies! Don't you bloody listen? I said I don't want to hear about it.' I could not help it. I was crying. Through my tears, the Politburo looked at one another. They knew that a weeping Stalin in Politburo signified some imminent eruption and they did not know what. '*The peasants act wisely by killing mad wolves,*' I added.

Stalin kept saying this during his last meeting with a foreign ambassador. Ormonde and Ogleton glanced nervously at each other. They did not understand me, thought I was senile.

'Who are the "mad wolves"?' asked Archie innocently. 'Are the wolves the reason Miss Snow's leaving?'

'Come on, Stalin. You know why she's going ...' began Ogleton. He was hectoring me, almost bullying me, just like Beria with old Stalin. I noticed the effect of my tears. They cleaned away thirty years of dictatorship; they were not afraid of me any more.

'That's it!' I shouted. 'I'm going to arrest the lot of you. Molotov. Kaganovich. Beria. I'm cleaning you lot out just as Stalin wanted. How dare you give Stalin such lip!'

But now they did dare. They sat there in silence. They were shaking their heads ...

I could not concentrate. I tried to think of Catalina, my consolation. But there was no consolation. After Miss Snow, I was hollow inside. I hadn't got the will any more.

Then Pahlavi just stood up and pointed a slender finger right at me. 'You drove out Miss Snow! I was listening. Yes, you fool, Stalin, you were under surveillance like everyone else. I heard everything, Conroy!'

'I didn't! I didn't!' But no one was convinced. Everyone seemed to be shouting at me. I had so trusted Pahlavi.

'What do you mean?' asked Ogleton. 'What had Stalin got to do with it?'

'Tell us!' Nonsuch, Archie and the rest were angry, truly angry. Everyone adored Miss Snow. 'Tell us! Poor Miss Snow!'

I stood up and threw my stool across the room at Ogleton.

'How easy it is for the imperialist gentlemen to intimidate you! I shall have to make it a question of "either – or". Either we shall liquidate them or after my death, they will liquidate you like blind kittens. Like blind kittens.'

I knew Stalin's last speech well. I stood still for a second, then I tottered, raised my hands to my heart. I fell to the floor. Its cold stone chilled me through my clothes. I lay with my eyes closed.

For a few moments, they did not dare do or say anything. Suppose this was one of Stalin's tricks to test their loyalty? But they had all noticed that Stalin's mind had been wandering lately. He did not look well. He was seventy-three years old. His memory had gone. And what ghastly deaths was he planning for them?

Ogleton, always the bravest, kneeled and took my hand: 'Joseph Vissarionovich? Soso? Koba? come back to us!'

Then he was briefly bolder.

'Wake up, you nasty reptile! You're finished, Stalin! How could you do that to Miss Snow?'

Just then, my eyes flickered open for a moment.

'Oh brave noble teacher, Generalissimo Stalin, our sun and moon, Second Lenin come back to us!' he shrieked cravenly. That was how Beria behaved at Stalin's deathbed.

But my eyes closed again.

'Call the doctors!' said Nonsuch, tears running down his cheeks.

'They're all under arrest,' snuffled Weeping Wharton.

'Well, get Matron then!' ordered Pahlavi, always collected in a crisis. 'Stalin's had a stroke ...'

'How do you know it's a stroke?' asked Archeamboye.

'It's in the history books, you thicky,' snapped Ogre. 'He's gone. He won't recover. Don't you see? The old gangster's croaking!'

'It can't be, it can't,' gasped Ormonde. 'Stalin! Stalin!' He was shaking the body by its lapels but the head, that famous head with its black hair now thin and grey, just lolled. The face was restful now – all my enemies forgotten. Even Miss Snow was forgotten momentarily.

'Kiss me, Hardie,' I sighed, opening my eyes again.

'S'truth! Now he thinks he's Admiral Nelson!' exclaimed Ogleton. 'By Jove, Ormonde, pass me that shoe rag. We can't risk him coming back again!' I tried to sit up but Ogleton covered my face, pressing with the rag. He was right anyway. After Miss Snow, there was no coming back. Stalin was too ill to struggle. His limbs quivered. Then they relaxed.

'He's gone,' said Ogre, removing the rag. 'Hard cheese, Stalin!'

'We're all alone now,' murmured Nonsuch. 'What will we do without him?'

Ormonde quoted Sholokhov:

> Farewell, Father!
> That sudden and terrible feeling
> of having become an orphan

That afternoon, the following statement was issued by the Central

Committee of the Coverdale Communist Party and pasted up on the board beside the First and Second Football Torpid teams for the game against Heathfield:

Dear Comrades and Friends

It is with a feeling of profound grief that the Central Committee, the Council of Ministers and the Presidium of the Supreme Soviet announce to the Party and all the workers of the Soviet Union that Joseph Vissarionovich Stalin, Chairman of the Council of Ministers and Secretary-General of the Central Committee, passed away on March 5 at 9.50 at night after a grave illness.

The heart of J. V. Stalin, Lenin's comrade-in-arms and the inspired continuator of his work, wise leader and teacher of the Communist Party and Soviet people, has stopped beating.

The immortal name of Stalin will always live in the hearts of the Soviet people and the hearts of all progressive humanity.

Long Live the great all-powerful doctrine of Marx-Engels-Lenin-Stalin!

PS: Lying in state tomorrow afternoon in Mr Trevelyan's Greenhouse! Funeral before tea – Camps!

PPS: Recite in chapel the Patriarch of the Russian Orthodox Church's prayer for Stalin instead of Lord's Prayer:

May the soul of your servant Joseph rest amongst the saints, Oh Lord.

PPPS: All Berks, Twits and Scallywags to attend. Or else Lubianka!

Signed: Central Committee.

That night, after Stalin died, there was a freak summer shower.

The storm gathered its strength and then tossed everything it had at Coverdale. We took Lenin's carpet and lay it out in the hay at the feet of the cows. It was warm there because the cows huddled together, breathing their sweet vapours onto us. When the rain ceased as suddenly as it had begun, we became so feverish in there that I took all my clothes off and she wrapped me in her greatcoat.

But it did not feel like a streak any more.

'Catalina, I have to leave Coverdale early. Tomorrow,' I said when the storm was quiet enough to whisper. I knew she would not mind too much. Being brought up in a school is like being brought up in a circus: everyone leaves in the end. So she was a law unto herself – what my mum called 'free and easy, easy-come-easy-go'. 'My parents called. They have discussed me with the Trevelyans. After Miss Snow. She's gone too.'

She lay back and rolled her green eyes.

'Miss Snow, Miss Snow,' she crooned carelessly, stretching herself. 'Maybe it was better that she knew the truth.'

'I don't think so.'

'My dead Stalin.' She gave that crooked smile. 'You do look good naked.'

'The body was laid on a stretcher,' wrote Stalin's daughter Svetlana when she saw her father laid out dead and naked. *'It was the first time I had seen my father naked. It was a beautiful body. I realised that body that had given me life no longer had life or breath in it, yet I would go on living.'*

39

THE FUNERAL

'Pssst! Stalin!' said Kildare.
'Shush,' I whispered without opening my eyes as I lay there in a flowerbed of Mrs Trevelyan's orchids.
'What are you doing, Conroy?'
'Hasn't anyone told you! I'm lying in state. Now buzz off!'

Merke rode the gun-carriage at Stalin's funeral. My catafalque was pulled by two dopey cows from the farm, against all the rules.

The Politburo lifted me, lying on the Old Pavilion's bloodied stretcher, gently off the cart and carried my stretcher on their shoulders. With my head on a pillow and my hands open but palm down, resting on my hips, I lay on the bier, wearing a false moustache. The body sported a Salvation Army jacket with red epaulettes and gold buttons, stolen by Ogleton from the theatrical cupboard.

As the 'gun-carriage' clanked away, they marched slowly to the funeral music of 'How Deep Is Your Love' by the Bee Gees, which brought most of them to the verge of tears. The Central Committee walked behind, wearing their wellington boots, Parka coats and white armbands of mourning. The marshals, including Zhukov, formed a guard of honour. But I could not resist glancing around a little: I was pleased to see Steady Pelham.

When Comrade Nonsuch played 'We are the Champions' on the ghetto blaster, even Ogleton started to sniff noisily. Their weeping was not merely collective hysteria at the death of the man they had regarded as a father, almost a god. They knew this was my goodbye. They were coming for me that evening to take me away from the school. We might never meet again.

Behind the Politburo, in solemn procession according to the

following order (worked out with typical orderliness by Comrade Pahlavi), marched the prefects, the captains of cricket, football and rugby, the keepers of golf and fives, the bloods, the First Elevens and First Fifteen, all bearing poster-sized pictures of Stalin, hastily prepared in the art school. The swimming, squash, rackets, golf and chess teams followed in slow steps. The hockey eleven, bearing their sticks like rifles, formed the ceremonial guard.

Dear Pelham represented the draughts team.

The Odd Jobsmen, ordinary workers carrying their brooms, were especially honoured as all knew that young Koba had once swept the leaves and built the bonfires.

The Bovverboys, Barry Blue-Eyes and Jug Ears, brought up the rear.

'Halt!' ordered Marshal Diggle.

The procession stopped abruptly.

That was when the masters arrived.

'Right everyone, back to the school,' Mr Trevelyan was shouting. His nimbus of ashen fuzz was now distinctly grey. He suddenly looked older than his seventy years, as if there had been a death in the family. But then in retrospect, he already knew more about Miss Snow than I did. 'I warned you. Come on, Ogleton! Conroy! This is over!' Then he pointed to me and said quietly, even gently, 'Are your cases packed, Conroy?'

The Mausoleum, where I was to be reunited with Lenin, lay under the Kremlin trees beside the wall of the school.

The Politburo formed up in their two lines as guardians. You have probably seen the photographs of the dead Stalin: there I am, in the middle, in my dashing uniform. I am surrounded by wreaths. The senior members of the Politburo stand vigil in two lines that form a passageway towards Stalin – Nonsuch, Ormonde, Pahlavi on one side; Ogleton, Archeamboye and Weeping Wharton on the other. They are staring right ahead, some wearing their Marshals' uniforms, others in dark suits, with their faces set in the frigid mask of tragedy.

How did I persuade them I was Stalin? By a kind of schoolboy black magic? By whipping up a Mephistophelian hysteria more compelling than any they had experienced? By believing, when they did not, sure the sheep would do anything to follow the flock? By offering them the power that most adults never even know: the Highest Measure of Punishment?

But when I opened my eyes again, something had changed. They no longer stood in line. Ogre was tickling Nonsuch. Ormonde had his yo-yo hidden in his right hand. Archeamboye was facing the wrong way. Only Weeping Wharton was still weeping. When they saw me, they collected themselves and straightened up again.

Then I looked once more. Ogre and Archeamboye were gone. Nonsuch still stood at attention. Then I saw it: Weeping Wharton was not weeping any more. He was laughing at something Ormonde was doing with his yo-yo. 'Watch this splendiferous yo-yo "round the world",' Ormonde was telling him.

'Supercadjerlocious!' said Wharton.

I closed my eyes and pretended I was indeed dead. In some ways, I wished I was. I had had a fine career as a little Stalin but, like him, I had poisoned the wells.

Tonight was the end of my life so far. I feared the world outside: at some larger school, I would be a Cabbage again.

Miss Snow was already long gone. Far gone. No one told me where she went and how. It was only years later that I discovered what I had done. But even before I knew, I never forgave myself. I used to see women in the street whom I thought I recognised. 'It's Miss Snow. I'm sure of it.' And I'd follow the woman through the streets until she turned ...

As I lay there in Stalin's Mausoleum, I firmly believed that I would wear the black spot of Cain until the end of my days.

'Goodbye, Conroy,' Steady Pelham said. I did not even know he was there. 'But don't worry. We all make mistakes. I'd probably have done the same. Even though I knew it was wrong. Everything heals, Conroy.' He was the only one of the boys I ever did see again.

When I heard the wind blow, I realised I was alone. Then I felt the weight of one leg and then another on the mattress. I smiled and the lips came down and crushed mine in a kiss.

It was Catalina, my devoted Valeshka Istomina, Stalin's last loyal retainer. She popped a profiterole into my mouth.

'So Stalin's dictatorship fell in the end?'

I wondered what would happen to Stalin's real empire – the Soviet Imperium. There was no sign of Brezhnev faltering. No, Stalin's empire would surely last for ever, long after I left Coverdale ... But what was all that worth if it was just a big crime perpetrated by one bloodthirsty murderer?

'Will you always love me?' asked Catalina teasingly.

'Love? Lurrve? I'll never love anyone. It's a stupid thing. It spoils everything.' I was thinking of Miss Snow.

I could never imagine not liking Catalina. But I was leaving Coverdale. My trunks were packed. The boys avoided my eyes in the corridors. The masters regarded me as a disgrace, almost to be pitied – like one of Stalin's non-persons as Mr Eye had warned on the day of the revolution. 'It will be as if you had never even existed,' he had said.

Perhaps we only have one true love in a lifetime and I had mine too soon. I never had another. Today, I am quite alone. My routine is simple, though tedious. But recently, I began to think about the past – my affair with Stalin. Would I be the same person if I had never known Marshal Stalin and Miss Snow? I want to think I would be different. But I doubt it.

When I left, the masters and the school, even Miss Snow, were frozen in time: they would remain for ever as I remembered them. Only the boys grew older. It is funny. When I was homesick, Marshal Stalin and Miss Snow comforted me. But I cried more when I left Coverdale than when I arrived.

'Will you always remember me?' Catalina asked, suddenly serious for the first time since she prematurely commenced my romantic education. She was losing another little friend. It was almost the hour for me to go to the Inner Sanctum. For the last time.

'Always!' I told her.

You see, for a child, always is not a very long time. But I was not lying. I have remembered her. I remember everything.

'One last question: how long do you think you would have lasted under the real Stalin before he had you shot?'

'Not as long as THIS.' And I kissed her.

EPILOGUE

Double, triple the guard around the tomb!
So that Stalin may never get out ...

Yevgeny Yevtushenko

APPENDIX I

Life Of Stalin: The Key Dates

21 December 1879	Stalin born Josef Djugashvili in Gori, Georgia.
1894	Djugashvili studies at Tiflis Theological College to become priest.
1899	'Koba' expelled for revolutionary tactics.
1904	Marries Keke Svanidze.
1906	Meets Lenin.
1907	Stalin robs Tiflis Stage Coach. Death of Keke.
1917	Russian Revolution. Stalin in Politburo. Commissar for Nationalities.
1919	Stalin marries Nadezhda aged eighteen.
1922	Lenin appoints Stalin Secretary-General.
1924	Lenin dies.
1925	Struggle for succession. Stalin defeats Trotsky. The city of Tsaritsyn renamed Stalingrad.
1927	Stalin defeats Zinoviev and Kamenev.
1929	Stalin defeats Bukharin. Begins Collectivisation. Trotsky expelled from USSR.
1932	Famine and liquidation of kulaks. Nadezhda Stalin commits suicide.
1934	Assassination of Stalin's heir apparent Kirov. Start of Purges under NKVD boss Yagoda.
1936–8	Yezhov appointed NKVD boss. Great Purge. Yezhovschina. Millions of innocent people killed. Zinoviev shot.
1938	The Great Trial. Bukharin shot. Yezhov sacked. Beria NKVD boss.

1939	Yezhov shot. Molotov-Ribbentrop Pact with Hitler.
1940	Stalin has Trotsky assassinated.
1941	Hitler invades. Stalin Prime Minister (Chairman of Council of People's Commissars), Supreme Commander in Chief, Minister of Defence, Chairman of State Defence Council.
1942–3	Battle of Stalingrad.
1945	Fall of Berlin. Stalin Generalissimo.
1946–	Cold War with West.
1947	Purge of actors, Jews, writers by Stalin's heir-apparent Zhdanov.
1948	Death of Zhdanov. Purge of Zhdanov's supporters.
1952	Doctors' Plot threatens second Great Purge of the Party and deportation and massacre of Russian Jews.
5 March 1953	Stalin dies. Embalmed with Lenin in Mausoleum. Succeeded initially by triumvirate of Molotov, Beria and Malenkov. They soon lose power to Khrushchev. Beria executed.
1956	Denounced by Khrushchev.
1961	Body removed from Mausoleum. Stalingrad renamed Volgagrad.
1964	Fall of Khrushchev. Succeeded by Brezhnev.
1985	Mikhail Gorbachev – last Secretary-General of Communist Party.
1991	Boris Yeltsin President of Russian Federation. FALL OF THE SOVIET UNION.